Python Programming Demystified

A Clear and Concise Guide
Your Key to Unlocking Career Opportunities

Sachin Kr Gupta
Praveen K Sharma
Gayathri Gopalakrishnan
Gaurav Aroraa

AF517997

ARCCHIE
www.arcchieonline.com

Python Programming Demystified

A Clear and Concise guide: Your Key to Unlocking Career Opportunities

SACHIN KR GUPTA
NOIDA, INDIA

PRAVEEN K SHARMA
GHAZIABAD, INDIA

GAYATHRI GOPALAKRISHNAN
BANGALORE, INDIA

GAURAV ARORAA
DELHI, INDIA

Copyright © 2024 Arcchie Publications, India

All rights reserved. No part of this publication may be reproduced, distributed, or transmitted in any form or by any means, including photocopying, recording, or other electronic or mechanical methods, without the prior written permission of the publisher, except in the case of brief quotations embodied in critical reviews and certain other noncommercial uses permitted by copyright law.

Arcchie Publications has made every effort to provide trademark information about all the companies and products mentioned in this book through the appropriate use of capitals. However, Arcchie Publications cannot guarantee the accuracy of this information.

Editor: Shambhu
Production Manager: Meghna
Cover design & creatives by Freepik
Formatting & Indexing: Gaurav

First Edition: June-2024

Reference: 2309011

Published by Arcchie Publications

ISBN-13 (paperback): 978-81-966127-0-2

www.arcchieonline.com

TABLE OF CONTENTS

FOREWORD

What if you could shape the future, make the tools used by the next generation, or make the entertainment you always wanted to have? Yes, it might even be videogames that get you into programming. It was for me, and it was for Elon Musk…

> *"I probably wouldn't have started programming if it wasn't for video games... I think video games are a very powerful force for getting young kids interested in technology."*
>
> — *Elon Musk*

Imagine if the path you're on right now is not just a journey but the most consistently profitable one you could be on. It's not a far-fetched idea. When you're shaping the future through coding and learning programming languages, you're gaining knowledge and opening doors to a world of opportunities and financial success.

I learned how to code in college. When I was in California at Fullerton College, I learned Visual Basic, Java, and C++. Later, at the DigiPen Institute of Technology in Washington State, I also learned Python and C#. My first job at Microsoft was writing the SDK for an early version of Microsoft Surface and touch computing. Over the last few decades, I got to help publish architectural content for developers to build applications on Microsoft Azure and Google Cloud. I've also had the privilege of co-authoring Learn to Program with Small Basic to teach kids 10+ how to code, Hands-On Microservices with C# 8 and .NET Core 3 with one of this book's authors (Dr. Gaurav Aroraa), Cloud Debugging and Profiling in Microsoft Azure also with Dr. Gaurav, and ASP.NET Core 5 for Beginners. I've also helped teach and organize others to teach thousands of students at Microsoft campuses and Bellevue College. Python has always impressed me by how easy it is to pick up and learn and how powerful and versatile it can be.

What you have in your hand right now is a door. I know what you're thinking, "Ed, this is a book, not a door." I mean, it's a door. If you read the book and truly learn from it, completing the exercises, then it's as if you're walking through a door. What's on the other side of the door? It's a big room with many opportunities that only exist once you open and walk through the door. And guess what? Inside that room are a lot more doors. Each door is another learning journey, and you'll find a new room with new opportunities each time. But don't take my word for it. Like many others, I'm just a child. Let's see what our parents have to say.

"Everyone should learn to code. It teaches you how to think."

– Steve Jobs

"Programming allows you to think about problems and find solutions in a structured way. It's a powerful tool for innovation and progress."

— Mark Zuckerberg

"Learning to write programs stretches your mind, and helps you think better, creates a way of thinking about things that I think is helpful in all domains."

– Bill Gates

There you have it. The more you learn to code, the more you'll learn to think, solve problems, and innovate. All this is true, but let's get down to some simple facts. You could be a marketing manager… or a marketing manager who learns how to code and builds a resume and reputation working in technical teams.

The latter could lead to you becoming a marketing manager who works for a big tech company, doing the same job as other marketing managers but making upwards of five times more money (and much better benefits). It's the same thing if you were going to be a lawyer, financial analyst, or even an administrative assistant. It's time to open a door and walk through it.

"At a time when people are saying "I want a good job - I got out of college and I couldn't find one," every single year in America there is a standing demand for 120,000 people who are training in computer science."

– President Bill Clinton

It's time to begin expanding your opportunities. You'll likely need a college degree and experience to get to your dream opportunity. So, this won't be the last door for you to walk through, to open up your future opportunities. However, it might be the most important one.

"Computer science empowers students to create the world of tomorrow."

– Satya Nadella, Microsoft

"To prepare humanity for the next 100 years, we need more of our children to learn computer programming skills, regardless of their future profession."

– Salman Khan, Khan Academy

"There's so much that's possible with technology, especially if you can learn how to code. You can create anything you want and reach everyone in the world."

– Jessica Alba, actress

"If we want America to stay on the cutting edge, we need young Americans to master the tools and technology that will change the way we do just about everything."

– President Barack Obama

Computer science can teach you not only how to think and solve problems but Not only can it provide the most consistently rewarding career today, but it's also your best shot at changing the world.

In Python Programming Demystified – A Clear and Concise Guide, Sachin, Dr. Gaurav, Gayathri, and Praveen take you on an easy and simple journey into coding with a professional and powerful programming language, Python.

Python is the easiest and best professional programming language to learn, and this book will provide you with basic programming concepts and hands-on exercises. You'll learn about functions, modules, exception handling, data structures, and how to build interfaces and databases, among many other topics.

You've taken the step and are about to open the door. It's time to learn Python programming. It's time to open a door for your future.

"Small minds are concerned with the extraordinary, great minds with the ordinary."

– Blaise Pascal

As Pascal mentioned 300 or so years ago, all you have to do is find an ordinary problem and solve it. Then you can help change the world.

Ed Price

Architecture Portfolio Lead, Google Cloud
Former Senior Program Manager of Architectural Publishing, Microsoft Azure
Co-Author of 7 Books, including **Meg the Mechanical Engineer**, **Hands-On Microservices with C# 8 and .NET Core 3** (co-written with Dr. Gaurav Aroraa), **The Azure Cloud Native Architecture Mapbook**, and **ASP.NET Core 5 for Beginners**

DEDICATED TO

To our beloved uncle, Lt Dr. Madhukar Achyutrao Kulkarni, his vision and understanding of life have always inspired me. His ideology has also helped me a lot while authoring the book. I want to dedicate this book to everything I learned from him to envision life and all the lovely memories that I spent with him in various temples of Maharashtra, Bharat.

- Sachin Kr Gupta

I want to dedicate this book to all my colleagues who helped and motivated me to write it. A special thanks to my friend Dr Gaurav Arora, who always acts as a catalyst for me.

- Praveen Kumar Sharma

To my loving son Shreyas Parasuram, who is pursuing MBBS, his caring nature and commitment to overcoming challenges have always admired me. With immense pride and endless support, I dedicate this book to him as he forge a legacy of healing and understanding.

- Gayathri Gopalakrishnan

I want to dedicate this book to Upendra Khatri, one of the most lovable members of our family. He always inspires me to believe in myself regardless of any situation. While writing this book, I faced numerous challenges, but his words always supported me. This book is a testament to his encouragement.

- Gaurav Aroraa

ACKNOWLEDGMENT

Writing and publishing a book is a project that requires the full dedication and effort of all authors and the publisher team. First and foremost, I would like to express my heartfelt gratitude to my dear friend and co-author, Dr. Gaurav Aroraa. This book is not just an outcome of our collaboration but a testament to his unwavering belief in me and his encouragement that I could be an author. I am also deeply indebted to my family and friends. Their support and constructive feedback were invaluable in helping me write this book. A special gratitude to ARCCHIE Publications for their support, expertise, and commitment to making this book a reality. Lastly, this book is for all the readers.

- Sachin Kr Gupta

ABOUT THE AUTHORS

Sachin Kr Gupta is a seasoned project manager with more than two and a half decades of industry experience in multiple domains, such as banking and telecommunications. His expertise lies in coordinating complex projects, ensuring timely delivery, and maintaining the highest quality standards.

Praveen K Sharma is a visionary leader with over two decades of industry experience in Database and Project management, Delivery, and customer relations. He has been involved in multiple on-site and offshore assignments, including client-facing interactions and Delivery. He has managed projects that drive a large workforce in multicultural environments across locations. With strong leadership skills, his expertise spans Strategy Consulting, Enterprise Transformation, Analyst Communications, and more.

Gayathri Gopalakrishnan is a results-driven solution architect with extensive experience in spreading solutions management, design, development, implementation, and testing. She is a recognized leader in applying high-impact technical solutions to significant business objectives with capabilities transcending boundaries. She is adept at working with management to prioritize activities and achieve defined project objectives, and she can translate business requirements into technical solutions. She received the IBM Tech 2023 Award for her extensive contribution to various disciplined technologies.

Gaurav Aroraa is a professional with over 27 years of industry experience. His impressive achievements, including being a MuleSoft Mentor, recipient of the Microsoft MVP award, and serving as a Mentor of Change with AIM NITI Aayog, Govt. of India, speak volumes about his expertise. Gaurav is also a Business Coach with Business Blaster, Govt. of NCT of Delhi, India. He holds a lifetime membership with the Computer Society of India (CSI) and serves as an advisory member and Senior Mentor at India Mentor. He is certified as a Scrum trainer and Coach, ITIL-F certified, and holds PRINCE-F and PRINCE-P certifications. He is also a certified Microsoft Azure architect, MuleSoft Platform Architect, MuleSoft Integration Architect, and a Microsoft Certified Azure Data Scientist Associate. He has authored books on various technologies. He actively mentors underprivileged students, and he is associated with the NGO SHIKSHA एक पहल.

You can reach Gaurav at:

Blog: ***https://gaurav-arora.com/blog/***

LinkedIn: ***https://linkedin.com/in/aroragaurav/***

ABOUT THE TECHNICAL REVIEWER

Ritu Mittal brings a wealth of experience, with a career spanning nearly 17 years in Engineering Software Systems across diverse industries. Her versatility is evident in her multiple roles and the successful delivery of a wide range of projects.

Currently, Ritu is working as a Project Manager in the Security space for IBM, leading a diverse and global team of more than 25+ on-role employees. She is responsible for server-level security for more than 150+ clients. In addition to this role, she has taken on the additional responsibility of guiding and mentoring multiple teams across various areas.

Ritu's commitment to uplifting diversity in IT is not just a role; it's a passion. As a leading member of her company's Diversity & Inclusion initiative for Delhi NCR, her impactful efforts have invariably been a source of pride and inspiration.

Her motto for leading via examples truly defies her journey.

ABOUT THE TECHNICAL EDITORS

Prasad Nutheti is a seasoned professional with over 15 years of experience in the industry. As a Senior Solution Architect specializing in SAP MM (Materials Management), Prasad has demonstrated exceptional expertise in designing and implementing robust solutions that drive business efficiency and innovation. His extensive knowledge and hands-on experience have made him a trusted advisor in the field, known for his strategic insights and practical approach to complex challenges.

Kaushal Mehta is an Associate Professor at Bhai Parmanand DSEU Shakarpur Campus-II, with over 28 years of experience in his field. His extensive knowledge and dedication to education have made him a respected figure in academia. Throughout his career, Kaushal has been committed to fostering a deep understanding of his subject matter among students and peers.

PREFACE

Welcome to Python Programming Demystified: A Clear and Concise Guide. This book has been meticulously crafted to be your reliable companion for learning Python.

This book aims to bridge the gap for those desiring to start their industry careers. It is based on a simple yet profound idea—to make Python learning accessible, practical, and enjoyable. We understand that diving into programming can be daunting, and we aim to make this transition as smooth as possible.

Unlike typical Python textbooks that often complicate concepts with jargon and theoretical examples, we've taken a distinct approach. Complex ideas are distilled into plain language, complemented by practical, real-world examples. Whether you're laying the foundation for your programming knowledge or honing your existing skills, this book provides comprehensive coverage to suit your needs.

Python Programming Demystified is designed for a diverse audience, including students, developers, and aspiring data analysts. No matter your background, if you're looking to harness the power of Python, you'll find valuable insights and guidance within these pages. Python's versatility and power can open a world of possibilities, and our book is here to guide you every step of the way.

This book is a testament to learners like you who want to learn and leverage Python's capabilities. Your desire for knowledge and dedication to learning Python inspire us. We thank you for embarking on this journey with us. Together, let's demystify Python and unlock its potential.

Let's embark on this journey of learning together.

What's Inside This Book

Chapter 1: Introduction to Python Programing sets the stage by emphasizing the importance of programming skills. It highlights Python's significance in the technical industry and provides an overview of what readers can expect from the book.

Chapter 2: Basics of Python dives into Python syntax, variables, data types, and basic operations. Learn how to handle user input and display output in Python programs.

Chapter 3: Program Flow in Python explores conditional statements and loops in Python and explains how to control program flow based on different conditions and loops.

Chapter 4: Functions and Modules delves into defining and using functions in Python and discusses modular coding, which uses modules to organize code efficiently.

Chapter 5: Exception Handling explains the importance of handling errors and exceptions in Python programs and describes techniques for ensuring smooth program execution, even in unexpected errors.

Chapter 6: File Handling discovers how to read from and write to files in Python. Understand file modes, manipulate text files, and work with file objects.

Chapter 7: Generators & Iterators delves into generators and iterators. Explains how to create efficient generators and work with iterators to handle data sequences.

Chapter 8: Data Structures explores essential data structures in Python, including lists, tuples, and dictionaries, and understands their properties and usage scenarios-wise.

Chapter 9: Collections explores the power of the Python collections module. Understand data structures like Deque, Counter, NamedTuple, and OrderedDict.

Chapter 10: GUI Development Using Python explains and helps to start with GUI development using Python. Explains different components of GUI in Python with a simple application.

Chapter 11: Basics of Database with Python delves into and explains how to interact with SQL databases using Python. It also explains different ways to query data and explains basic database operations.

Chapter 12: Introduction to Python Threading explores the concept of multithreading in Python and explains how to create and manage threads for concurrent programming.

Chapter 13: Regular Expression: an overview uncovers the world of regular expressions for text pattern matching. Explains how to use regex for various tasks.

Chapter 14: Basics of Artificial Intelligence provides an introductory glimpse into the world of artificial intelligence using Python and explains fundamental concepts and their use cases.

For Whom This Book Is Intended

This book is designed for:

- Beginners and individuals with no prior programming experience.
- Students are seeking to build a robust foundational understanding of Python.
- Professionals from non-technical backgrounds are looking to start in Python programming.
- Developers are looking to transition to Python from other languages.
- Professionals in diverse industries are eager to leverage Python skills.

Download the source code and colored images:

To download the source code bundle

and the colored images, please follow the link

OR

scan the QR Code

https://l1nq.com/9788196612702

Errata

At **ARCCHIE Publications**, we are committed to delivering the highest-quality content in all our publications. We follow best practices to ensure the accuracy of our content to provide our readers with an indulgent reading experience. We believe and understand that our readers are our best judges, and we always use their input and feedback from time to time to improve human errors, if any, that may occur during the publishing processes involved. We invite you to participate in our errata submission process to ensure our books remain accurate and up to date. Please help us reach out to readers who might have difficulties due to unforeseen errors. Please write to us at ***errata@arcchieonline.com***.

When submitting errata, please include the following information:

- Book Title
- Reference#
- Author(s)
- Page Number
- Description of the Error
- Suggested Correction (if applicable)

The **ARCCHIE Publications** Family highly appreciates your support, suggestions, and feedback.

Sharing Your Perspective and Providing Feedback

Your perspective is invaluable to us, as it helps us enhance our content and gather your feedback. We warmly welcome all forms of feedback. Please feel free to send us an email at **feedback@arcchieonline.com**, mentioning the book title in the subject line of your message.

Book Review Invitation

We kindly invite you to share your thoughts. After you've read and engaged with this book, consider leaving a review on the platform where you acquired it. Your impartial feedback can greatly assist potential readers in making informed decisions. Your reviews provide valuable insights for us at **Arcchie**, helping us better understand your perspectives on our products, and they offer authors the chance to appreciate your feedback on their work.

PIRACY

Should you encounter unauthorized reproductions of our publications in any digital format on the internet, we kindly request your assistance in pinpointing their locations or website sources. Please reach out to us at **copyright@arcchieonline.com** and include a link to the infringing material.

If you possess expertise in a particular subject and wish to participate in the creation or contribution to a book, please visit ***authors.arcchieonline.com***. We welcome you and assist you to start your authorship journey with **ARCCHIE PUBLICATIONS**.

JOIN US ON THE ARCCHIE PUBLICATIONS DISCORD SERVER

Connect with fellow readers, authors, and enthusiasts to discuss all things related to our publications and the exciting world of AI, programming, and learning. Share your insights, ask questions, and engage in vibrant discussions to expand your knowledge and inspire creativity. Take advantage of this opportunity to be part of a dynamic community dedicated to exploring the frontiers of technology and innovation. Join our Discord Server today and be part of the ARCCHIE Publications community!

https://discord.gg/z26SenmpEt

Notes

Date:

Chapter 1 Introduction to Python Programming

In today's digital age, programming skills have become indispensable. Whether you're a student, a professional, or someone with a keen interest in technology, having a solid understanding of programming opens a world of opportunities. From developing software applications to automating tasks and analyzing data, programming skills empower individuals to innovate, problem-solve, and create solutions for real-world challenges.

Python has emerged as one of the most popular and versatile programming languages. Known for its simplicity, readability, and extensive libraries, Python has found its place in various domains, including web development, data science, artificial intelligence, and more. Its user-friendly syntax makes it an ideal choice for beginners, while its powerful features make it a favorite among seasoned developers.

In this book, we aim to equip you with the fundamental knowledge and practical skills needed to become proficient in Python programming. Whether you're a complete novice or someone looking to enhance your existing skills, this book will guide you through the basics of Python, provide hands-on examples, and introduce you to advanced topics to help you excel in your programming journey.

In this chapter, we will cover:

- Importance of Programming Skills
- The Role of Python in the Technical Industry
- Getting Started with Python

Importance of Programming Skills

When we talk about programming skills, it is important to note that technical industry in a lot of things to finalize the and automating the various processes. Which requires not only business knowledge but also skills in programming. Here are the few points which guides what is the importance of Programming skills:

- `Problem-solving`: Programming skills enable individuals to break down complex problems into smaller, more manageable components and develop algorithms to solve them. For example, a software engineer might use programming skills to develop an algorithm for optimizing route planning in a transportation system.
- `Automation`: Programming allows individuals to automate repetitive tasks, saving time and reducing errors. For instance, a data analyst might use programming skills to automate the process of cleaning and analysing large datasets.
- `Innovation`: Programming skills empower individuals to innovate and create new solutions to address various challenges. For example, a software developer might use programming skills to create a mobile app that revolutionizes how people manage their finances.
- `Career Opportunities`: Proficiency in programming opens a wide range of career opportunities across industries such as software development, data science, cybersecurity, and artificial intelligence. For example, a machine learning engineer with strong programming skills might develop algorithms to improve recommendation systems for an e-commerce platform.
- `Critical Thinking`: Programming encourages individuals to think critically and logically, helping them develop problem-solving skills that are valuable in various aspects of life, not just in the technical field. For example, a student learning programming might develop logical thinking skills that benefit them in mathematics and science subjects.

To understand these points in more detail let's consider an example- suppose you're a marketing analyst tasked with analyzing customer data to identify trends and insights. By learning programming skills, you can automate data analysis processes, perform advanced statistical analysis, and visualize data more effectively, leading to more informed marketing strategies and improved business outcomes.

The role of Python in the Technical Industry

Python has gained immense popularity in the technical industry due to its versatility, simplicity, and extensive libraries. Its role in various domains includes:

- `Web Development`: Python frameworks like Django and Flask are widely used for building web applications. Example: Instagram, a popular social media platform, uses Django for its backend development.
- `Data Science and Machine Learning`: Python's rich ecosystem of libraries such as NumPy, pandas, and scikit-learn make it the preferred choice for data analysis, machine learning, and artificial intelligence applications. Example: Spotify uses machine learning algorithms developed in Python to personalize music recommendations for its users.
- `Scientific Computing`: Python is used extensively in scientific computing for tasks such as simulation, data analysis, and visualization. Example: NASA uses Python for data analysis and visualization in space exploration projects.
- `Automation and Scripting`: Python's simplicity and readability make it ideal for automating tasks and writing scripts. Example: System administrators use Python scripts to automate routine system maintenance tasks and manage infrastructure.
- `Education and Research`: Python's ease of learning and extensive documentation make it a popular choice for teaching programming and conducting research in academia. Example: Universities use Python in computer science courses to teach fundamental programming concepts.

Suppose you're a data scientist working for a retail company. You can leverage Python's libraries like pandas and scikit-learn to analyze sales data, forecast future demand, and build predictive models to optimize inventory management and pricing strategies.

Getting started with Python programming

In this section, we will set up an environment to start with Python Programming. If you already have environment setup, you can skip this section.

- In this step, we will install Python on Windows Operating System (you can choose your operating system; steps maybe differ). Go to ***https://www.python.org/*** click on download, refer **`Figure 1.1`**

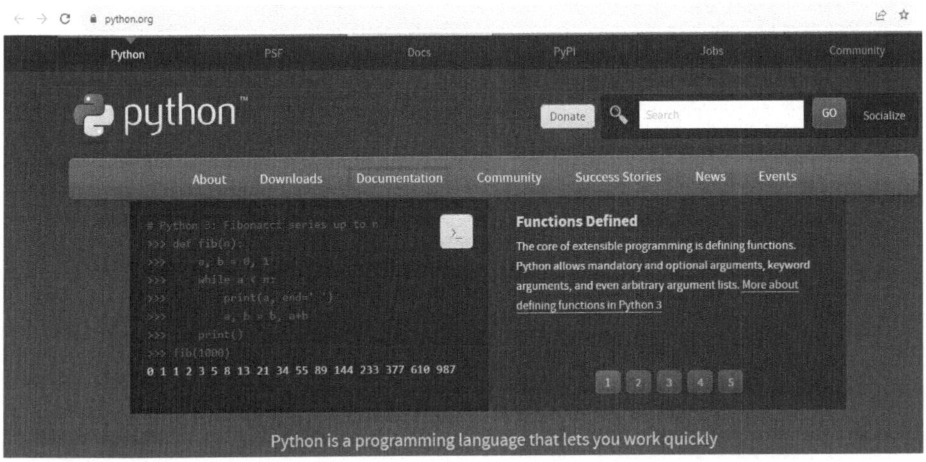

***Figure 1.1**: Official website of Python*

- Select on Python version under Download for Windows, refer **Figure 1.2**

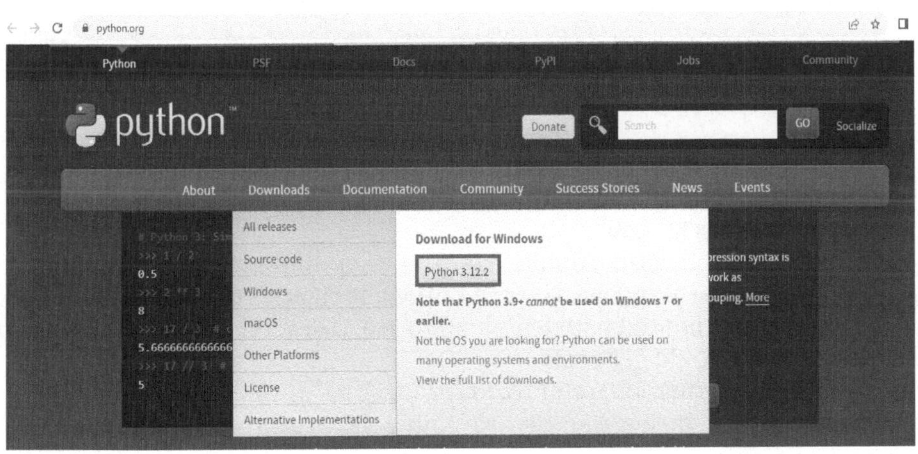

***Figure 1.2**: Download for Windows*

- Go to your download folder and click **Python executable**; it opens the installation wizard.
- Click the check boxes **Use admin privileges** when installing **py.exe** – it is required to elevated privileges during installation; and Add **python.exe** to

path - by checking this option you can run python commands from anywhere within your operating system (e.g. **`console window`**) ,
Refer **`Figure 1.3`**

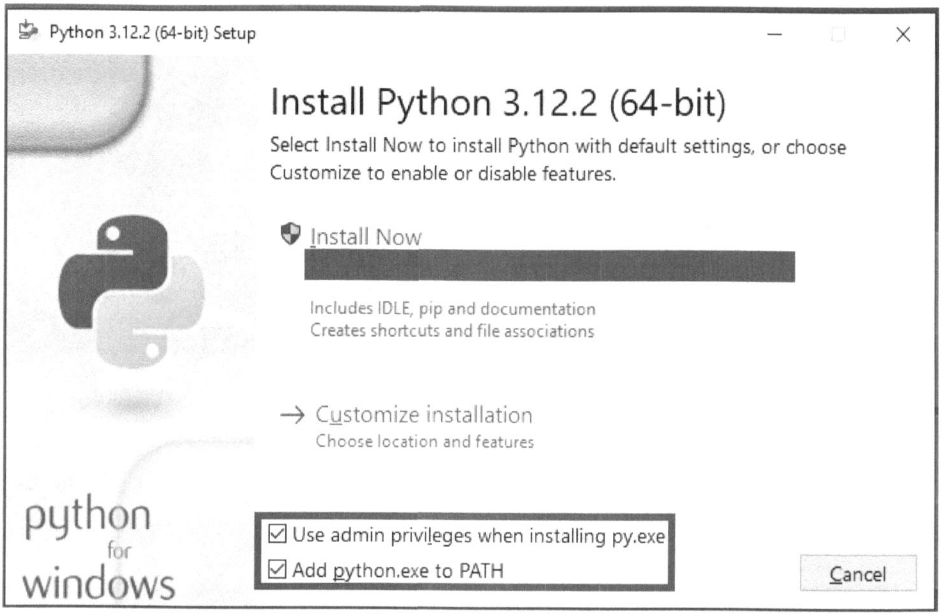

`Figure 1.3`: *Install Python*

- Optionally you can Customize installation.
- Click on **`Install Now`**
- You will see the Setup complete (**`Figure 1.4`**) windows once installation is completed. For Windows you can optionally remove the **`MAX_PATH`** limitations. Windows has limited path length up to **`260 characters`** hence for longer path length; you would get error.
- For more information, refer to: ***`https://docs.python.org/3/using/windows.html#removing-the-max-path-limitation`***

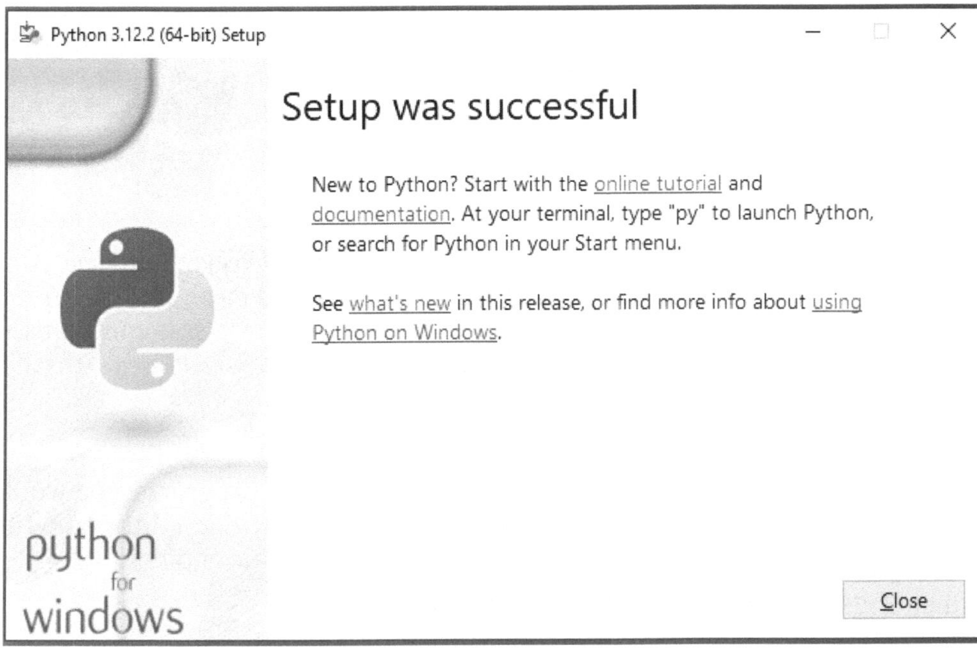

Figure 1.4: *Setup completed*

- Verify the installation with one liner code. At this stage, do not think about the syntax or code, we will discuss in next **Chapter 2 Basics of Python**.
- Open notepad and type following code. Save file as **firstcode.py**

```
print("Hello there, Python is installed on your System.")
```

- Open Windows Command prompt, go to the folder/directory where you saved **firstcode.py** file and type following; you would see output as appeared in **Figure 1.5**

```
python firstcode.py
```

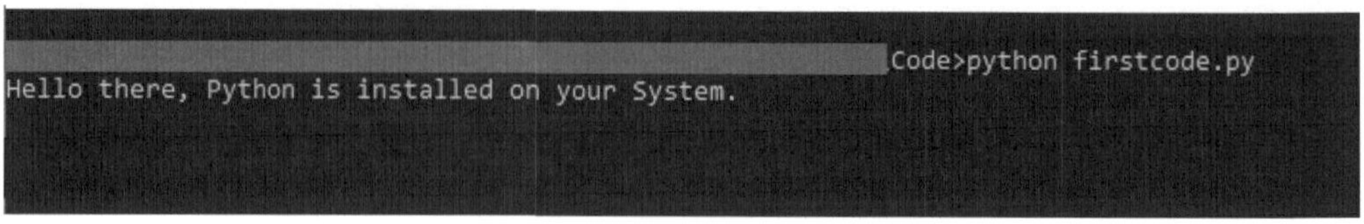

Figure 1.5: *Output of firstcode.py*

In the last step you may encounter a long file path error, if you missed selecting the relevant option, discussed in preceding steps. In this case, you can either rerun the installation and select the appropriate option or you can edit the installation settings as detailed here: ***https://docs.python.org/3/using/windows.html#removing-the-max-path-limitation***

We used notepad to write our short code but for complex programs; you would require a code editor like **Visual Studio code** (I used VS Code editor to write code examples in the book). You can use any editor of your choice.

To Install **Visual Studio Code**; follow these steps:

- Go to ***https://code.visualstudio.com/***
- Click on Download for Windows, refer **Figure 1.6**

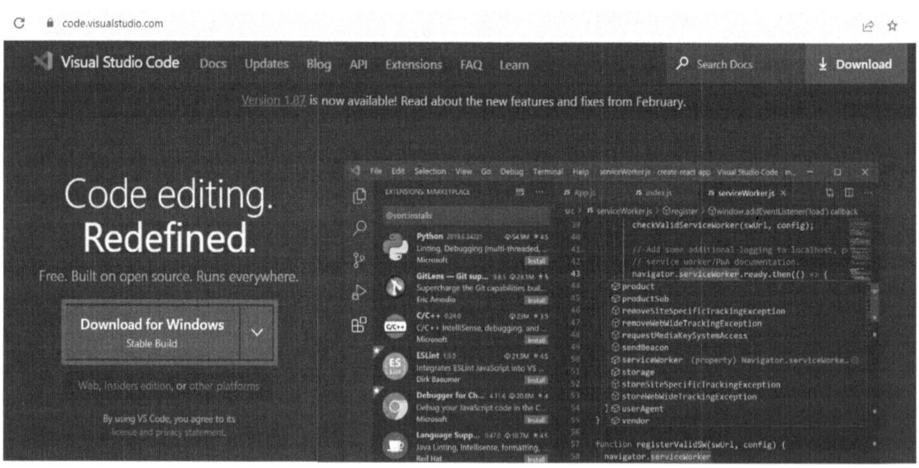

Figure 1.6: *Download Visual Studio Code*

- Go to the folder where you downloaded the setup file and double click on the setup file to start Setup wizard. Check **I accept the agreement** and click on **Next**, refer **Figure 1.7**

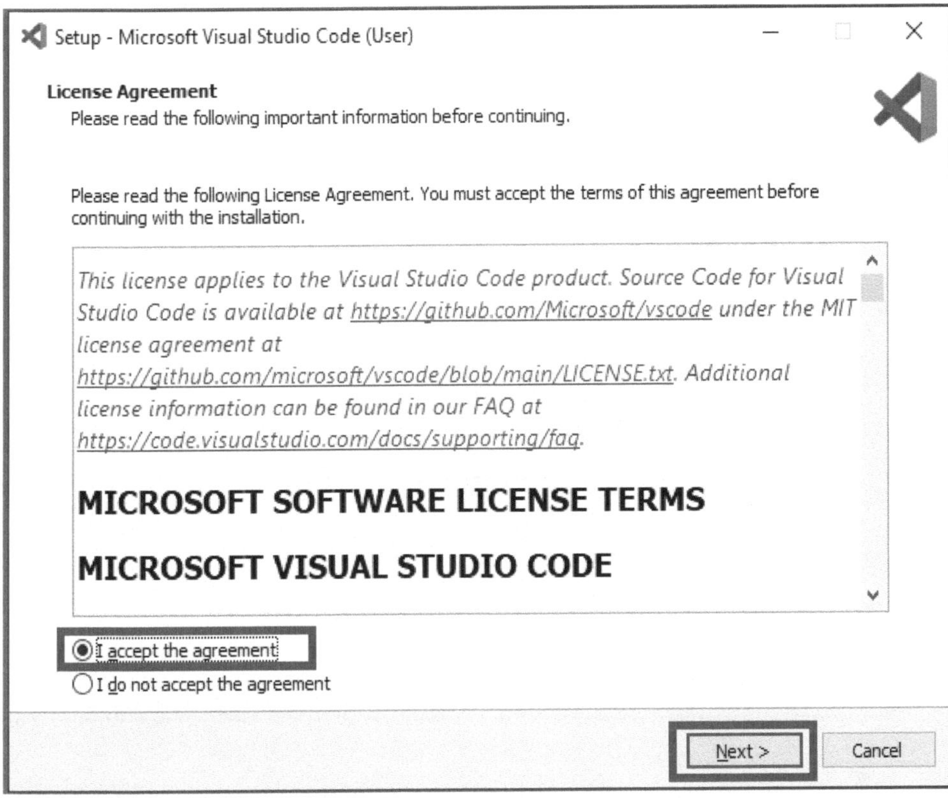

Figure 1.7: *Accept agreement*

- Select all checkboxes and click on **Next**, refer **Figure 1.8**

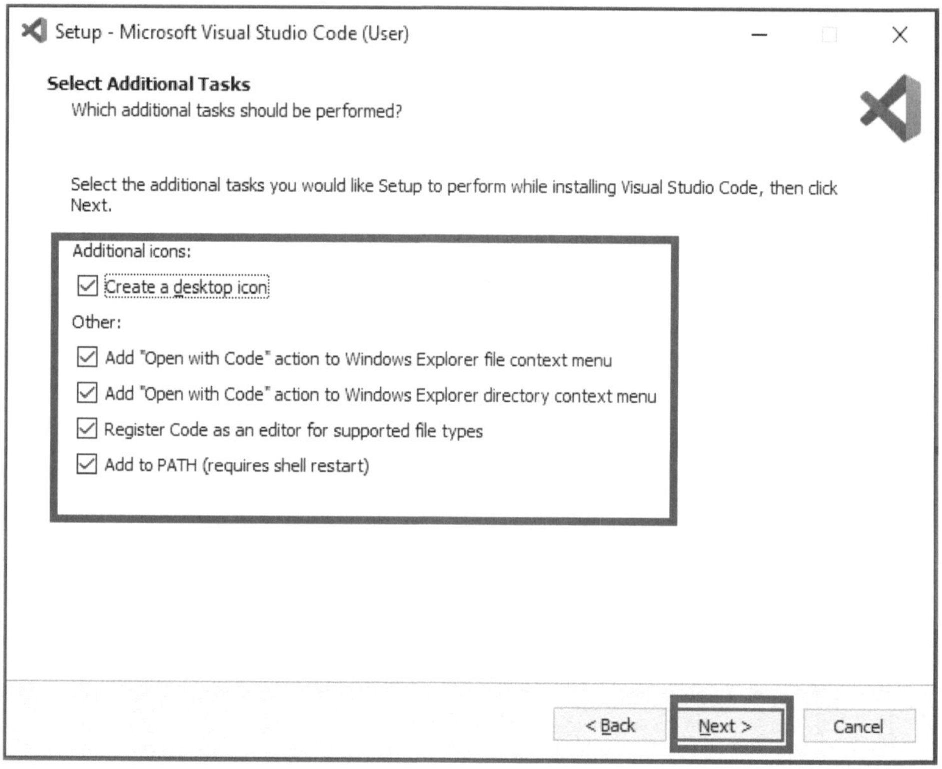

Figure 1.8: *Select additional tasks and start installation*

- Next, ready to install screen will appear, verify, and click on **Install**, refer **Figure 1.9**

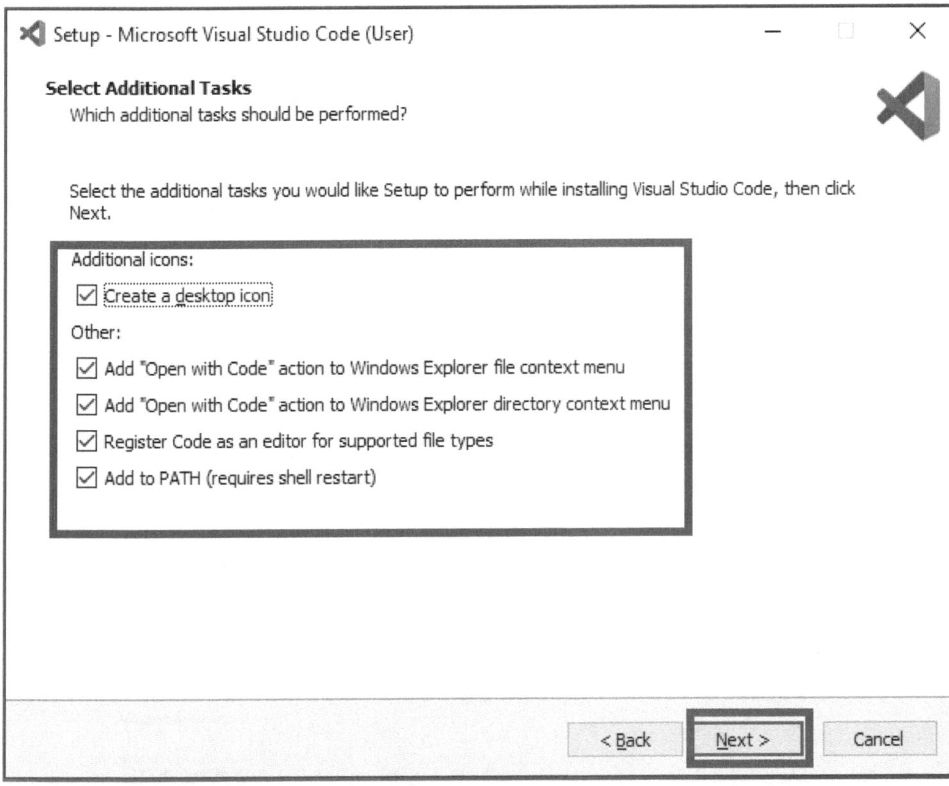

Figure 1.9: *Ready to Install*

- Click on **Finish**, keep **Launch Visual Studio Code** checkbox checked, refer **Figure 1.10**

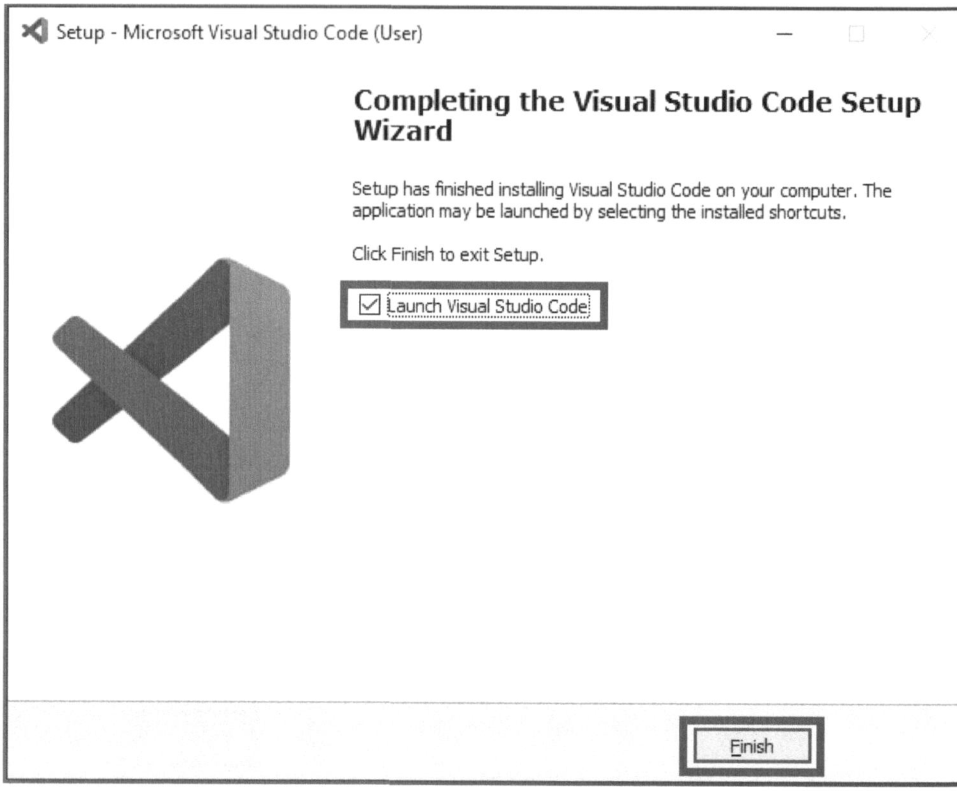

Figure 1.10: *Complete the Visual Studio Code Setup Wizard*

- From **Visual Studio Code** click on **File** | **Open File** or **ctrl+O** and select the file **firstcode.py** from the folder where you saved this file. You may be prompted for trust file issue, ignore this warning, and click on **Open**, refer **Figure 1.11**

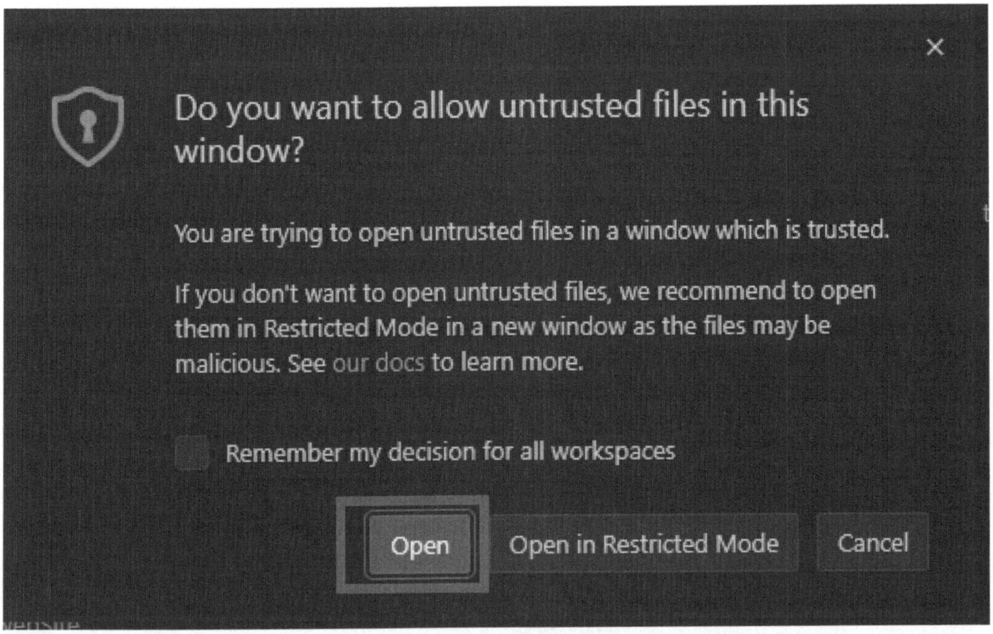

Figure 1.11: *Allow file (untrusted files warning)*

- You may prompt to install the Python plugin/extension. Go to extension and install **Python**, refer **Figure 1.12**

Figure 1.12: *Python Extension*

- Move to your **firstcode.py** tab from **Visual Studio Code**
- Click on **Run** | **Run Without Debugging** or press **crtl+F5**
- You would see the result in **Terminal window**, refer **Figure 1.13**

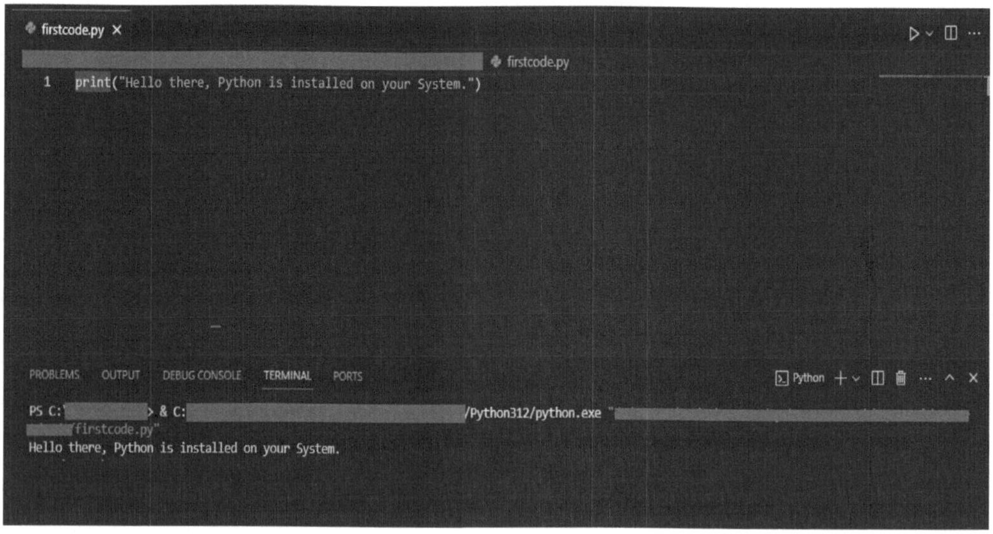

Figure 1.13: *Output of Python Program*

In this section, we have setup **Python** and **Visual Studio Code** as our preferred Editor to write Python programs.

Conclusion

In the growing technical era, Python Programming is one of the best choices which covers a broad spectrum of technologies. In this chapter, we get introduced with Python Programming and understood its various aspects by covering:

- Understanding the Role of Programming Skills: We delved into why programming skills are essential in today's digital landscape and how they can empower individuals to tackle complex problems and drive innovation.
- Recognizing Python's Relevance: We explored why Python has become the go-to language for developers worldwide, its applications across different industries, and the advantages it offers over other programming languages.

In next chapter, we will understand more about Python programming and will cover basics of Python with the help of code examples; including getting started with Python, learning the basics of Python syntax, working with data structures, and exploring advanced concepts such as object-oriented programming and web development.

Exercise: Test Your Understanding

Answer the following questions and test your understanding of learning from `Chapter 1`:

`Q. 1.` Why are programming skills essential in today's job market?

`Q. 2.` How do programming skills contribute to problem-solving abilities?

`Q. 3.` What impact do programming skills have on innovation?

`Q. 4.` How can programming skills improve efficiency in the workplace?

`Q. 5.` In what ways can programming skills enhance collaboration and communication within a team?

`Q. 6.` Why is Python considered a crucial programming language in the technical industry?

`Q. 7.` How does Python contribute to the field of data science and analytics?

`Q. 8.` What are some key industries that heavily rely on Python for their operations?

`Q. 9.` In what ways has Python influenced the development of artificial intelligence and machine learning?

`Q. 10.` What makes Python an attractive language for startups and new tech companies?

`Q. 11.` What are the first steps to take when starting to learn Python?

`Q. 12.` Which resources are recommended for beginners learning Python?

`Q. 13.` How can beginners practice their Python skills effectively?

`Q. 14.` What are some common pitfalls to avoid when learning Python for the first time?

`Q. 15.` How important is it to understand Python libraries and frameworks early in the learning process?

Notes Date:

Chapter 2

Basics of Python

In this chapter, we will lay the foundation by exploring the basics of Python syntax, variables, data types, and input/output operations. Whether you're new to programming or looking to refresh your knowledge, this chapter will equip you with essential skills to write and understand Python code effectively.

Python, known for its simplicity and readability, is a versatile programming language used in a wide range of applications, from web development to data science and artificial intelligence. Understanding the basics of Python is crucial for building a solid programming foundation and unlocking the full potential of this powerful language.

Throughout this chapter, we will dive deep into the core concepts of Python syntax and structure. You will learn about the rules and conventions that govern Python code, including indentation, comments, and statement structure. By grasping these fundamental principles, you'll be able to write clean, organized, and easily understandable Python code.

Next, we will explore variables and data types in Python. Variables are placeholders that store data values, and understanding how to define and manipulate variables is essential for writing dynamic and flexible programs. We will cover different data types in Python, including integers, floats, strings, lists, tuples, and dictionaries, and learn how to perform operations on them.

Basic operations and operators play a crucial role in Python programming, allowing us to perform arithmetic, comparison, logic, and assignment operations on data. We will delve into the various operators available in Python and understand how to use them effectively to manipulate data and control program flow.

Handling user input and displaying output are essential skills in Python programming. We will learn how to prompt users for input, process their responses, and present results in a clear and user-friendly manner. Understanding input/output operations will enable you to create interactive and engaging Python programs that interact with users effectively.

Throughout the chapter, we will explore code examples and practical exercises to reinforce your understanding of Python fundamentals. By the end of this chapter, you will have mastered the basics of Python syntax, variables, data types, and input/output operations, setting the stage for your journey into more advanced Python programming concepts.

In this chapter, we will cover:

- Python Syntax and Structure
- Variables and Data Types
- Basic Operations and Operators
- Input and Output Handling

Python Syntax and Structure

Python syntax and structure form the backbone of the Python programming language, defining the rules and conventions for writing code that the Python interpreter can understand and execute. Understanding Python syntax is essential for writing clear, concise, and efficient code that accomplishes desired tasks effectively.

At its core, Python syntax is designed to be simple and easy to read, making it accessible to beginners and experienced programmers alike. One of the key principles of Python syntax is the use of indentation to define code blocks. Unlike other programming languages that use braces or keywords to delineate blocks of code, Python uses indentation with spaces or tabs to indicate the beginning and end of code blocks. This indentation-based syntax enhances code readability and encourages consistent coding practices.

Python statements are written one per line and do not require semicolons to terminate them, contributing to the language's clean and minimalist syntax. Additionally, Python is case-sensitive, meaning that uppercase and lowercase letters are treated as distinct characters. Therefore, variable names, function names, and keywords must be spelled and capitalized consistently throughout the code.

Python syntax also includes various elements such as variables, data types, operators, and control structures that enable programmers to manipulate data and control program flow. Variables are used to store and manipulate data values, while data types define the nature of the data being stored, such as integers, floats, strings, lists, tuples, dictionaries, and more. Python provides a rich set of built-in data types and allows users to define custom data types through classes and objects.

Python syntax also encompasses control structures, including conditional statements (if, elif, else) and loops (for, while), which allow programmers to make decisions and execute code repetitively based on specific conditions. Conditional statements evaluate conditions and execute different code blocks accordingly, while loops iterate over sequences or execute code until a certain condition is met. Mastering control structures is essential for writing flexible and efficient Python programs that respond dynamically to changing inputs and conditions.

Consider the below code:

```
# Program to calculate the area of a rectangle


# Define the dimensions of the rectangle

length = 5

width = 3


# Calculate the area of the rectangle

area = length * width


# Display the result

print("The area of the rectangle is:", area)
```

Explanation of Python Syntax and Structure based on the preceding code-example:

- Comments: Comments in Python are denoted by the '#' symbol. They are used to provide explanations or annotations within the code. In the above program, comments are used to describe the purpose of each section of code.
- Variables: Variables are used to store data values. In the program, 'length' and 'width' are variables that store the dimensions of the rectangle.
- Assignment Operator (=): The assignment operator (=) is used to assign values to variables. For example, 'length = 5' assigns the value 5 to the variable 'length'.
- Expressions: Expressions are combinations of values and operators that evaluate to a single value. In the program, 'length * width' is an expression that calculates the area of the rectangle by multiplying the length and width.
- Print Statement: The print() function is used to display output to the console. In the program, the print statement displays the calculated area of the rectangle.
- Indentation: Python uses indentation to define code blocks. In the program, the lines of code within the main block are indented by four spaces. This indentation indicates that they are part of the main block of code.
- Syntax Rules: Python syntax follows specific rules and conventions. For example, statements must be written one per line, and indentation must be consistent throughout the code. Failure to adhere to these rules can result in syntax errors.

You can try to execute the code and try variations of the code by changing the values.

Variables and Data Types

In Python programming, variables are used to store and manipulate data values.

Variables

A variable is like a container that holds a particular piece of information, allowing programmers to reference and modify it throughout the program. Variables provide a way to manage and work with data dynamically, enabling programs to perform calculations, make decisions, and interact with users.

Declaring Variables

In Python, variables are declared by assigning a value to a name using the assignment operator (=).

Consider following code-snippet:

```
num = 10

name = "Sachin Gupta"
```

In the preceding code-snippet, `num` and `name` are variables, and 10 and "Sachin Gupta" are their respective values. Python is dynamically typed, meaning that variable types are determined automatically based on the values assigned to them.

Rules to naming variables

To ensure proper usage and adherence to coding conventions, there are certain rules and guidelines to follow when naming variables:

Variable Names

Variable names can consist of letters (`a-z, A-Z`), digits (`0-9`), and underscores (_). Variable names cannot start with a digit. They must begin with a letter or an underscore. Variable names are case-sensitive, meaning 'name', 'Name', and 'NAME' are treated as distinct variables.

Naming Conventions

Variables should have descriptive names that reflect their purpose or content. Use lowercase letters for variable names to improve readability and consistency. For multi-word variable names, use underscores to separate words (e.g., `'first_name', 'total_count'`). Avoid using reserved keywords or built-in function names as variable names to prevent conflicts and confusion.

Readability and Clarity

Choose meaningful and intuitive variable names that convey the purpose or intent of the variable. Avoid using single-letter variable names (e.g., 'x', 'y') except in cases where their meaning is clear from context (e.g., loop counters).

Use camelCase or PascalCase conventions for naming variables in situations where it aligns with the coding style or project guidelines.

Consistency

Maintain consistent naming conventions throughout the codebase to enhance readability and maintainability. Follow established naming conventions and coding standards adopted by the project or development team.

Examples of Valid Variable Names:

```
name = "Sachin Gupta"

age = 30

total_students = 100

is_active = True

first_name = "Sachin"

last_name = "Gupta"
```

Examples of Invalid Variable Names:

```
3name = "Sachin"  # Variable name cannot start with a digit

my-variable = 10  # Hyphens are not allowed in variable names

class = "Python"  # 'class' is a reserved keyword
```

By adhering to these rules and best practices, developers can write clean, readable, and maintainable Python code, facilitating collaboration and reducing the likelihood of errors or misunderstandings. Consistent and meaningful variable naming is essential for creating code that is easy to understand, debug, and maintain over time.

Data Type

Python supports various built-in data types, each representing different kinds of data and allowing different operations to be performed on them.

Some common data types in Python include:

Data Type	Description	Example
Int	Integer numbers (whole numbers)	10, -5, 100
float	Floating-point numbers (real numbers with decimals)	3.14, -0.5, 2.0
str	Strings (sequences of characters)	"hello", 'Python', "123"
bool	Boolean values (True or False)	True, False
list	Ordered collections of items (mutable)	[1, 2, 3], ['a', 'b', 'c']
Tuple	Immutable collections of items	(1, 2, 3), ('a', 'b', 'c')
Dict	Key-value pairs	{'name': Sachin, 'age': 30}
Set	Unordered collections of unique elements	{1, 2, 3}, {'a', 'b', 'c'}

Table 2.1: Data types in Python

Consider the following code:

```
# Integer

integer_var = 10



# Float

float_var = 3.14



# Complex

complex_var = 3 + 4j
```

```
# String
string_var = "hello"

# List
list_var = [1, 2, 3, "a", "b", "c"]

# Tuple
tuple_var = (4, 5, 6, "d", "e", "f")

# Dictionary
dict_var = {'name': 'Sachin', 'age': 30, 'city': 'New Delhi'}

# Set
set_var = {1, 2, 3, 4, 5}

# Boolean
bool_var = True

# None
none_var = None

# Displaying the values and types of variables
print("Integer:", integer_var, type(integer_var))
print("Float:", float_var, type(float_var))
```

```
print("Complex:", complex_var, type(complex_var))

print("String:", string_var, type(string_var))

print("List:", list_var, type(list_var))

print("Tuple:", tuple_var, type(tuple_var))

print("Dictionary:", dict_var, type(dict_var))

print("Set:", set_var, type(set_var))

print("Boolean:", bool_var, type(bool_var))

print("None:", none_var, type(none_var))
```

This program initializes variables of each main data type in Python and prints out their values and types. By running this program, you can see how each data type is represented and used in Python.

```
D:\Code>python code-data-type.py

Integer: 10 <class 'int'>
Float: 3.14 <class 'float'>
Complex: (3+4j) <class 'complex'>
String: hello <class 'str'>
List: [1, 2, 3, 'a', 'b', 'c'] <class 'list'>
Tuple: (4, 5, 6, 'd', 'e', 'f') <class 'tuple'>
Dictionary: {'name': 'Sachin', 'age': 30, 'city': 'New Delhi'} <class 'dict'>
Set: {1, 2, 3, 4, 5} <class 'set'>
Boolean: True <class 'bool'>
None: None <class 'NoneType'>
```

Figure 2.1: *output of code-data-type.py*

The preceding `Figure 2.1` displays the output of all the variables declared in the program.

Basic Operations and Operators

In Python programming, basic operations and operators are fundamental concepts that allow programmers to perform various mathematical and logical operations on data values. Understanding these operations and operators is essential for writing effective and efficient Python code.

Arithmetic Operators

Python supports the following arithmetic operators for performing mathematical calculations:

- `Addition (+)` Adds two operands together to produce their sum.
- `Subtraction (-)` Subtracts the second operand from the first operand to produce their difference.
- `Multiplication (*)` Multiplies two operands together to produce their product.
- `Division (/)` Divides the first operand by the second operand to produce their quotient.
- `Floor Division (//)` Divides the first operand by the second operand and returns the integer quotient (rounded down).
- `Modulus (%)` Divides the first operand by the second operand and returns the remainder.
- `Exponentiation (**)` Raises the first operand to the power of the second operand.

Consider following Code-snippet:

```
x = 10

y = 3

print("Addition:", x + y)         # Output: 13

print("Subtraction:", x - y)      # Output: 7

print("Multiplication:", x * y) # Output: 30

print("Division:", x / y)         # Output: 3.3333333333333335

print("Floor Division:", x // y)# Output: 3

print("Modulus:", x % y)          # Output: 1

print("Exponentiation:", x ** y)# Output: 1000
```

Comparison Operators

Comparison operators are used to compare the values of two operands and return a Boolean value (`True or False`) based on the comparison result. Common comparison operators include:

- **`Equal to (==)`** Returns True if the operands are equal, otherwise False.
- **`Not equal to (!=)`** Returns True if the operands are not equal, otherwise False.
- **`Greater than (>)`** Returns True if the first operand is greater than the second operand, otherwise False.
- **`Less than (<)`** Returns True if the first operand is less than the second operand, otherwise False.
- **`Greater than or equal to (>=)`** Returns True if the first operand is greater than or equal to the second operand, otherwise False.
- **`Less than or equal to (<=)`** Returns True if the first operand is less than or equal to the second operand, otherwise False.

Consider following code-snippet:

```
a = 5

b = 10

print("Equal to:", a == b)            # Output: False

print("Not equal to:", a != b)        # Output: True

print("Greater than:", a > b)         # Output: False

print("Less than:", a < b)            # Output: True

print("Greater than or equal to:", a >= b) # Output: False

print("Less than or equal to:", a <= b)    # Output: True
```

Logical Operators

Logical operators are used to perform logical operations on Boolean values. The common logical operators include:

- **`Logical AND (and)`** Returns True if both operands are True, otherwise False.
- **`Logical OR (or)`** Returns True if at least one of the operands is True,

otherwise False.

- `Logical NOT (not)` Returns the opposite Boolean value of the operand.

Consider following code-snippet:

```
x = True

y = False

print("Logical AND:", x and y)     # Output: False

print("Logical OR:", x or y)       # Output: True

print("Logical NOT:", not x)       # Output: False
```

Understanding and mastering basic operations and operators in Python is crucial for performing mathematical calculations, making logical decisions, and controlling the flow of program execution. These fundamental concepts serve as building blocks for writing complex and efficient Python programs.

Input and Output Handling

Input and output (I/O) handling in Python refers to the process of interacting with external sources of data (input) and displaying information to the user (output) within a Python program. Effective I/O handling is essential for building interactive and user-friendly applications that can accept user input, process it, and provide meaningful output.

Input Handling

Input handling involves obtaining data from external sources such as the user, files, or other programs, and incorporating that data into the Python program for processing. The most common method of obtaining user input in Python is through the `input()` function. When called, the `input()` function displays a prompt to the user and waits for them to enter data from the keyboard. Once the user presses the `Enter` key, the input data is returned as a string and can be assigned to a variable for further processing.

Consider following code-snippet:

```
name = input("Enter your name: ")

print("Hello,", name)
```

In this example, the `input()` function prompts the user to enter their name, and the input data is stored in the variable `name`. The program then prints a greeting message using the user's input.

Output Handling

Output handling involves presenting information, results, or messages to the user in a readable format. Python provides several methods for outputting data, including the `print()` function, file operations, and standard output redirection.

The `print()` function is the most commonly used method for displaying output in Python. It takes one or more arguments and prints them to the standard output (usually the console) separated by spaces. Additionally, the `print()` function supports formatting options such as string concatenation and formatting specifiers for precise control over the output format.

Consider following code-snippet:

```
age = 30

print("Your age is:", age)
```

File I/O Handling

Python also supports reading from and writing to files, enabling programs to interact with external files for data storage, retrieval, and manipulation. File I/O handling involves opening files, reading data from them, writing data to them, and closing files once the operation is complete. Python provides built-in functions such as `open(), read(), write(), and close()` for file I/O operations. This topic will be discussed in detail in upcoming `Chapter 6 File Handling`

Conclusion

In this chapter, we embarked on a journey to explore the fundamentals of Python programming. We delved into Python syntax and structure, learning how to write clean and readable code. By understanding variables and data types, we gained the ability to store and manipulate different types of data efficiently. Basic operations and operators allowed us to perform mathematical and logical operations on our data, empowering us to solve a variety of problems. Furthermore, we mastered input and output handling, enabling us to interact with users through our programs and display information effectively.

Through code examples and practical exercises, we solidified our understanding of Python fundamentals and sharpened our programming skills. By grasping fundamental Python syntax, understanding variable usage, performing operations on data types, and mastering input and output operations, we laid a strong foundation for our Python journey ahead.

In the next chapter, we will dive deeper into the realm of program flow in Python. We will explore conditional statements such as if, elif, and else, learning how to control the flow of our programs based on different conditions. Additionally, we will delve into the concept of loops, including for and while loops, to automate repetitive tasks and iterate over collections of data. By understanding if-else statements, using logical operators, and implementing loops effectively, we will gain the ability to create more complex and dynamic Python programs. Through examples and practical usage, we will apply our newfound knowledge to solve real-world problems and further expand our Python skills.

Exercise: Test Your Understanding

Answer the following questions and test your understanding of learning from **Chapter 2**:

Q. 1. What is the significance of indentation in Python, and how does it affect the code structure?

Q. 2. How would you write a simple if-else statement in Python to check if a number is positive or negative?

Q. 3. What are the different data types available in Python?

Q. 4. Write a Python program to add two numbers.

Q. 5. What is the difference between the == operator and the = operator in Python?

Q. 6. Write a simple program in Python that takes user input and displays it on the screen.

Notes

Date:

Chapter 3
Program Flow in Python

In this chapter, we will delve into the fascinating realm of program flow in Python. Program flow is the sequence in which instructions are executed within a program, and mastering it is crucial for writing efficient and logical code. Throughout this chapter, we will explore conditional statements and loops, which are fundamental constructs for controlling the flow of execution in Python programs.

Throughout this chapter we will understand and learn the concepts of:

- Understanding if-else statements and logical operators for decision-making.
- Implementing loops for automating repetitive tasks.
- Exploring the interaction between conditional statements and loops to dictate program flow.

Program flow in Python refers to the sequence in which instructions are executed within a program. Controlling program flow is essential for writing efficient and logical code that performs tasks in a specific order and responds appropriately to different conditions. In Python, program flow is primarily managed through conditional statements and loops.

Conditional statements, such as if, elif, and else, allow programs to make decisions based on certain conditions. These statements evaluate expressions and execute different blocks of code based on the outcome. For example, an if statement can be used to check if a condition is true and execute a specific block of code if it is, while an else statement can be used to execute a different block of code if the condition is false. Additionally, elif statements provide a way to check multiple conditions sequentially.

Loops are another crucial aspect of program flow in Python. They allow programs to repeat a block of code multiple times, automating repetitive tasks and processing collections of data. Python supports two main types of loops: for loops and while loops. For loops iterate over a sequence of elements, such as lists or strings, executing a block of code for each item in the sequence. On the other hand, while loops continue iterating as long as a specified condition remains true, providing more flexibility in looping behavior.

By effectively using conditional statements and loops, programmers can control the flow of execution in their Python programs, directing the program's actions based on different conditions and requirements. This ability to manage program flow enables the creation of more dynamic, responsive, and versatile applications that can adapt to various scenarios. Understanding program flow is essential for writing clean, maintainable, and efficient Python code, and mastering these concepts is a crucial step in becoming a proficient Python programmer.

In this chapter, we will cover:

- Conditional Statements
- Looping with for and while
- Control Flow in action

Conditional Statements

Conditional statements in Python are essential constructs that allow programmers to control the flow of execution in their programs based on certain conditions. These statements enable the creation of dynamic and responsive programs that can adapt to different scenarios. In this note, we will explore the concept of conditional statements in Python, including how to write programs using conditional statements, the different types of conditional statements available, and how flow statements can affect the execution of code.

Exploring Types of Conditional Statements

In this section, we will delve into different conditional statements and understand their working with the help of small code snippets:

- The **if** Statement

The **if** statement is the most basic form of conditional statement in Python. It allows you to execute a block of code only if a specified condition is true.

Consider following code:

```
# Get input from the user

number = int(input("Enter a number: "))


# Check if the number is positive

if number > 0:

    print("The number is positive.")


# Check if the number is negative

if number < 0:

    print("The number is negative.")


# Check if the number is zero

if number == 0:

    print("The number is zero.")
```

The preceding program prompts the user to enter a number using the **input()** function. The input is then converted to an integer using the **int()** function and stored in the variable number.

The **if** statement is used three times in succession to independently check if the number is positive, negative, or zero. Each **if** statement checks a single condition:

- The first **if** statement checks if the number is greater than 0 (number > 0). If true, it prints "**The number is positive.**"
- The second **if** statement checks if the number is less than 0 (number < 0). If true, it prints "**The number is negative.**"
- The third **if** statement checks if the number is equal to 0 (number == 0). If true, it prints "**The number is zero.**"

Here every **if** statement checks condition independently, so multiple messages may be printed depending on the value of the input number.

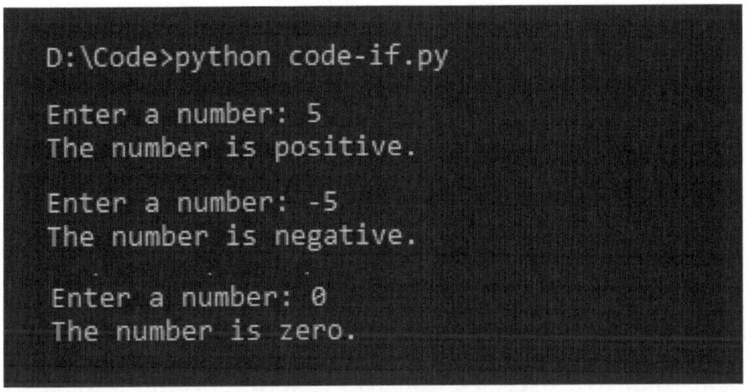

***Figure 3.1**: output of code-if.py*

The preceding **Figure 3.1** displays the output for all the possible 3-inputs from the user; the result may differ as per your input to the above program.

- The **else** Statement

The 'else' statement follows an 'if' statement and provides an alternative action to take if the condition specified in the 'if' statement is false. It is used to execute a block of code when the 'if' condition evaluates to false.

Consider the following code:

```
# Get input from the user
number = int(input("Enter a number: "))

# Check if the number is positive or Zero
if number >= 0:
    print("The number is positive or Zero.")

# else the number is negative
else:
    print("The number is negative.")
```

The preceding code has 3 main blocks:

- **`Get input from the user`**: The **`input()`** function prompts the user to enter a value. The value entered by the user is then converted to an integer using the **`int()`** function to ensure it can be treated as a numerical value. The result is stored in the variable number.

- **`Check if the number is positive or Zero`**: The '**`if`**' statement is used to evaluate a condition. In this case, the condition is number >= 0, which checks if the value of number is greater than or equal to 0. If the condition evaluates to True (meaning the number is greater than or equal to 0), the indented block of code under the 'if' statement is executed. In this block, the program prints the message "The number is positive or Zero." indicating that the number entered by the user is either positive or zero.

- **`Else the number is negative`**: If the condition specified in the 'if' statement evaluates to False (meaning the number is less than 0), the indented block of code under the 'else' statement is executed. In this block, the program prints the message "The number is negative." indicating that the number entered by the user is negative.

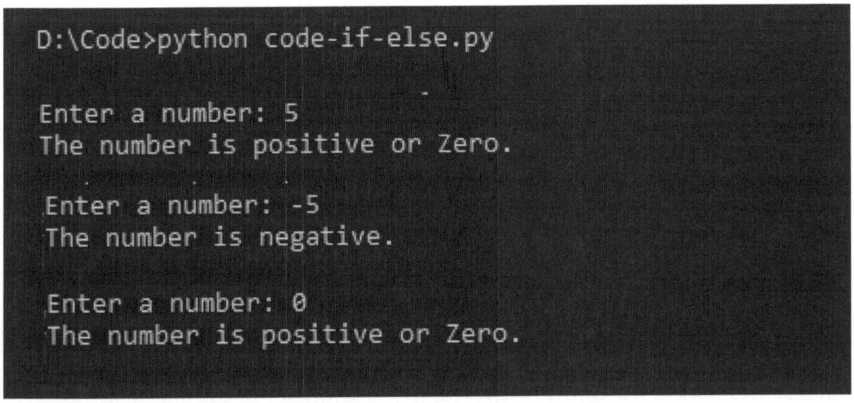

`Figure 3.2`: *output of code-if-else.py*

The preceding **`Figure 3.2`** displays the output for all the possible 3-inputs from the user; the result may differ as per your input to the above program.

- Nested **`if..else`** Statements

Nested if...else statements in Python allow for the creation of conditional structures within other conditional structures. This means that you can have an if...else statement inside another if or else block.

Consider the following code:

```
# Get input from the user

number = int(input("Enter a number: "))


# Check if the number is positive, negative, or zero

if number >= 0:

    # Check if the number is positive

    if number > 0:

        print("The number is positive.")

    # If the number is not positive, it must be zero
```

```
    else:
        print("The number is zero.")
else:
    print("The number is negative.")
```

The program prompts the user to enter a number using the **input()** function, and the input is converted to an integer using the **int()** function. The result is stored in the variable number.

The outer **if...else** statement checks if the number is greater than or equal to 0. If true, it means the number is either positive or zero, and the corresponding block of code is executed.

Inside the outer if block, there is another **if...else** statement. This nested **if...else** statement checks if the number is greater than **0**. If true, it prints "**The number is positive**." If false, it means the number is zero, so it prints "**The number is zero**."

If the outer if statement evaluates to false, it means the number is negative, so the else block of the outer **if...else** statement is executed, printing "**The number is negative**."

Nested **if...else** statements can be useful for handling more complex conditional logic where different levels of conditions need to be evaluated.

However, it's essential to maintain readability and avoid excessive nesting to keep the code clean and understandable.

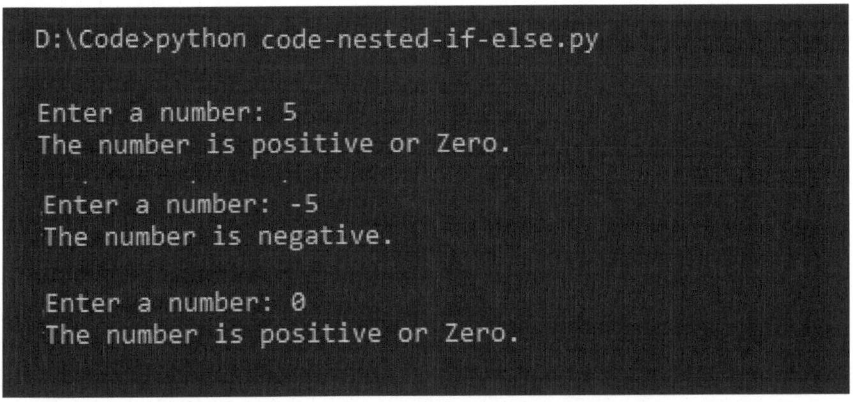

`Figure 3.3`: *output of code-nested-if-else.py*

The preceding **`Figure 3.3`** displays the output for all the possible 3-inputs from the user; the result may differ as per your input to the above program.

- The **`if-elif-else`** Statement
  The 'elif' statement allows you to specify additional conditions to check if the condition in the 'if' statement is false. It stands for "else if". It is used when you have multiple conditions to evaluate.

Consider the following code:

```
# Get input from the user

number = int(input("Enter a number: "))


# Check if the number is positive, negative, or zero

if number > 0:

    print("The number is positive.")

elif number < 0:

    print("The number is negative.")
```

```
else:

    print("The number is zero.")
```

The program prompts the user to enter a number using the input() function. The input is then converted to an integer using the int() function and stored in the variable number.

The 'if' statement is used to check the value of the number variable. The condition number > 0 checks if the number is greater than 0. If the condition is true, the corresponding block of code under the 'if' statement is executed, printing "The number is positive."

If the condition in the 'if' statement is false, the 'elif' statement is evaluated. The condition number < 0 checks if the number is less than 0. If true, it prints "The number is negative."

If neither the 'if' nor 'elif' conditions are true, the 'else' statement is executed, printing "The number is zero." This covers the case when the number entered by the user is exactly 0.

This program effectively demonstrates the use of the 'if' statement to make decisions based on conditions and provides a simple example of how to determine the sign of a number.

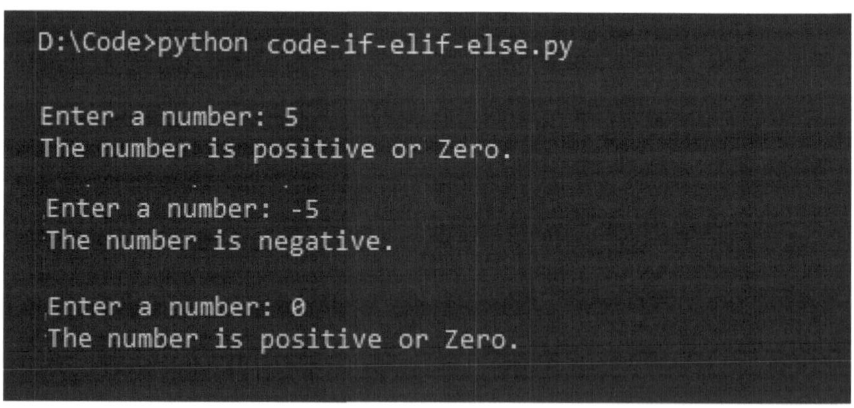

Figure 3.4: *output of code-if-elif-else.py*

The preceding **Figure 3.4** displays the output for all the possible 3-inputs from the user; the result may differ as per your input to the above program.

- Ternary Expression
  A ternary expression, also known as a conditional expression, is a concise way to write conditional statements in Python. It allows you to evaluate a condition and return one of two values based on the result of the condition.

Consider the following code:

```
# Get input from the user

number = int(input("Enter a number: "))


# Check if the number is positive, negative, or zero

result = "The number is positive or Zero." if number >= 0 else "The number is negative."


# Print the final output

print(result)
```

The preceding code has three blocks, explained as:

- **Get input from the user**: The program uses the input() function to prompt the user to enter a number. The input() function displays the message "Enter a number: " to the user, and the user is expected to enter a numerical value. The entered value is then converted to an integer using the int() function to ensure that it can be treated as a numerical value. The result is stored in the variable number.

- **Check if the number is positive, negative, or zero**: The program uses a ternary expression to evaluate the condition number >= 0. If the condition is true (i.e., if number is greater than or equal to 0), the expression "The number is positive or Zero." is assigned to the variable result. If the condition is false (i.e., if number is negative), the expression "The number is negative." is

assigned to the variable result.
The ternary expression serves as a concise way to perform the conditional check and assign a value to the variable result based on the condition.

- `Print the result`: The program then prints the value of the variable result using the print() function. Depending on the value of number, the printed message will indicate whether the number is positive or zero if it's non-negative, or it will indicate that the number is negative if it's less than 0.

```
D:\Code>python code-ternary.py

Enter a number: 5
The number is positive or Zero.

Enter a number: -5
The number is negative.

Enter a number: 0
The number is positive or Zero.
```

***Figure 3.5**: output of code-if-elif-else.py*

The preceding `Figure 3.5` displays the output for all the possible 3-inputs from the user; the result may differ as per your input to the above program.

Best Practices to Use Conditional Statements

When writing code that involves conditional statements, it's essential to follow best practices to ensure readability, maintainability, and reliability.

Here are some recommendations for using conditional statements effectively:

- `Use meaningful variable names and clear conditions`: Choose descriptive names for your variables that convey their purpose and the condition they represent. This makes your code more readable and understandable for other developers. Additionally, ensure that your conditions are clear and concise, avoiding ambiguity.
- `Avoid excessive nesting`: Excessive nesting of conditional statements can make code difficult to understand and maintain. Whenever possible, refactor

nested if...else statements into separate functions or use logical operators to simplify conditions. This helps reduce complexity and improves the overall structure of your code.

- `Use comments for complex logic`: If you encounter complex conditions or unusual logic in your code, use comments to explain the reasoning behind them. This helps other developers (and your future self) understand why certain decisions were made and how the code operates. Clear and informative comments can significantly enhance the readability and maintainability of your codebase.
- `Test thoroughly`: Before deploying your code to production, ensure that you thoroughly test it under different scenarios and edge cases. This includes testing for both expected and unexpected inputs to verify that your conditional statements behave as intended. Testing helps uncover bugs and ensures that your code functions correctly in various situations, providing confidence in its reliability.

By following these best practices, you can write cleaner, more readable code that is easier to understand, maintain, and debug. Effective use of conditional statements contributes to the overall quality and robustness of your software, leading to better outcomes for both developers and end-users.

Looping with `for` and `while`

Looping with 'for' and 'while' statements in Python provides a powerful mechanism for iterating over sequences of data, performing repetitive tasks, and controlling program flow. These constructs allow you to execute blocks of code repeatedly, either for a fixed number of times or until a specific condition is met.

The `for` Loop

In Python, the '`for`' loop is a fundamental construct used for iterating over sequences of data, such as lists, tuples, strings, and dictionaries. It allows you to execute a block of code repeatedly, once for each item in the iterable object. The 'for' loop is versatile and widely used for various programming tasks, including data processing, iteration, and automation.

Consider following code-example:

```
# Iterate over a list of numbers
numbers = [1, 2, 3, 4, 5]
for num in numbers:
    print(num)
```

In the preceding code example, the 'for' loop iterates over each element in the list 'numbers'. In each iteration, the variable 'num' takes on the value of the current element, and the 'print()' function is called to print the value of 'num'. As a result, this loop will print each number in the list 'numbers' on a separate line.

The for loop can also be used iterate the characters in a string; consider following code-snippet:

```
# Iterate over a string
text = "Hello, World!"
for char in text:
    print(char)
```

This loop will iterate over each character in the string 'text' and print it on a separate line. It demonstrates the flexibility of the 'for' loop in handling different types of iterable objects.

Consider the following code snippet, which uses range() built-in-function to generates a sequence of numbers:

```
# Iterate over a range of numbers
for num in range(1, 6):
    print(num)
```

In the preceding code-example, the '`range()`' function generates a sequence of numbers from `1` to `5` (inclusive), and the '`for`' loop iterates over each number in the sequence, printing it on a separate line. The '`range()`' function is useful for creating sequences of numbers with specific start, stop, and step values.

The `for` loop can also be used with `enumerate()` - The '`enumerate()`' function is used to iterate over both the index and value of items in a sequence simultaneously. It returns a tuple containing the index and value of each item in the sequence. This is useful when you need to access both the index and value of elements in a list or other `iterable` object:

Consider the following code-snippet:

```
# Define a list of fruits

fruits = ["apple", "banana", "cherry", "date"]


# Iterate over the list using enumerate() and a for loop

for index, fruit in enumerate(fruits):

    print("Index:", index, "Fruit:", fruit)
```

In the preceding code-example, we have a list called fruits containing several fruit names. We use the `enumerate()` function within a '`for`' loop to iterate over the fruits list. The `enumerate()` function returns an iterator containing tuples, where each tuple consists of an index and the corresponding item from the `iterable`. Inside the '`for`' loop, we unpack each `tuple` into two variables: `index` and `fruit`. The `index` variable holds the index of the current item in the list, and the `fruit` variable holds the value of the current item. We then print the `index` and the `fruit` name for each iteration of the loop.

The while Loop

The 'while' loop in Python is a versatile construct used to execute a block of code repeatedly if a specified condition evaluates to true. It allows programmers to create iterative processes where the loop continues until a certain condition becomes false. This makes the 'while' loop suitable for scenarios where the number of iterations is not predetermined or when the loop needs to run indefinitely until a condition is met.

One common use case of the 'while' loop is implementing iterative processes that require dynamic termination conditions. For example, suppose we want to find the smallest integer 'n' such that the sum of integers from 1 to 'n' exceeds a certain threshold.

We can use a 'while' loop to achieve this:

```
threshold = 100

total = 0

n = 0


while total <= threshold:

    n += 1

    total += n


print("The smallest integer n such that the sum exceeds", threshold,
"is", n)
```

In the preceding example, the loop continues to execute as long as the 'total' sum is less than or equal to the 'threshold' value. Inside the loop, we increment the value of 'n' and add it to the 'total' sum. Once the sum exceeds the threshold, the loop terminates, and the program prints the value of 'n'. Another common use of the 'while' loop is creating interactive programs that prompt the user for input until a specific condition is met.

For instance, consider a simple guessing game where the user must guess a secret number:

```
import random


secret_number = random.randint(1, 100)
```

```
guess = 0

while guess != secret_number:
    guess = int(input("Guess the secret number (between 1 and 100): "))
    if guess < secret_number:
        print("Too low! Try again.")
    elif guess > secret_number:
        print("Too high! Try again.")

print("Congratulations! You guessed the secret number:", secret_number)
```

In the preceding example, the loop continues until the user correctly guesses the secret number. Inside the loop, the program prompts the user for input, compares the guess with the secret number, and provides feedback based on the comparison. Once the guess matches the secret number, the loop terminates, and the program congratulates the user.

It's essential to ensure that the loop's termination condition eventually becomes false to prevent infinite loops, which can lead to program crashes or freezes. Additionally, care should be taken to avoid off-by-one errors or unintentional infinite loops by thoroughly testing the loop's logic and termination conditions.

The **'break'**, **'continue'**, and **'pass'** statements are used to control the flow of execution within loops and conditional blocks.

Break Statement

The **'break'** statement is used to exit a loop prematurely, stopping further iterations even if the loop's condition has not been met. When the 'break' statement is encountered within a loop (such as a 'for' or 'while' loop), the loop is immediately terminated, and control is transferred to the next statement after the loop.

Consider the following code-snippet:

```
for num in range(5):
    if num == 3:
        break
    print(num)
```

In the preceding code-snippet, the loop will print numbers from `0` to `2` and then terminate when `'num'` becomes equal to `3`.

Continue Statement

The **`'continue'`** statement is used to skip the current iteration of a loop and proceed to the next iteration. When the 'continue' statement is encountered within a loop, the remaining code in the loop's body for the current iteration is skipped, and the loop proceeds to the next iteration.

Consider the following code-snippet:

```
for num in range(5):
    if num == 2:
        continue
    print(num)
```

In the preceding code-snippet, the loop will print numbers from 0 to 4, skipping the number 2.

Pass Statement

The `'pass'` statement is a null operation that does nothing when executed. It is used as a placeholder where syntactically a statement is required but no action needs to be taken. The `'pass'` statement is often used as a placeholder for code that will be added later.

Consider the following code-snippet:

```
for num in range(5):
    if num == 2:
        pass
    else:
        print(num)
```

In the preceding code-snippet, the 'pass' statement is used to indicate that no action should be taken when num is equal to `2`, while the **'else'** block prints all other numbers from `0` to `4`.

Best Practices to Use Loop Statements

When using loop statements in Python programs, it's essential to follow best practices to ensure code readability, maintainability, and efficiency.

Here are some recommended practices for using loop statements effectively:

- Use Meaningful Variable Names: Choose descriptive variable names that accurately convey the purpose of the loop and the variables used within it. This makes the code easier to understand for other developers and for future reference.
- Keep the Loop Body Concise: Write concise and focused code within the loop body, avoiding unnecessary complexity or nesting. Each loop iteration should ideally perform a single task or operation, enhancing readability and maintainability.
- Avoid Infinite Loops: Ensure that loop termination conditions are correctly defined to prevent infinite loops. Check that the condition will eventually become false or that there is a mechanism to break out of the loop when necessary.
- Minimize Redundant Code: Refactor duplicate or redundant code outside of the loop whenever possible. This reduces code duplication and enhances efficiency.
- Use Built-in Functions and Tools: Leverage built-in functions and tools provided by Python, such as list comprehensions, generator expressions, and the itertools module, to simplify and optimize loop constructs.
- Consider Performance: Be mindful of the performance implications of loop constructs, especially when dealing with large datasets or performance-sensitive applications. Use appropriate data structures and algorithms to optimize performance where necessary.

- Use Generators for Memory Efficiency: When dealing with large datasets or infinite sequences, consider using generator functions or generator expressions instead of traditional loops to conserve memory and improve efficiency.
- Test Thoroughly: Test loop constructs thoroughly with various inputs and edge cases to ensure correctness and robustness. Consider using automated testing frameworks to streamline the testing process and catch potential issues early.
- Document Complex Logic: If the loop contains complex logic or unusual behavior, consider adding comments or docstrings to explain the purpose and functionality of the loop. This helps other developers understand the code and facilitates future maintenance.
- Follow PEP 8 Guidelines: Adhere to the Python Enhancement Proposal (PEP) 8 guidelines for code style and formatting, including indentation, spacing, and naming conventions. Consistent code style improves readability and consistency across projects.

Refer: **`https://peps.python.org/pep-0008/`** for complete information.

By following these best practices, you can write clean, efficient, and maintainable loop constructs in your Python programs, enhancing code quality and developer productivity.

Control Flow in Action

Control flow in Python refers to the order in which statements are executed in a program. It allows developers to control the flow of execution based on conditions, loops, and function calls. Understanding control flow is essential for writing programs that perform different actions based on specific conditions or requirements. In previous sections we have already discussed Conditional and Loop Statements which are Control Flow Statement in Python.

In this section, we will write a Python program using all the control flow discussed in this chapter. Consider the following program:

```
def main():

    while True:

        print("Select a control statement:")

        print("1. If statement")
```

```
print("2. For Loop")
print("3. While Loop")
print("4. Break statement")
print("5. Continue statement")
print("6. Pass statement")
print("Press 'x' to exit")

choice = input("Enter your choice: ")

if choice == 'x':
    print("Exiting program...")
    break
elif choice == '1':
    # If statement
    num = int(input("Enter a number: "))
    if num > 0:
        print("Number is positive")
    elif num < 0:
        print("Number is negative")
    else:
        print("Number is zero")
elif choice == '2':
    # For Loop
    fruits = ["apple", "banana", "cherry"]
```

```
        for fruit in fruits:
            print(fruit)
    elif choice == '3':
        # While loop
        count = 0
        while count < 5:
            print("Count:", count)
            count += 1
    elif choice == '4':
        # Break statement
        for i in range(5):
            if i == 3:
                break
            print(i)
    elif choice == '5':
        # Continue statement
        for i in range(5):
            if i == 2:
                continue
            print(i)
    elif choice == '6':
        # Pass statement
        for i in range(5):
            if i == 2:
```

```
                pass
            else:
                print(i)
    else:
        print("Invalid choice. Please try again.")
if __name__ == "__main__":
    main()
```

This program presents a menu to the user, allowing them to choose a specific control statement to execute. If the user enters 'x', the program exits. Otherwise, the program executes the chosen control statement and returns to the menu. Each control statement is demonstrated with a relevant example.

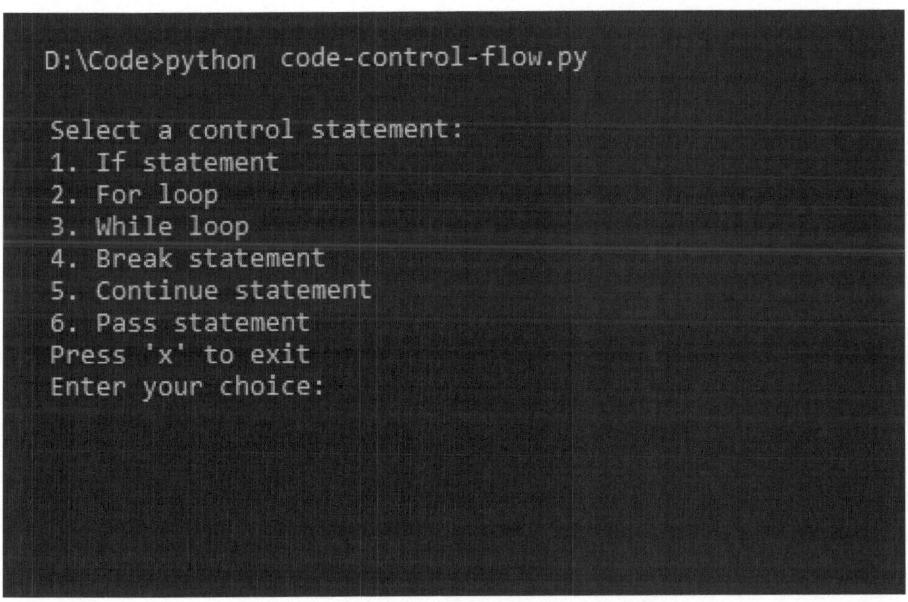

Figure 3.6: *output of code-control-flow.py*

The preceding `Figure 3.6` displays the output for all the possible inputs from the user; the result may differ as per your input to the above program.

Conclusion

Throughout this chapter, we explored the essential concepts of program flow in Python, including conditional statements and loops. We learned how to use if-else statements and logical operators to make decisions within our programs, as well as how to implement loops for automating repetitive tasks.

Through code examples and practical exercises, we solidified our understanding of Python fundamentals and sharpened our programming skills. By grasping fundamental Python syntax, understanding variable usage, performing operations on data types, and mastering input and output operations, we laid a strong foundation for our Python journey ahead.

In the next chapter, we will delve into defining and using functions in Python. Also, learn about modular coding using modules to organize code efficiently.

Exercise: Test Your Understanding

Answer the following questions and test your understanding of learning from `Chapter 3`:

`Q. 1.` What is a conditional statement, and why is it used in programming?

`Q. 2.` How does an if-else statement work in Python?

`Q. 3.` What is the purpose of elif in Python's conditional statements?

`Q. 4.` How can nested conditional statements be used in Python?

`Q. 5.` What are logical operators and how are they used in conditional statements?

`Q. 6.` What is a for loop and how does it work in Python?

`Q. 7.` What is the difference between a for loop and a while loop?

`Q. 8.` How can you use a break statement in a loop?

`Q. 9.` What is the purpose of the continue statement in a loop?

`Q. 10.` How do you use a while loop to create an infinite loop and how can you break out of it?

`Q. 11.` How do conditional statements and loops work together to control the flow of a program?

`Q. 12.` What is a nested loop and how can it be used in a program?

`Q. 13.` How can you use control flow statements to implement a simple menu-driven program?

`Q. 14.` How does the else clause work with loops in Python?

`Q. 15.` Can you provide an example of using both a for loop and a while loop within the same program?

Notes

Date:

JOIN US ON THE

ARCCHIE PUBLICATIONS

DISCORD SERVER

Connect with fellow readers, authors, and enthusiasts to discuss all things related to our publications and the exciting world of AI, programming, and learning. Share your insights, ask questions, and engage in vibrant discussions to expand your knowledge and inspire creativity. Take advantage of this opportunity to be part of a dynamic community dedicated to exploring the frontiers of technology and innovation. Join our Discord Server today and be part of the ARCCHIE Publications community!

https://discord.gg/z26SenmpEt

Chapter 4

Functions and Modules

In this chapter we will explore the foundational concepts of defining and using functions in Python. Functions are the building blocks of readable, maintainable, and reusable code. You will learn how to create functions, pass arguments, and return values. In addition to functions, this chapter covers Python modules, which allow for the modular organization of code for enhanced maintainability and readability.

In this chapter, we will cover:

- Introduction to Functions
- Defining and Calling Functions
- Function Parameters and Return Values
- Modular Coding with Modules
- Reusability and Organization

Introduction to Functions

Functions in Python are defined using the def keyword and are used to encapsulate a block of code that performs a specific task. This section introduces the concept of functions, why they are used, and the benefits they offer in terms of code organization and reusability.

In Python, a function is a block of code which only runs when it is called. Functions can receive data via parameters and can return data as a result.

Functions are defined using the **def** keyword, and they help in making code more organized, reusable, and scalable.

Following are the important 3-areas where functions play an important role:

- **Modularity**: Breaking down complex processes into smaller, manageable pieces.
- **Reusability**: Writing code once and using it many times.
- **Organization**: Keeping code separated and organized by functionality.

Basic Syntax of a Function:

```
def function_name(parameters):

    """Docstring explaining the function."""

    # code to execute

    return output
```

- def tells Python that you are defining a function.
- function_name is the name of the function.
- parameters are the variables to hold the input values.
- The indented block of code is the body of the function.
- return sends back the result of the function. If omitted, the function will return None.

Example 1: A Simple Function

Let's create a simple function that prints a greeting.

```
def greet():

    """Print a simple greeting."""

    print("Hello, welcome to Python functions!")
```

Code explanation:

- The greet function takes no parameters and prints a string when called.
- To call the function, you simply use its name followed by parentheses.
- Now, you can use or call this function as `greet()`

Example 2: Function with Parameters

Now, let's define a function that uses parameters to personalize the greeting.

```
def personalized_greet(name):

    """Print a personalized greeting."""

    print(f"Hello, {name}! Welcome to Python functions.")
```

Explanation:

- name is a parameter, which acts as a variable within the function.
- When calling this function, you provide a value for name.
- Call the function `personalized_greet("Praveen").`

Example 3: Function with Return Value

A function can also return a value back to the caller. Here's how you can return the greeting as a string instead of printing it.

```
def return_greeting(name):

    """Return a greeting string."""

    return f"Hello, {name}! This is a returned greeting."
```

Code explanation:

- The return statement sends the formatted string back to the caller.
- This allows the result to be stored in a variable or used in other expressions.
- Call function `return_greeting("Praveen")`

In these examples, you've seen how functions encapsulate behaviour that can be reused throughout your programs. Functions with parameters are more flexible, and functions that return values allow for more dynamic and interactive coding patterns.

Defining and Calling Functions

In Python, defining a function requires you to specify what task the function is meant to perform. This is done by encapsulating the task within a block of code. Once defined, the function can be executed, or "called," to perform its task whenever needed.

When you define a function, you are essentially creating a mini program within your program that can be executed on demand.

Example 1: Defining a Function to Add Two Numbers

```
def add(a, b):

    """Return the sum of two numbers."""

    sum = a + b

    return sum
```

Code explanation:

- add is the function name.
- a and b are parameters that the function expects to receive when it is called.
- The calculation a + b is performed within the function.
- The return keyword sends the result of the calculation back to the caller.
- To execute the function, you use the function name followed by parentheses and include the necessary arguments inside the parentheses.

Example 2: Calling the Add Function

```
result = add(5, 3)

print(result)
```

Code explnation:

- `add(5, 3)` calls the add function with arguments `5` and `3`.
- The function executes and returns the sum, which is stored in the result variable.
- `print(result)` then prints the value of result to the console.

Functions Without Return Values

Not all functions need to return a value. Some might perform an action that doesn't require sending data back.

Example 3: A Function That Prints Instead of Returns

```
def say_hello(name):

    """Print a greeting message to the console."""

    print(f"Hello, {name}!")
```

Code explanation:

- say_hello accepts a single parameter name.
- It does not return anything; instead, it directly prints a greeting message.
- Call function say_hello("Sachin")

Functions with Multiple Parameters

Functions can also be designed to take multiple parameters, allowing for more complex interactions.

Example 4: A Function with Multiple Parameters

```
def create_email(sender, recipient, subject, message):

    """Create a simple email format."""

    email = f"From: {sender}\nTo: {recipient}\nSubject: {subject}\n\
n{message}"

    return email
```

Code explanation:

- create_email takes four parameters.
- It constructs a string that formats these parameters into a simple email structure.
- The formatted email string is returned.

Through defining and calling functions, you can see how you can encapsulate complex logic within a simple interface, making your code more modular and maintainable. Functions can vary from performing a simple task like printing to the console, to carrying out complex operations with multiple parameters and returning sophisticated data structures.

Function Parameters and Return Values

Functions often take data, known as parameters, which influence their behavior. Similarly, they can return data as a result. This section explains how to define functions with parameters and what return values are, along with their significance.

Function parameters and return values are essential in Python as they allow functions to operate on different data and produce results. This section provides a deeper understanding of how to work with them effectively.

Parameters

Parameters are the variables listed inside the parentheses in the function definition. They act as placeholders for the data you can pass into the function. Parameters allow functions to accept input values at runtime, making them dynamic and reusable for different scenarios.

Example 1: Function with Parameters

```
def multiply(x, y):

    """Return the product of two numbers."""

    return x * y
```

Code explanation:

- multiply is a function that takes two parameters, x and y.
- These parameters are used within the function to calculate the product.
- The result of x * y is returned to the caller.

Default Parameters

You can also define default values for parameters. These are used if no argument is passed during the function call.

Example 2: Function with Default Parameters

```
def power(base, exponent=2):

    """Return the base raised to the power of exponent."""

    return base ** exponent
```

Code explanation:

- power function takes base and an optional exponent parameter, which defaults to 2 if not provided.
- It calculates the exponentiation using ** operator.

Keyword Arguments

When calling functions, you can specify arguments by the name of their corresponding parameters, allowing you to skip over default values or input them out of order.

Example 3: Using Keyword Arguments

```
def describe_pet(animal_type, pet_name):

    """Display information about a pet."""

    print(f"I have a {animal_type}. Its name is {pet_name}.")

describe_pet(animal_type='hamster', pet_name='Harry')

describe_pet(pet_name='Willow', animal_type='dog')
```

Return Values

The return statement in a function sends the function's result back to the caller. A function can return any type of object.

Example 4: Function Returning Multiple Values

Python functions can return multiple values in the form of tuples, lists, or dictionaries, which can be useful when you need to get several related items from a single function.

```
def get_user_info(username):

    """Return a tuple containing user information."""

    # Imagine that this function fetches user information from a
database

    email = f'{username}@example.com'
```

```
    user_id = username.upper()

    return email, user_id

# Unpacking the tuple returned by get_user_info

user_email, user_id = get_user_info('alice')

print(user_email, user_id)
```

Code explanation:

- `get_user_info` takes a username and simulates fetching associated email and user ID from a database.
- It returns both the email and user ID, which are unpacked into `user_email` and `user_id` variables.

Modular Coding with Modules

Modules are files containing Python definitions and statements intended for reuse. Discover how to create your own modules, import them into your scripts, and organize your codebase in a clean and efficient manner.

Modular coding is a practice that involves structuring your code into separate parts, each with a specific task or functionality. In Python, these parts are often contained in what are called modules. Modules are simply files with a .py extension that contain Python definitions and statements. They can define functions, classes, and variables that you can reuse in other Python scripts.

Followings are advantages with the use of Module:

- **Organization**: Keep your code organized by grouping related code into modules.
- **Reusability**: Use the functions, classes, or variables defined in a module in any Python program.
- **Namespace**: Avoid conflicts between identifiers of global objects.

Creating a Module

To create a module, simply save your code in a new file with a `.py` extension.

Example 1: Creating a Module

Suppose we have a file named math_operations.py with the following content:

```
# math_operations.py

def add(a, b):

    return a + b

def subtract(a, b):

    return a - b

def multiply(a, b):

    return a * b
```

Code explanation:

- math_operations.py defines three functions: add, subtract, and multiply.
- Each function performs a basic arithmetic operation.

Using a Module

You can use the module by importing it into your script. The import statement allows you to access the functions defined in the module.

Example 2: Importing and Using a Module

```
# main_program.py

import math_operations

result_add = math_operations.add(10, 5)

result_subtract = math_operations.subtract(10, 5)


print(result_add)         # Output: 15

print(result_subtract)    # Output: 5
```

Code explanation:

- import math_operations imports the module we created earlier.
- We then call the functions using math_operations.function_name.

Importing Specific Functions

Instead of importing the entire module, you can import specific functions from the module.

Example 3: Importing Specific Functions

```
from math_operations import add, multiply

result = add(20, 15)          # No need to use module name here

print(result)                 # Output: 35
```

Code explanation:

- from math_operations import add, multiply imports only the add and multiply functions.
- You can then use these functions directly without prefixing them with math_operations.

Module Initialization with __init__.py

In packages (a directory of modules), an __init__.py file is used to initialize a Python package. This file can be empty, or it can contain code to execute when the package is imported.

Example 4: Initializing a Package

Imagine you have the following package directory:

```
math_package/
|-- __init__.py
|-- arithmetic.py
|-- algebra.py
```

In `__init__.py`, you might want to import specific modules so that they are available when the package is imported:

```
# __init__.py in math_package
```

```
from .arithmetic import add, subtract

from .algebra import solve_quadratic
```

Now, when you import **math_package**, you can directly access add, subtract, and **solve_quadratic**.

Example 5: Importing from a Package

```
# main_program.py

from math_package import add, solve_quadratic

sum = add(3, 4)

solution = solve_quadratic(1, -5, 6)

print(sum)           # Output: 7

print(solution)      # Output: (3.0, 2.0)
```

Code explanation:

- from **math_package** import add, **solve_quadratic** makes use of the objects imported in **__init__.py**.
- We can use add and **solve_quadratic** directly.

Renaming Imports with as

You can also rename imports using the as keyword to prevent naming conflicts or simply for convenience.

Example 6: Renaming an Imported Function

```
from math_operations import multiply as m

result = m(10, 5)

print(result)  # Output: 50
```

Code explanation:

- from math_operations import multiply as m imports the multiply function and renames it to m.
- result will now hold the product of 10 and 5.

Reusability and Organization

Dive into the principles of DRY (Don't Repeat Yourself) and code organization. Understand how functions and modules contribute to a maintainable codebase and learn strategies to avoid redundancy and keep your code modular.

The principles of reusability and organization are critical for writing efficient and maintainable code. In Python, these principles are enforced using functions and modules, which help to prevent repetition, facilitate the sharing of code, and promote the organization of logic.

Reusability

Code reusability means writing code in a way that helps to avoid duplication and allows the same code to be used in different contexts. This is one of the fundamental benefits of using functions and modules.

Example 1: Writing Reusable Functions

```
# utils.py

def calculate_area(radius):

    """Calculate the area of a circle given its radius."""

    pi = 3.14159

    return pi * (radius ** 2)

def calculate_perimeter(radius):

    """Calculate the perimeter of a circle given its radius."""

    pi = 3.14159

    return 2 * pi * radius
```

Code explanation:

- We have defined two functions in utils.py module: calculate_area and calculate_perimeter.
- These functions can be reused wherever we need to calculate the area or perimeter of a circle.

Organization

Organizing code into modules helps in maintaining a clean and navigable codebase. Functions related to a particular functionality can be grouped together in a single module.

Example 2: Organizing Code in Modules

Imagine a project with the following structure:

```
project/
|-- main.py
|-- utils.py
|-- data/
    |-- __init__.py
    |-- processing.py
    |-- cleanup.py
```

- utils.py contains utility functions used throughout the project.
- The data package contains modules for processing and cleaning up data.

Using Organized Code

```python
# main.py

from data.processing import process_data

from utils import calculate_area

processed_data = process_data(raw_data)

area = calculate_area(radius)
```

Code explanation:

- process_data function from the processing.py module is used to process raw_data.
- calculate_area function from the utils.py module is used to calculate the area.

Maintainability

A well-organized codebase is easier to maintain. When changes are required, the impact is localized, reducing the risk of introducing bugs into unrelated parts of the program.

DRY Principle (Don't Repeat Yourself)

The DRY principle is a best practice in programming that recommends reducing repetition of information. Repeating code can lead to inconsistencies and bugs, and it makes maintenance more challenging.

Example 3: DRY Principle in Action

```
# bad_example.py

# Repetitive code for calculating the area of circles

area1 = 3.14159 * (radius1 ** 2)

area2 = 3.14159 * (radius2 ** 2)

area3 = 3.14159 * (radius3 ** 2)


# Good example with DRY principle

# main.py

from utils import calculate_area

# Reusable function call for calculating the area of circles

area1 = calculate_area(radius1)

area2 = calculate_area(radius2)

area3 = calculate_area(radius3)
```

Code explanation:

- In the bad example, the formula for the area of a circle is repeated for each calculation.
- In the good example, we define the calculation once in a function and reuse that function, adhering to the DRY principle.

Conclusion

In this chapter, we went through the Functions with Python. We learned creation of functions with code-snippet. With the explanation of code snippet, we went inside of the code and discussed the functions. Following by we discussed modular programming with examples.

In next chapter, we will understand the exceptions and learn to handle the exceptions in Python.

Exercise: Test Your Understanding

Answer the following questions and test your understanding of learning from `Chapter 4`:

Q. 1. What is the function in Python?

Q. 2. How do you define a function in Python?

Q. 3. How can you call a function with no parameters?

Q. 4. What does the return statement do in a function?

Q. 5. Can a function return more than one value?

Notes

Date:

Do You Know?

Python is named after the British comedy series "Monty Python's Flying Circus," and not after the snake! The creator, Guido van Rossum, wanted a short, unique, and slightly mysterious name.

Chapter 5
Exception Handling

Python, a versatile and widely used programming language, is acclaimed for its simplicity and readability, making it an excellent choice for both beginners and seasoned programmers. One of the fundamental aspects of Python programming is error handling, a critical component for writing reliable and robust applications. In this guide, we'll delve into the nuances of handling errors and exceptions in Python, ensuring that your programs not only function correctly but also gracefully handle unexpected situations.

Error handling is not just about preventing crashes; it's about foreseeing potential pitfalls and managing them effectively. By mastering this skill, you'll be able to write programs that are not only efficient but also resilient to unforeseen errors.

In this chapter we will discuss:

- Understanding Exceptions
- Handling Exceptions with try-except
- Multiple Exception Handling
- Writing Robust Code
- Error Messages and Debugging

Understanding Exceptions

In Python, exceptions are events that occur during the execution of a program that disrupts its normal flow. This disruption often happens when the Python interpreter encounters an error. Unlike syntax errors that prevent code from running at all, exceptions can occur during runtime and, if not handled, lead to program termination.

Understanding exceptions is crucial as it allows developers to anticipate and manage potential errors, leading to more reliable and maintainable code.

Types of Exceptions

Python has several built-in exceptions, such as ValueError, TypeError, IndexError, and FileNotFoundError, each representing different error types. For instance, ValueError is raised when a function receives an argument of correct type but inappropriate value.

ValueError

Raised when a function receives an argument of the correct type but an inappropriate value.

Consider following code-snippet:

```
try:

    number = int("not_a_number")

except ValueError as e:

    print("ValueError:", e)
```

The preceding code attempts to convert an invalid string to an integer, which raises a `ValueError` exception. The `except` block catches this exception and prints an error message, preventing the program from crashing.

TypeError

TypeError occurs when an operation or function is applied to an object of an inappropriate type.

```
try:
    result = 'a' + 1
except TypeError as e:
    print("TypeError:", e)
```

Code explanation:

- The `try` block attempts to execute the invalid operation.
- A `TypeError` is raised because you can't concatenate a string and an integer.
- The `except` block catches the `TypeError` and prints an error message, preventing the program from crashing and providing feedback about what went wrong.

IndexError

`IndexError` occurs when trying to access an item at an invalid index, such as accessing beyond the length of a list.

```
try:
    lst = [1, 2, 3]
    print(lst[5])
except IndexError as e:
    print("IndexError:", e)
```

Code explanation:

- Creates a list lst with three elements: [1, 2, 3].
- Attempts to access the element at index 5, which is out of range.
- Catches the resulting IndexError and prints an error message.

FileNotFoundError

`FileNotFoundError` is raised when trying to access a file that does not exist.

Consider following code-snippet:

```
try:

    with open('non_existent_file.txt', 'r') as file:

        content = file.read()

except FileNotFoundError as e:

    print("FileNotFoundError:", e)
```

In the preceding code, it attempts to open a file that does not exist, resulting in a **`FileNotFoundError`**.

Custom Exceptions

Python also allows the creation of custom exceptions. These are particularly useful in larger applications where you might need to handle errors that are specific to your application's context.

```
class MyCustomError(Exception):

    pass

try:

    raise MyCustomError("This is a custom error message.")

except MyCustomError as e:

    print("MyCustomError:", e)
```

The code defines a custom exception class (**`MyCustomError`**) and raises it with a custom message, which is then caught and handled.

Exception Hierarchy

In Python, all exceptions are derived from the base class **BaseException**. The Exception class is the base class for all built-in, non-exit exceptions. Custom exceptions should also be derived from this class.

```
BaseException
├── SystemExit
├── KeyboardInterrupt
├── GeneratorExit
└── Exception
    ├── ArithmeticError
    │   ├── FloatingPointError
    │   ├── OverflowError
    │   └── ZeroDivisionError
    ├── AttributeError
    ├── EOFError
    ├── ImportError
    │   └── ModuleNotFoundError
    ├── LookupError
    │   ├── IndexError
    │   └── KeyError
    ├── NameError
    │   └── UnboundLocalError
    ├── OSError
    │   ├── FileNotFoundError
    │   ├── PermissionError
    │   └── TimeoutError
    ├── TypeError
    ├── ValueError
    │   └── UnicodeError
    │       ├── UnicodeDecodeError
    │       ├── UnicodeEncodeError
    │       └── UnicodeTranslateError
    └── RuntimeError
        └── RecursionError
```

Figure 5. 1: *Visualizing Exception Hierarchy*

Understanding this hierarchy is important for catching exceptions correctly. For example, using except Exception will catch most exceptions, but not system-exiting exceptions like **SystemExit** or **KeyboardInterrupt**, which are derived directly from **BaseException**.

The Importance of Specificity

Specificity in Python programming is crucial for writing clear, efficient, and error-free code. It helps in ensuring that the program does exactly what is intended and is easy to understand and maintain.

Consider following code-snippet:

```
# Non-specific variable names

x = 10

y = 20

z = x + y

# Specific variable names

length = 10

width = 20

area = length + width
```

Code explanation:

- Non-specific variable names like x, y, and z make it hard to understand the purpose of the variables.
- Specific variable names like length, width, and area make the code more readable and self-explanatory.

Handling Exceptions with try-except

The `try-except` statement in Python is used to catch and handle exceptions, providing a way to write safer and more robust code. When the code within the `try` block raises an exception, the flow is immediately passed to the `except` block. If the exception matches the type specified in the except block, the code within that block is executed.

Using `try-except` effectively can prevent your program from crashing due to unhandled exceptions and can also provide more user-friendly error messages.

Basic try-except Structure

The simplest form of a `try-except` block involves trying to execute some code and catching a general exception if one occurs.

```
try:
    # Trying to divide by zero
    result = 10 / 0
    print("This will not be printed.")
except ZeroDivisionError as e:
    # Handling the ZeroDivisionError
    print("Caught an exception:", e)
print("Program continues here.")
```

Code explanation:

- The `try` block contains code that might raise an exception.
- The `except` block catches and handles the `ZeroDivisionError`, preventing the program from crashing.
- The program prints messages to indicate the caught exception and continues running.

Catching Multiple Exceptions

You can catch multiple exceptions using a single except block by specifying the exceptions as a tuple. This allows you to handle different types of exceptions in the same way.

Consider following code-snippet:

```
try:
    # Some code that may raise exceptions
    result = 10 / 0
except (ZeroDivisionError, TypeError) as e:
    # Handling both ZeroDivisionError and TypeError
    print(f"An error occurred: {e}")
```

In the preceding code-snippet. the **except** block catches both **ZeroDivisionError** and **TypeError**. If either of these exceptions is raised in the **try** block, the code inside the **except** block will be executed.

Finally Block

The **finally** block can be used along with try-except to execute code regardless of whether an exception occurred or not. This is often used for clean-up actions.

```
try:

    # Code that may raise an exception

    x = 1 / 0  # This will raise a ZeroDivisionError

except ZeroDivisionError:

    print("Cannot divide by zero!")

finally:

    print("This will always execute, regardless of exceptions.")
```

In the preceding code-snippet, even though the division by zero raises an exception, the **finally** block is still executed, printing "This will always execute, regardless of exceptions."

The **finally** block is useful for releasing external resources like files or network connections, ensuring that these resources are properly closed or cleaned up, even if an exception occurs.

Multiple Exception Handling

In Python, you can handle multiple exceptions in a single try block, allowing for more precise and differentiated handling of various error conditions. This approach is beneficial when a segment of code might raise more than one type of exception, and each requires a different response or handling mechanism.

Catching Multiple Exceptions Separately

You can specify multiple except blocks after a try block, each catching and handling a different type of exception.

```
try:

    # Code that may raise exceptions

    x = int(input("Enter a number: "))

    y = 10 / x

    print("Result:", y)

except ValueError:

    print("Invalid input. Please enter a valid number.")

except ZeroDivisionError:

    print("Cannot divide by zero. Please enter a non-zero number.")

except Exception as e:

    print("An error occurred:", e)
```

In this example, we have three **except** blocks:

- The first except block (**ValueError**) handles the **ValueError** that may occur if the user enters something that is not a valid integer when using int().
- The second except block (**ZeroDivisionError**) handles the **ZeroDivisionError** that may occur if the user enters zero as input, which would cause division by zero.
- The last except block (**Exception**) is a generic catch-all block that catches any other exceptions that were not handled by the previous except blocks. It also demonstrates how to access the exception object (**e**) for further analysis or logging.

Using multiple except blocks allows you to handle different types of exceptions differently, providing more specific error messages or handling logic for each case.

Catching Multiple Exceptions in One Block

You can also catch multiple exceptions in a single block using a tuple. This is useful when you want to handle different exceptions in the same way.

```
try:

    # Code that might raise exceptions

    x = 1 / 0  # Raises ZeroDivisionError

    y = int('abc')  # Raises ValueError

except (ZeroDivisionError, ValueError) as e:

    print(f"An error occurred: {e}")
```

In the preceding code-snippet, the **except** block catches both **ZeroDivisionError** and **ValueError**. If either of these exceptions occurs in the try block, the corresponding error message will be printed.

This approach is useful when you want to handle different types of exceptions in the same way, such as logging the error or displaying a generic error message to the user.

Nested try-except Blocks

Nested try-except blocks can be used for more complex error handling scenarios, where an exception handler itself might cause another exception.

```
try:
   # Outer try block
   num1 = int(input("Enter a dividend: "))
   num2 = int(input("Enter a divisor: "))

    try:

        # Inner try block

        result = num1 / num2
```

```
        print("Result:", result)

    except ZeroDivisionError:

        print("Cannot divide by zero!")

    except ValueError:

        print("Please enter valid numbers.")


except Exception as e:

    print("An error occurred:", e)
```

Code-snippet explanation:

- The outer try block encompasses the entire code segment where exceptions might occur.
- Inside the outer try block, there's another try block (the inner try block). This inner block is nested within the outer one.
- The inner try block specifically handles exceptions that might occur during the division operation (ZeroDivisionError) and during the conversion of inputs to integers (ValueError).
- If a ZeroDivisionError occurs inside the inner try block (i.e., when attempting to divide by zero), it's caught and the corresponding error message is printed.
- If a ValueError occurs inside the inner try block (i.e., when the input cannot be converted to an integer), it's caught and the corresponding error message is printed.
- If any other exception occurs inside the outer try block, it's caught by the outermost except block, and a generic error message along with the exception information is printed.

Nested try-except blocks provide a structured way to handle different types of exceptions at different levels of your code, allowing for more specific error handling and cleaner code organization.

Writing Robust Code

Writing robust code in Python means anticipating potential issues and ensuring that the program behaves sensibly in all scenarios, especially unexpected ones. This involves not only handling exceptions effectively but also using programming practices that minimize the likelihood of errors. Robust code is reliable, maintainable, and resilient to both foreseen and unforeseen problems.

Validating Inputs

One key aspect of robust code is validating inputs before processing them. This can prevent many types of errors.

Using Assertions

Assertions can be used to check the state of the program and ensure it is as expected. They are mainly used for debugging and can help catch bugs early.

Handling Resources with Context Managers

Proper management of resources like file handles is crucial in robust coding. Context managers ensure that resources are correctly cleaned up after use.

Graceful Degradation

Robust programs should degrade gracefully under failure conditions, providing useful feedback rather than crashing.

Writing robust code in Python is about more than just handling exceptions. It involves proactive measures such as input validation, using assertions for debugging, managing resources properly with context managers, and ensuring that the program can gracefully handle failure scenarios. These practices lead to the development of reliable, maintainable, and user-friendly applications.

Error Messages and Debugging

Error messages and debugging are crucial aspects of Python programming. Effective debugging involves understanding error messages, which are Python's way of indicating that something has gone wrong. These messages often provide valuable information about the nature and location of the problem, enabling the programmer to diagnose and fix issues more efficiently.

Python error messages typically consist of the type of error and a traceback that shows where the error occurred. Reading and interpreting these messages is key to successful debugging.

In larger applications, it's often useful to log errors instead of or in addition to printing them. Python's logging module can be used for this purpose.

Conclusion

This chapter has provided a comprehensive overview of exception handling in Python. We began by understanding the concept of exceptions and how they disrupt the normal flow of a program. We then delved into the try-except block, which allows us to handle exceptions gracefully, ensuring that our programs continue to run smoothly even in the presence of errors.

Additionally, we explored the concept of multiple exception handling, which allows us to handle different types of exceptions in a single except block, streamlining our code and making it more readable. We also discussed the importance of writing robust code that anticipates and handles exceptions effectively, thus enhancing the reliability and stability of our programs.

Finally, we touched upon the significance of error messages and debugging in the development process. By providing informative error messages and using effective debugging techniques, we can quickly identify and rectify errors in our code, ensuring that it functions as intended.

In the next chapter, we will discuss and learn File handling in Python.

Exercise: Test Your Understanding

Answer the following questions and test your understanding of learning from

Chapter 5:

Q. 1. What type of error in Python is raised when an operation or function is applied to an object of an inappropriate type?

Q. 2. What Python keyword is used to create a custom exception?

Q. 3. If you want to explicitly raise an exception in your code, which statement do you use?

Q. 4. What base class do most built-in exceptions in Python extend from?

Q. 5. Name an exception in Python that is raised when trying to access an item at an index that does not exist in a list?

Notes

Date:

Unlock Your Potential

Imagine being able to automate your daily tasks, analyze complex data, or even build a web application from scratch. Python makes all this possible with its simple and readable syntax. As you dive deeper into the chapters, you'll unlock your potential and discover Python's endless possibilities.

Chapter 6

File Handling

Files play a crucial role in programming, allowing us to store, access, and manipulate data. In Python, file handling is a fundamental skill that every programmer should master. This chapter will take you on a journey through the intricate world of file manipulation in Python. We will delve deep into opening and closing files, understanding different file modes, reading and writing text files, working with file objects, and handling exceptions during file operations.

In this chapter, we will discuss:

- Working with Files in Python
- File Modes and Operations
- Reading and Writing Text Files
- File Objects and Context Managers
- Handling Exceptions in File Operations

Working with Files

File handling is a fundamental aspect of many Python programs. It involves reading from and writing to files, which are crucial for data storage and retrieval.

File handling is an essential aspect of programming in Python, used in a variety of applications ranging from data analysis to web development. It involves creating, reading, updating, and deleting files — operations that are crucial for the persistent storage and retrieval of data.

Let us discuss the importance of File handling:

- Data Persistence: File handling allows data to be stored persistently. Unlike variables that lose their data when a program ends, files retain their data, making them essential for long-term data storage.
- Data Exchange: Files can be used as a means to exchange data between different programs or systems. They act as a common medium understandable by various software.
- Configuration and Logging: Many applications use files for configuration (storing settings) and logging (recording events and errors), which are crucial for maintaining and debugging software.

Basic Operations

The fundamental operations in file handling are:

- **Opening a File**: This is the first step in file handling. Python uses the built-in **open()** function to access a file.
- **Reading a File**: After opening a file, you can read its contents. This is typically done for files that store data for your program to process.
- **Writing to a File**: This involves adding or modifying the content of a file. It's crucial for tasks like saving program outputs, creating logs, etc.
- **Closing a File**: It's essential to close a file after your operations are completed. This ensures that resources are freed, and changes are properly saved.

Consider the following code-snippet:

```
# Opening a file

file = open('example_to_read.txt', 'r')  # Open a file in read mode

content = file.read()  # Read the content of the file

file.close()  # Always close the file

print(content)
```

Opening a File:

file = open('example_to_read.txt', 'r'): This line uses the open() function to open a file.

'example_to_read.txt' is the name of the file to be opened.

'r' indicates the mode, which in this case is "read." This means we are opening the file for reading.

The open() function returns a file object, which is stored in the variable file.

Reading from a File:

content = file.read(): This line reads the content of the file.

The read() method is called on the file object. It reads the entire contents of the file and stores it in the variable content.

Closing the File:

file.close(): This line closes the file.

Closing a file is crucial. It ensures that the connection between the file and the program is terminated, freeing up system resources and ensuring that all data is written to the file.

Printing the Content:

print(content): This line prints the content read from the file.

It's always good to verify the file's content, especially when learning file operations.

Figure 6.1: *output of opening_a_file.py*

The preceding `Figure 6.1` displays the output of opening a file.

Let us have a quick look at best practices for file handling:

- Always Close Files: Ensure that every file opened is closed to prevent resource leaks and data corruption.
- Handle Exceptions: Use try-except blocks to handle potential errors, such as attempting to open a file that doesn't exist.
- Use Context Managers: Python's context managers (with statement) are preferred for file handling as they automatically take care of closing the file.
- Check File Existence: Before attempting to read a file, check if it exists to prevent errors.
- Be Mindful of File Paths: Understand the difference between absolute and relative paths and use them correctly.
- Consider File Permissions: Be aware of file permissions, especially when dealing with writing or modifying files.

Mastering file handling is a steppingstone towards proficiency in Python. It is a fundamental skill that underpins many practical applications in real-world programming. Understanding how to effectively and safely manipulate files allows developers to handle data efficiently and securely.

File Modes and Operations

Python supports various file modes for different operations like reading, writing, and appending.

File operations in Python are highly versatile, allowing programmers to interact with files in various ways. The mode in which a file is opened determines the type of operations that can be performed on it. Understanding these modes and operations is crucial for efficient and safe file manipulation.

Understanding File Modes

When opening a file using Python's open() function, the mode specified as an argument determines how the file will be used. The common modes are:

- Read ('r'): Opens a file for reading. This is the default mode.
- Write ('w'): Opens a file for writing. Creates a new file if it doesn't exist or truncates the file if it exists.
- Append ('a'): Opens a file for appending at the end of the file without truncating it. Creates a new file if it does not exist.
- Read and Write ('r+'): Opens the file for both reading and writing.
- Binary Mode ('b'): This can be appended to other modes to handle

binary files (e.g., 'rb', 'wb').

Each mode is designed for specific use cases, and choosing the right mode is fundamental to the task at hand.

File Operations

File operations include reading from, writing to, or appending to a file. The mode in which a file is opened dictates which operations can be performed.

Reading: Involves extracting data from a file. This is usually done in 'r' or 'r+' mode.

Writing: Involves inserting or modifying data in a file. This can be done in 'w', 'w+', or 'r+' mode.

Appending: Adds new data to the end of the file without affecting the existing content. This is done in 'a' or 'a+' mode.

Closing: After completing operations, closing the file is essential to free up resources.

```
# Writing to a file

with open('example_to_write.txt', 'w') as file:

    file.write("Hi, Python!")

# Appending to a file

with open('example_to_write.txt', 'a') as file:

    file.write("\nAppending a new line to existing file.")
```

Writing to a File

with open('example_to_write.txt', 'w') as file:

This line opens 'example_to_write.txt' in write mode ('w'). If the file doesn't exist, it's created. If it exists, it's truncated to zero length.

The with statement is used to handle the file object, ensuring that the file is properly closed after its suite finishes.

as file assigns the file object to the variable file for further operations.

file.write("Hi, Python!"):

This writes the string "Hi, Python!" to the file. The write() method writes the specified string to the file.

Appending to a File

with open('example_to_write.txt', 'a') as file:

This line opens 'example.txt' in append mode ('a'). If the file doesn't exist, it's created. If it exists, the write operations append data at the end.

file.write("\nAppending a new line to existing file."):

This appends the string "\nAppending a new line to existing file." to the file. The newline character '\n' ensures that the new string is written on a new line.

```
Hi, Python!
Appending a new line to existing file.
```

Figure 6.2: *output of writing_to_a_file.py*

The preceding **Figure 6.2** displays the output of writing to a file.

Best Practices in File Modes and Operations

- Choose the Right Mode: Always select the file mode that best suits your needs to avoid data loss or corruption.
- Use Context Managers: Utilize with statements for better management of file resources.
- Handle Exceptions: Implement try-except blocks to handle I/O errors, like a file not being accessible.
- Ensure File Closure: Always make sure that files are closed after operations are completed, either manually or using context managers.
- Be Careful with Write Mode: Remember that opening a file in 'w' mode will erase the existing content.
- Prefer Append Mode for Logs: When dealing with log files, use append mode to keep existing logs intact.

Use cases to understand each of the modes

Providing detailed use cases for each file mode helps in understanding the practical applications of these modes in real-world scenarios. Let's delve into common situations where different file modes in Python are particularly useful.

Read Mode ('r')

Use Case: Data Analysis

In data analysis, you often need to read data from files such as CSV or text files. Opening a file in read mode allows you to access and analyze this data without the risk of modifying the original file.

Example: A Python script reads a log file to generate a report on user activity.

Use Case: Configuration Files

Many applications use configuration files (like .ini or .json files) to load settings. Read mode is used to access these settings without altering them.

Example: A web application reads database connection details from a configuration file at startup.

Write Mode ('w')

Use Case: Generating Reports

When you need to create a new report or overwrite an existing one with new data, write mode is appropriate. It's useful when the previous data is no longer relevant.

Example: A script that generates a daily summary report, overwriting the previous day's report.

Use Case: Creating Initialization Files

In scenarios where you need to create initialization or setup files from scratch, write mode is ideal.

Example: An installation script that creates initial configuration files for a software application.

Append Mode ('a')

Use Case: Logging

Append mode is crucial for logging systems where new log entries are added without disturbing the existing logs.

Example: An error logging system for a web application where each new error is added to the end of a log file.

Use Case: Continuous Data Collection

For applications that continuously collect and record data, such as sensor readings over time, append mode ensures that new data is added sequentially without overwriting old data.

Example: A weather monitoring application that periodically appends the latest weather data to a file.

Read and Write Mode ('r+')

Use Case: File Modification

This mode is useful when you need to read and modify the contents of a file. It's ideal for scenarios where you don't want to discard the entire file content.

Example: A script that reads a configuration file, updates certain settings, and writes the changes back to the same file.

Use Case: Database File Operations

In lightweight database systems where data is stored in files, 'r+' mode allows for reading and updating records without the need to rewrite the entire file.

Example: A simple file-based database system that updates specific records based on user input.

Binary Mode ('b')

Use Case: Image Processing

When working with binary files like images or executable files, binary mode is used to read and write data correctly.

Example: A script that opens an image file in binary mode to apply a filter or watermark.

Use Case: Data Serialization and Deserialization

Binary mode is used for serialization (saving data structures like objects) and deserialization (restoring them) in a binary format.

Example: A game that saves and loads game state in a binary file format.

Handling binary files, such as images or videos, is a common task in many Python applications. These files are stored in binary format, meaning they contain data in a non-textual form that represents the file's contents. Processing binary files requires careful handling to ensure data integrity.

Understanding Binary Files

Binary files can include a variety of data types, from images and videos to executables and archives. Unlike text files, binary files are not human-readable and require specific software to interpret their contents. When dealing with binary files in Python:

Binary Mode: Files must be opened in binary mode ('b'). This mode ensures that the file's data is not modified or corrupted due to encoding issues. For example, 'rb' for reading, 'wb' for writing, and 'ab' for appending.

Reading and Writing Bytes: Operations on binary files deal with bytes rather than strings. This is crucial when processing data like images or videos, where every byte represents part of the file's content.

Use Cases in Image and Video Processing

Image Processing: Reading an image file, modifying its content (like applying filters or resizing), and saving the modified image back to disk.

Video Processing: Reading video files, extracting frames, editing, or converting them, and possibly recompiling them into a new video.

Example Code: Reading and Writing an Image File

Let's consider a simple example of opening an image file, reading its content, and writing it back to a new file. This example doesn't modify the image; it simply demonstrates the process of reading and writing binary data.

The file types supported are:

- JPEG (.jpg, .jpeg)
- PNG (.png)
- GIF (.gif)
- BMP (.bmp)

The file size supported for reading and writing in Python is generally limited by the system's available memory and storage. When an image (or any file) is read using methods like file.read(), the entire content is loaded into the memory. Therefore, if an image file's size exceeds the available RAM, it may lead to memory errors.

For very large images, it's advisable to either:

- Ensure that the system has sufficient RAM to handle the file size.
- Use libraries that support efficient loading and processing of large images, possibly by reading portions of the image into memory rather than the entire file at once.

```
# Read an image file

with open('input_image.jpg', 'rb') as file:

    image_data = file.read()

# Write the image data to a new file

with open('output_image.jpg', 'wb') as file:

    file.write(image_data)
```

Reading the Image

open('input_image.jpg', 'rb') as file: This line opens an image file named 'input_image.jpg' in binary read mode ('rb'). The file is opened as a binary file, ensuring the data is read as bytes.

image_data = file.read(): Reads the entire content of the image file into the variable image_data. This variable now contains the binary data of the image.

Writing the Image:

open('output_image.jpg', 'wb') as file: Opens a new file named 'output_image.jpg' in binary write mode ('wb'). If this file doesn't exist, it's created; if it does, it's overwritten.

file.write(image_data): Writes the binary data stored in image_data to the new file. This effectively creates a copy of the original image.

Figure 6.3: *output of reading_an_image.py*

The preceding **Figure 6.3** displays the output of reading an image file.

Understanding file modes and operations is vital for any Python developer, as it forms the basis of data handling in many applications. Mastery of these concepts enables developers to manage file I/O efficiently and safely, a critical component in the world of programming.

Encoding considerations

When working with text files in Python, understanding file encoding is crucial. Encoding determines how characters are represented in bytes, and different encodings can represent the same characters using different byte sequences. Common encodings include ASCII, UTF-8, and UTF-16. Misalignment between the encoding used to write and read a file can lead to errors or garbled text. For instance, UTF-8 encoded files might display incorrectly if read with ASCII encoding. Python defaults to UTF-8, but you can specify encoding when opening files, like open('file.txt', 'r', encoding='utf-16'). Being mindful of encoding is especially important in applications dealing with international text or transferring files between different systems, where encoding standards may vary. Understanding and correctly applying encodings ensures data integrity and readability across diverse environments.

Performance considerations

Performance considerations in file operations are crucial, especially in applications dealing with large files or high-frequency file I/O operations. The way files are handled can significantly impact system resources and overall performance.

Here are key factors to consider:

File Size and Memory Usage

Reading Large Files: Reading an entire large file into memory with file.read() can be resource-intensive, potentially leading to memory issues. Instead, reading in chunks or line-by-line using file.readline() or a loop can be more memory-efficient.

Writing Large Files: Similar to reading, writing large files all at once can be demanding. Writing in smaller chunks can help manage memory usage better.

Buffering

Buffered I/O: Python's file I/O operations are buffered by default, meaning data is first written to a buffer and then flushed to disk. This improves performance by reducing the number of disk writes. However, the buffer size and flush frequency can affect performance.

Unbuffered I/O: For real-time or log file writing, unbuffered I/O (open(file, 'w', buffering=0)) ensures immediate writing to disk but can be slower due to frequent disk access.

File Access Patterns

Sequential vs Random Access: Sequential access (e.g., reading a file from start to end) is generally faster than random access (e.g., seeking specific positions in a file) due to the way storage devices work. Optimizing access patterns based on application needs can enhance performance.

I/O Bound vs CPU Bound

I/O Bound Operations: In scenarios where file I/O is the bottleneck (e.g., reading from a slow network drive), optimizing I/O operations (like asynchronous I/O) can improve performance.

CPU Bound Operations: If processing the data is the bottleneck, optimizing the computation (e.g., using faster algorithms or parallel processing) rather than the file operation itself may yield better performance improvements.

Concurrent File Access

Thread and Process Safety: When multiple threads or processes access the same file, ensuring thread-safe operations is vital to prevent data corruption. Locking mechanisms or atomic file operations can be employed.

Read-Write Conflicts: In applications with concurrent read and write operations, managing access to prevent conflicts (e.g., using reader-writer locks) is important for data integrity and performance.

File Caching and OS Considerations

Operating System Caching: Modern operating systems cache file operations, which can significantly speed up repeated read/write operations to the same file.

File System Type: The type of file system (e.g., NTFS, FAT32, ext4) can also impact file operation performance due to different underlying architectures and features.

Network File Operations

Latency and Bandwidth: When dealing with files over a network (e.g., cloud storage), network latency and bandwidth become significant factors. Strategies like data compression before transfer or batched I/O operations can help mitigate these issues.

Effective file handling in Python is more than just reading and writing data. It involves a comprehensive understanding of how different file operations and patterns affect system performance and resource utilization. By considering these factors, developers can optimize their applications for better efficiency and reliability, especially in data-intensive environments.

Reading and Writing Text Files

Reading and writing text files are the most common file operations. Python provides simple methods for these tasks.

Python provides simple and efficient means of handling text files, making it a preferred choice for many developers dealing with file input/output operations. Text files are one of the most common file types in programming, used for a variety of purposes like storing logs, configurations, or data for processing.

The Basics of Text Files in Python

Text files are files containing data in a format readable by humans – usually in a character encoding like ASCII or UTF-8. In Python, reading and writing text files involves opening a file, performing operations, and then closing it.

Reading Text Files

Reading files in Python is straightforward. The built-in open() function is used to open a file, and various methods like read(), readline(), or readlines() are used to read its content.

Whole File: read() reads the entire file content into a single string.

Line by Line: readline() reads the next line from the file.

All Lines as List: readlines() reads all lines into a list of strings.

Writing to Text Files

Writing to files is similarly simple. Opening a file in write ('w') or append ('a') mode and using the write() or writelines() methods allows you to add text to the file.

Write Method: write() writes a specified string to the file.

Writelines Method: writelines() writes a list of strings to the file.

Context Managers for File Operations

Python's context managers simplify the process of handling files by automatically taking care of opening and closing files, even if an error occurs during file operations.

```
# Reading a text file

with open('example.txt', 'r') as file:

    content = file.read()

    print(content)


# Writing to a text file

with open('newfile.txt', 'w') as file:

    file.write("Writing new content.")
```

Reading from a File

with open('example.txt', 'r') as file

with is a context manager that ensures the file is properly closed after the block's execution.

open('example.txt', 'r') opens 'example.txt' in read mode ('r').

as file assigns the file object to the variable file.

content = file.read()

file.read() reads the entire content of the file into the variable content.

print(content)

This prints the content of 'example.txt' to the console.

Writing to a File

with open('newfile.txt', 'w') as file:

Opens 'newfile.txt' in write mode ('w'). If the file doesn't exist, it's created; if it does exist, its content is erased.

The with statement ensures the file is closed after the block.

file.write("Writing new content.")

file.write() writes the string "Writing new content." to 'newfile.txt'.

Figure 6.4: *output of reading_an_text_file.py*

The preceding **Figure 6.4** displays the output of reading an text file.

Use Cases for Reading and Writing Text Files

- Configuration Files: Reading settings from a configuration file at the start of an application.
- Data Processing: Writing processed data to a file for later use or analysis.
- Logging: Writing logs to a text file for debugging and record-keeping.
- Scripting and Automation: Reading input data from a file for batch processing or automation scripts.

Best Practices and Tips

- Use UTF-8 Encoding: When dealing with text files, it's good practice to explicitly set the encoding to UTF-8 unless you have a specific reason to use a different encoding.
- Handle Exceptions: Use try-except blocks to handle potential errors, such as file not found or permission issues.
- Avoid Resource Leaks: Always ensure files are closed after operations. Context managers (with statement) are a best practice for this.
- Large Files Handling: For large files, read/write in chunks or line by line to avoid memory issues.
- File Paths: Be mindful of file paths – absolute vs. relative paths – and how they are resolved in your application's environment.

File Objects and Context Managers

Context managers in Python are useful for resource management and can simplify file handling by automatically closing files.

In Python, file handling is a critical aspect of many programs, and understanding file objects and the use of context managers is essential for efficient and safe file operations.

Understanding File Objects

A file object in Python is an entity that provides a way for programs to work with files. It's created using the built-in open() function, which returns a file object. This object then provides methods and attributes to perform various operations on the file, such as reading or writing data.

The Role of File Objects

- Interface to Files: File objects act as the interface between your Python program and the file system, allowing you to read from or write to files.
- Buffering: They handle buffering, which means they temporarily hold data before it's written to or read from the file, enhancing performance.
- File Positioning: File objects keep track of the current position in the file, which is crucial for operations like reading or writing data at specific locations.

Context Managers and the with Statement

Context managers in Python are a powerful feature for resource management. They are typically used with the with statement to wrap the execution of a block of code. For file operations, context managers ensure that files are properly closed after their use, even if an error occurs within the block.

- Automatic Resource Management: When a file is opened using a context manager, it takes care of opening and closing the file, which prevents resource leaks.
- Error Handling: It also ensures that files are closed properly even if an error occurs, which is crucial for data integrity and application stability.

```
# Using context manager for file operations

with open('example.txt', 'r') as file:

  for line in file:

        print(line.strip())
```

with open('example.txt', 'r') as file

with open('example.txt', 'r'): This statement opens 'example.txt' in read mode ('r'). The open() function returns a file object.

as file: The file object returned by open() is assigned to the variable file. This variable is used to interact with the file.

The with statement ensures that the file is automatically closed when the block under it is exited, even if an error occurs.

for line in file

This is a for loop that iterates over the file object. Python file objects are iterable, and iterating over a file object yields its lines one by one.

line: In each iteration of the loop, line holds the current line read from the file.

print(line.strip())

line.strip(): This method removes any leading and trailing whitespace from the string line, including the newline character (\n) at the end of each line.

print(...): Prints the processed line to the console. This results in the content of the file being printed line by line, without extra leading or trailing spaces.

`Figure 6.5`: *output of using_context_manager_for_file.py*

The preceding **`Figure 6.5`** displays the output of using context manager for file.

Why Use Context Managers for File Operations?

- Resource Efficiency: Automatically managing file resources prevents scenarios where files remain open unnecessarily, consuming system resources.
- Error Resilience: By ensuring files are closed after use, context managers prevent data corruption that could occur if a program crashes or an exception is raised.
- Code Clarity and Maintenance: The use of context managers leads to cleaner, more readable code, which is easier to maintain and less prone to errors.

Advanced File Operations with Context Managers

- Context managers can be used for more than just opening and closing files. They can be extended to handle more complex scenarios such as:
- Transactional File Operations: Implementing operations that should either completely succeed or fail without causing side effects.
- Working with Temporary Files: Automatically handling the creation and deletion of temporary files used during program execution.
- Managing File Locks: Ensuring that file locks are appropriately acquired and released in applications where concurrent file access is involved.

Best Practices in Using File Objects and Context Managers

- Always Use Context Managers for File I/O: This is considered a best practice in Python as it leads to better resource management and error handling.
- Explicitly Specify Encoding: When dealing with text files, it's good practice to explicitly specify the file encoding, like open('file.txt', 'r', encoding='utf-8').
- Handle Exceptions Gracefully: Implement error handling within the context manager to deal with unexpected issues like file access errors or read/write failures

- Avoid Holding Files Open Unnecessarily: Open files only when needed and rely on the context manager to close them as soon as the operations are done.
- Be Mindful of File Modes: Choosing the correct file mode (read, write, append) is crucial to ensure that file operations perform as expected.

File objects and context managers are fundamental components in Python file handling, offering a robust and efficient way to perform file operations. Understanding and utilizing these features not only leads to more reliable and maintainable code but also ensures efficient use of resources and better error handling. As a core aspect of Python programming, mastering file objects and context managers is essential for any developer working with file I/O.

Handling Exceptions in File Operations

Exception handling is crucial in file operations to manage errors like file not found or read/write permissions.

In Python, handling exceptions during file operations is crucial for writing robust and reliable programs. Exception handling ensures that your program behaves predictably and safely, even when encountering unexpected situations like missing files, permission issues, or corrupted data.

Understanding Exceptions in File Operations

When performing file operations, several issues can arise:

- File Not Found: Attempting to open a file that does not exist.
- Permission Denied: Trying to read or write to a file without the necessary permissions.
- File Already Exists: Creating a file that already exists, depending on the mode.
- Disk Space Issues: Running out of disk space while writing to a file.
- Corrupted File Data: Encountering unreadable or corrupted data in a file.

Handling these exceptions prevents your program from crashing and allows for graceful recovery or error reporting.

Types of File Exceptions

Python's built-in exception types that are most relevant to file operations include:

- FileNotFoundError: Raised when a file or directory is requested but doesn't exist.

- PermissionError: Raised when trying to perform an operation without adequate access rights.
- OSError: Raised for system-related errors, like a full disk or an inaccessible file.
- IOError: Raised when an I/O operation (like reading or writing) fails for an I/O-related reason.

The Role of the try-except Block

The try-except block in Python is used to catch and handle exceptions. The try block contains the code that might raise an exception, and the except block contains the code that executes if an exception occurs.

```
# Exception handling in file operations
try:
    with open('nonexistent.txt', 'r') as file:
        content = file.read()
except FileNotFoundError:
    print("File does not exist.")
```

Code Breakdown

try::

This statement begins a block of code that might raise an exception. It's a signal that the following code is to be attempted, but it might lead to an error.

with open('nonexistent.txt', 'r') as file

Attempts to open a file named 'nonexistent.txt' in read mode ('r').

If the file does not exist, this line will raise a FileNotFoundError.

The with statement ensures that the file is properly closed after its suite finishes, even if an exception is raised.

content = file.read()

Reads the entire content of the file and stores it in the variable content.

If the file cannot be read due to some error, an IOError (or a subclass of it) might be raised.

except FileNotFoundError

This block of code will execute if and only if a FileNotFoundError is raised in the try block.

It's a way to gracefully handle the error instead of letting the program crash.

print("File does not exist.")

This line prints a message to the console, indicating that the file was not found.

`Figure 6.6`: *output of exception_handling.py*

The preceding Figure 6.6 displays the output of exception handling

It's a simple way of notifying the user or logging the error, as opposed to allowing the program to terminate with an unhandled exception.

Handling Permission Denied

```
try:

    with open('protected_file.txt', 'w') as file:

        file.write("Some data")

except PermissionError:

    print("You do not have permission to write to this file.")
```

Explanation of the preceding code-snippet:

- try:: Begins a block where we expect an exception might occur.
- with open('protected_file.txt', 'w') as file:: Tries to open a file named 'protected_file.txt' in write mode. If the file is protected or read-only, a PermissionError will be raised.
- file.write("Some data"): Attempts to write some data to the file.
- except PermissionError:: Catches the PermissionError.
- print("You do not have permission to write to this file."): Prints an error message indicating a lack of permission.

`Figure 6.7`: *output of handling_protected_file.py*

The preceding `Figure 6.7` displays the output of handling protected files.

Handling File Already Exists

```
import os

filename = "existing_file.txt"

try:

    if os.path.exists(filename):

        raise FileExistsError("File already exists")

    with open(filename, 'w') as file:

        file.write("Some data")

except FileExistsError as e:

    print(e)
```

Explanation of the code-snippet:

- import os: Imports the os module, which provides a method to check if a file exists.
- filename = "existing_file.txt": Defines the file to be created.
- try:: Begins a try block.
- if os.path.exists(filename):: Checks if the file already exists.
- raise FileExistsError("File already exists"): Raises a FileExistsError if the file exists.
- with open(filename, 'w') as file:: Opens the file for writing if it doesn't exist.
- file.write("Some data"): Writes data to the file.
- except FileExistsError as e:: Catches the FileExistsError.
- print(e): Prints the error message.

Figure 6.8: *output of handling_existing_files.py*

The preceding **Figure 6.8** displays the output of handling protected files.

Handling Disk Space Issues

Handling disk space issues programmatically is challenging as Python does not provide a built-in exception for this. Usually, an OSError is raised, but it's not specific to disk space. Monitoring disk space requires OS-level checks before writing large files.

Handling Corrupted File Data

Handling corrupted file data involves reading the file and catching exceptions that indicate unreadable or corrupted data. Python's built-in exceptions might not directly signal corruption, so you might need to implement additional checks based on the expected file format.

Each of these examples demonstrates handling specific file-related exceptions in Python. Proper error handling is key to developing resilient applications that can gracefully handle unexpected scenarios.

Importance of Exception Handling in File Operations

- Robustness: Exception handling makes your program more robust and less likely to crash in the face of errors.
- User Experience: It allows for a better user experience by providing clear error messages instead of cryptic stack traces.
- Data Integrity: Proper error handling can protect against data corruption or loss, especially in write operations.
- Debugging Ease: Handling exceptions with informative messages can make debugging easier when something goes wrong.

Exception handling in file operations is a key aspect of writing effective and reliable Python code. It not only prevents crashes but also provides a mechanism for dealing with and reporting errors gracefully. By understanding and correctly applying Python's exception handling mechanisms, developers can create more resilient and user-friendly applications.

Conclusion

While Python's file handling functions are versatile enough to read and write various image file types, practical limitations like system memory and storage, and the capabilities of any additional image processing libraries used, will dictate the actual file types and sizes that can be effectively handled.

Exercise: Test Your Understanding

Answer the following questions and test your understanding of learning from **Chapter 6**:

Q. 1. What function is used to open a file in Python?

Q. 2. Why is it important to close a file after operations?

Q. 3. What happens if you don't close a file in Python?

Q. 4. Can you read from and write to a file without closing it between operations?

Q. 5. What is the default mode for opening a file using the open() function?

Q. 6. What file mode should you use to append data to an existing file?

Q. 7. What happens if you open a file in write mode ('w') that already exists?

Q. 8. What is the difference between 'w' and 'a' mode in file operations?

Q. 9. Can you explain the difference between 'r' and 'r+' modes?

Q. 10. What file mode allows you to handle a file as a binary file?

Q. 11. How do you read the entire content of a file as a single string?

Q. 12. What method would you use to write a list of strings to a file?

Q. 13. How can you read a file line by line in Python?

Q. 14. What is a potential issue with using read() on very large files?

Q. 15. How would you write data to a file without overwriting its existing content?

Q. 16. What is the advantage of using a context manager for file operations?

Q. 17. How does Python mark the end of a context manager block for file operations?

Q. 18. What keyword is used in Python to implement a context manager?

Q. 19. Can file objects be used outside the context manager block?

Q. 20. What happens if an error occurs within a context manager block?

Q. 21. Which exception is raised when trying to open a non-existent file for reading?

Q. 22. How would you handle a situation where you don't have permission to read a file?

Q. 23. What type of exception should you catch for general I/O errors?

Q. 24. Is it possible to execute a certain block of code regardless of whether an exception was raised or not?

Q. 25. How can you handle multiple different exceptions in a single try-except block?

Notes Date:

Chapter 7

Generators & Iterators

In the realm of Python programming, efficiency and simplicity often go together. One of the powerful yet underutilized features of Python is the concept of generators and iterators. These tools are not only elegant in their design but also remarkable in their ability to handle data sequences efficiently. This book delves deep into the world of generators and iterators, exploring how to create and utilize them for various applications. Our journey will begin with understanding the core concepts, followed by exploring the intricacies of generator functions, the magic of the yield statement, and the practicality of iterating through sequences. Each topic will be accompanied by a detailed introduction, ensuring a comprehensive grasp of these concepts.

In this chapter we will discuss the following topics:

- Understanding Generators and Iterators
- Creating Generator Functions
- The yield Statement
- Iterating through Sequences
- Practical Applications

Understanding Generators and Iterators

Generators and iterators are fundamental concepts in Python that allow for efficient and concise handling of sequences of data. They are particularly useful in situations where you need to process large datasets or streams of data that wouldn't fit entirely in memory. This chapter aims to demystify these concepts, providing a solid foundation for understanding how they work and why they are beneficial in Python programming.

What are Iterators?

An iterator in Python is an object that can be iterated upon, meaning it returns data, one element at a time. Python iterator objects must implement two special methods, `__iter__()` and `__next__()`. The `__iter__()` method returns the iterator object itself and is implicitly called at the start of loops. The `__next__()` method returns the next item in the sequence and raises the **StopIteration** exception when there are no more items..

Here's a simple example of creating a custom iterator:

```
class ReverseCounter:

    def __init__(self, start_value):

        self.value = start_value

    def __iter__(self):

        # The iterator object itself is returned

        return self

    def __next__(self):

        # Check if the countdown has reached or passed zero

        if self.value <= 0:

            # Signals the end of the iteration

            raise StopIteration

        else:
```

```
            # Save the current value to return
            current = self.value
            # Decrement the counter
            self.value -= 1
            return current
# Example of how to use this class
for num in ReverseCounter(3):
    print(num)
```

In this code a class ReverseCounter is defined that acts as a custom iterator. This class counts down from a specified start value to 1.

Let's break down each part of the code to understand how it works:

Class Definition: ReverseCounter

`__init__(self, start_value):`

This is the constructor of the class. It initializes a new instance of ReverseCounter.

start_value: This parameter sets the initial value from which the countdown begins.

self.value: This attribute stores the current state of the countdown, initialized to start_value.

`__iter__(self):`

This method is required to make an object iterable. According to Python's iterator protocol, the __iter__() method must return the iterator object itself. Here, it returns self, allowing Python's iteration mechanisms (like loops) to use the ReverseCounter object as an iterator.

`__next__(self):`

This method is also a requirement of the iterator protocol. It's called automatically by Python's iterators (like in a for loop) to get the next item.

If `self.value` is 0 or less, the method raises a StopIteration exception. This is how Python iterators signal that they are exhausted, i.e., there are no more elements to provide.

If there are still numbers to count down, the method stores the current value of self.value in the variable current, decrements self.value by 1, and returns current.

The example shows how to use the `ReverseCounter` class in a for loop. The for loop automatically calls the `__iter__()` and `__next__()` methods.

```
for num in ReverseCounter(3):
```

This line creates an instance of `ReverseCounter` starting from `3`.

The loop iterates over the `ReverseCounter` instance. On each iteration, it prints the current number as the countdown progresses from `3` to `1`.

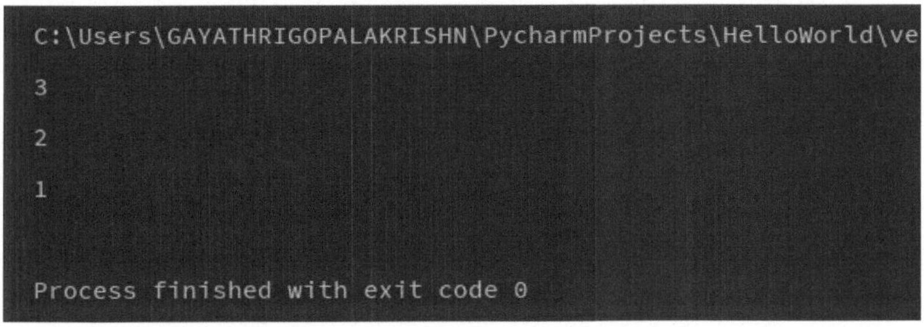

Figure 7.1: *output of creating a custom iterator*

The preceding **Figure 7.1** displays the output of creating a custom iterator.

What are Generators?

Generators are a simple way of creating iterators. A generator is a function that behaves like an iterator, i.e., it can be used in a for loop. The defining feature of a generator is the yield keyword. When a generator function calls yield, the state of the generator is "frozen," and the value is returned. The next time the generator is called, it resumes from where it left off.

The beauty of generators is that they allow for the generation of values on the fly and thus do not require all the values to be held in memory. This makes them extremely efficient when dealing with large datasets.

Here's an example of a generator function:

```
def reverse_string(string):

    length = len(string)

    for i in range(length - 1, -1, -1):

        yield string[i]


# Example usage

for char in reverse_string(“hello”):

    print(char)
```

In the `reverse_string` generator, the yield statement returns the next character in the string in reverse order. Each iteration of the for-loop in the example usage calls the generator, which resumes where it left off and yields the next character.

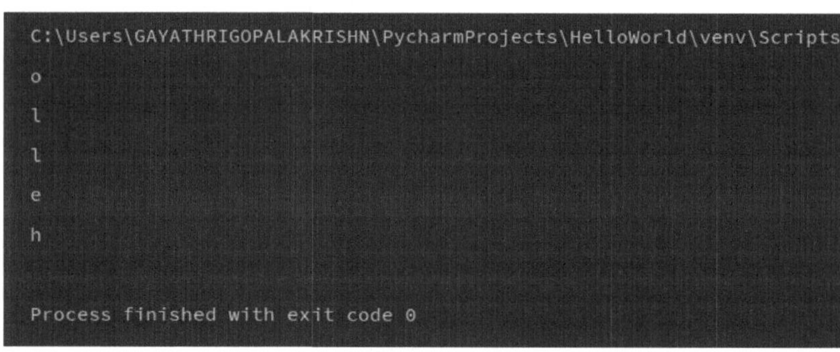

Figure 7.2: *output of a generator function*

The preceding **Figure 7.2** displays the output of a generator function.

Comparing Generators and Iterators

An iterator is defined by a class with __iter__() and __next__() methods, while a generator is created with a function that uses the yield keyword to produce values on the fly.

When comparing iterators and generators in Python, it's useful to contrast their creation mechanisms (using classes vs. functions), and how they handle local variables.

Here's a detailed comparison:

Creation Mechanism

To create an iterator, you define a class that implements the `__iter__()` and `__next__()` methods. The `__iter__()` method returns the iterator object itself, and the `__next__()` method returns the next item in the sequence. When there are no more items to return, `__next__()` must raise a `StopIteration` exception.

```
class BackwardSequence:

    def __init__(self, sequence):

        self.sequence = sequence

        self.position = len(sequence)  # Sets the initial position at
the end of the sequence


    def __iter__(self):

        # This method ensures the class can be iterated over by
returning the iterator object itself

        return self


    def __next__(self):

        # This method retrieves the next item in the sequence, moving
backwards

        if self.position == 0:
```

```
            # If position is at the beginning, end the iteration

            raise StopIteration

        self.position -= 1  # Move the position back by one

        return self.sequence[self.position]  # Return the element at the
new position
```

- Class Name: BackwardSequence clearly indicates that this class provides a way to iterate over a sequence in reverse order.
- Method and Variable Names: The names sequence and position are straightforward and describe their purpose, helping maintain clarity in the code.
- Functionality: The functionality remains the same; it iterates through the given sequence in reverse order. The iterator starts at the end of the sequence and moves backwards with each call to __next__, returning the current element before decrementing the index.

Generator Functions

Generators are created by defining a function with at least one yield statement. When the function is called, it returns a generator iterator but does not start execution immediately. Each call to the generator's `__next__()` method resumes the function until it hits a yield statement, which pauses the function and returns a value. The function ends when the generator function completes, automatically raising **`StopIteration`**.

```
def reverse(data):

for index in range(len(data) - 1, -1, -1):

yield data[index]
```

This example shows a generator function that accomplishes the same as the class-based iterator above but with less code.

Local Variables

In class-based iterators, local variables are stored as instance attributes. You have full control over the state, and you can manipulate the attributes in each call to `__next__()`. The state persists across method calls, allowing you to track the iteration's progress and any other necessary data.

Persistence: The state of the iterator (including local variables) is explicitly managed, making it clear how and when state changes occur.

Generator Functions

In generator functions, local variables are maintained automatically by the generator's execution frame. When execution is paused at a yield statement, the function's local state, including the local variables, execution point, and internal state, is automatically saved.

Persistence: The generator's state is implicitly maintained between yields. This automatic handling simplifies the code but offers less explicit control over the state compared to class-based iterators.

Efficiency of Generators and Iterators

Generators and iterators are highly efficient when dealing with large datasets. Instead of loading the entire dataset into memory, they allow processing of one item at a time, thereby reducing memory usage. This makes them ideal for tasks such as reading large files, processing streams of data, or generating infinite sequences.

Understanding generators and iterators is crucial for writing efficient Python code, especially when dealing with large data sequences. They not only provide a memory-efficient way of iterating over data but also offer a clean and maintainable approach to handle sequential data. As we progress through the following chapters, we will dive deeper into creating generator functions, using the yield statement, and iterating through sequences with practical examples and applications.

Creating Generator Functions

Generator functions are a cornerstone of Python's approach to handling iterables efficiently. Unlike regular functions that return a single value and terminate, generator functions are designed to yield a sequence of values over time, pausing and resuming their execution between each value generated. This ability to maintain state between outputs makes generator functions an invaluable tool in Python programming, especially when dealing with large datasets or complex iterative processes.

The Basics of Generator Functions

A generator function is defined like a normal function, but instead of returning a value and exiting, it uses the yield statement to pass back a value and pause its execution. The function can then be resumed right after the last yield run. This behavior turns the function into a generator object, capable of producing a sequence of results over time rather than a single result.

Here's a basic example of a generator function:

```
def simple_counter(max):

    count = 0

    while count < max:

        yield count

        count += 1

# Example usage

for i in simple_counter(3):

    print(i)
```

In this `simple_counter` function, the yield statement is used to return a value and pause the function. Each call to the generator's `__next__()` method resumes the function where it left off, until max is reached.

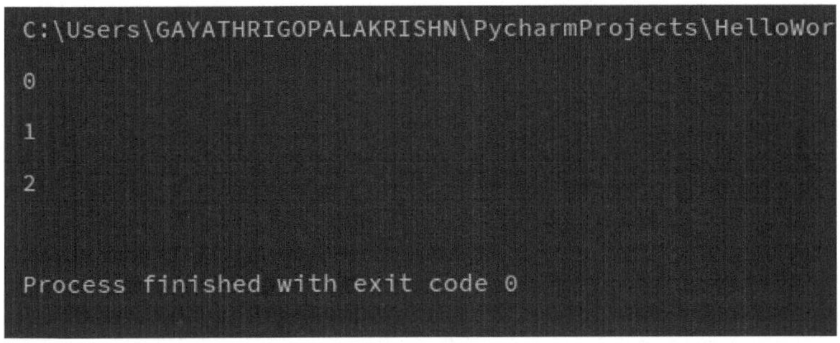

`Figure 7.3`: output of a simple counter function

The preceding `Figure 7.3` displays the output of a simple counter function.

Advantages of Generator Functions

Generator functions have several advantages:

- **Memory Efficiency**: They allow for the generation of values on the fly and do not require all the values to be held in memory. This is particularly beneficial for processing large datasets.
- **Lazy Evaluation**: Generators compute the next value only when needed, which can lead to performance improvements in your programs.
- **Maintain State**: Generators maintain their local state and execution context between calls, making them useful for managing complex sequences.

Creating Complex Generators

Generator functions can be as complex as needed. They can include multiple yield statements, control structures like loops and conditionals, and can even be used to create infinite sequences.

Consider the following complex generator that generates Fibonacci numbers:

```
def fibonacci_sequence(n):

    a, b = 0, 1

    cnt = 0

    while cnt < n:
```

```
        yield a

        a, b = b, a + b

        cnt += 1

# Example usage

for fib in fibonacci_sequence(5):

    print(fib)
```

In this example, the **fibonacci_sequence** function yields the next number in the Fibonacci sequence each time it's called, up to **n** numbers. The use of multiple variables and a while loop illustrates how generators can handle more complex logic.

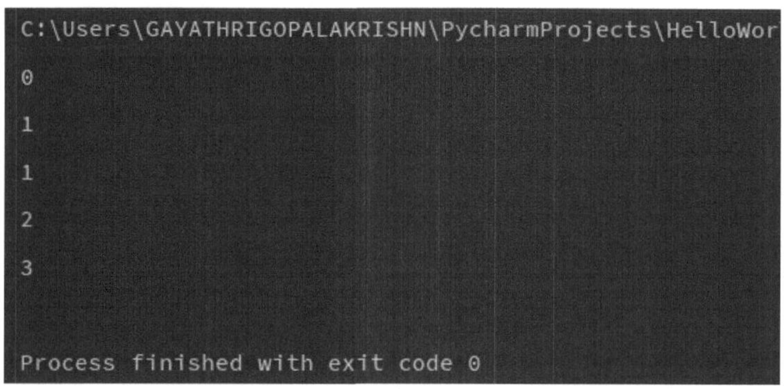

Figure 7.4: *output of Fibonacci series*

The preceding **Figure 7.4** displays the output of Fibonacci series.

Generators with External State

Generators can interact with external state, making them extremely flexible. They can read from files, interact with network resources, or communicate with other parts of your program, pausing and resuming as needed.

Here's an example of a generator that reads lines from a file:

```
def fetch_lines_from_file(filepath):

    """Generator function that iteratively reads and yields each line from a specified file,
```

```
    stripping any leading or trailing whitespace.”””
    with open(filepath, ‘r’) as file_handle:
        for line_content in file_handle:
            yield line_content.strip()
# Demonstrating how to use the generator function
for content in fetch_lines_from_file(‘sample.txt’):
    print(content)
```

This **fetch_lines_from_file** generator function reads a file line by line. Each call to the generator yields the next line in the file, making it memory efficient for reading large files.

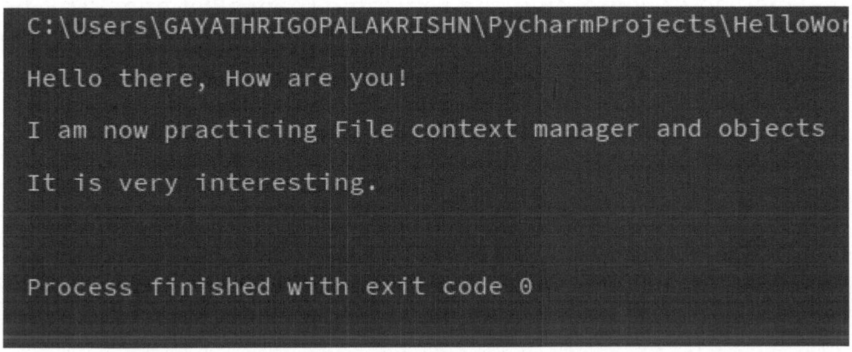

Figure 7.5: *output of generator that reads lines from a file*

The preceding **Figure 7.5** displays the output of generator that reads lines from a file.

Generator functions are a powerful feature in Python, offering an efficient and elegant way to generate sequences of values. They are particularly useful for handling large datasets, complex iterative logic, and situations where maintaining state between iterations is necessary. Understanding how to create and use generator functions is essential for Python programmers, especially in data processing and streaming applications. As we progress, we will explore the yield statement in more detail and see how it plays a pivotal role in the behavior of generator functions.

The yield Statement

In Python, the yield statement is what differentiates a generator function from a regular function. It is the cornerstone of generator functionality, enabling functions to send back a value and pause their execution, to be resumed later. This chapter explores the intricacies of yield, how it works, and its implications for memory and performance in Python programs.

Understanding yield

When a generator function calls yield, it effectively 'freezes': the state of the function is saved, including local variables and the point of execution. The next time the generator is called, it 'thaws' and continues execution from the point it left off, right after the yield statement.

The yield statement thus allows a function to generate a sequence of values over time, instead of computing and returning them all at once. This behavior is crucial for working with large data sets or streams of data where you want to use or process one item at a time.

Basic Usage of yield

Let's start with a simple example to illustrate the basic usage of yield

```
def reverse_count(start):

    “””Generator that counts down from the given starting number to 1, yielding each value.”””

    while start > 0:

        yield start

        start -= 1

# Demonstrating how to use the generator

for value in reverse_count(3):

    print(value)
```

In this countdown generator, the yield statement is used inside a while loop. Each iteration of the loop yields the current count, then decrements it. When used in a for-loop, the generator resumes where it left off after each yield, counting down until it reaches zero.

Figure 7.6: *output of basic usage of yield*

The preceding **Figure 7.6** displays the output of basic usage of yield

yield in a Complex Scenario

yield can be used in more complex scenarios, such as iterating over a nested structure or handling sophisticated data processing.

Here's an example of using yield to flatten a nested list:

```
def flatten(nested_list):

    for sublist in nested_list:

        for item in sublist:

            yield item

# Example usage

nested_list = [[1, 2, 3], [4, 5], [6]]

for number in flatten(nested_list):

    print(number)
```

In this flatten generator, there are two nested loops. The yield statement is placed in the inner loop, yielding items from each sublist in turn. This approach is memory-efficient and elegant, especially for very large or deeply nested lists.

Figure 7.7: *output of usage of yield in a complex scenario*

The preceding **Figure 7.7** displays the output of usage of yield in a complex scenario.

yield and State Preservation

One of the key features of yield is its ability to preserve the state of a function. This means that local variables and their states are remembered between successive calls to the generator. This state preservation is what allows generators to produce a series of outputs over time.

Consider this generator function that maintains state internally:

```
def accumulator():

    total = 0

    while True:

        value = yield total

        if value is None: break

        total += value
```

```
# Example usage

acc = accumulator()

next(acc)  # Start the generator

print(acc.send(1))  # Send a value and print the total

print(acc.send(2))
```

In the accumulator example, the generator maintains the total variable state between calls. Each time a value is sent to it using the `send()` method, it adds to the total and yields the updated total.

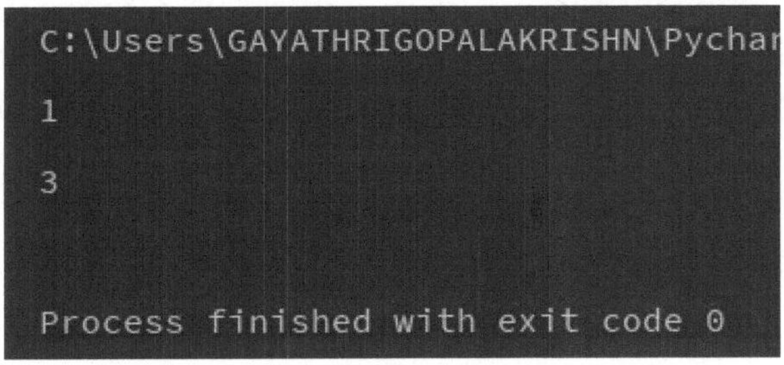

***Figure 7.8**: output of usage of yield and state preservation*

The preceding **Figure 7.8** displays the output of usage of yield and state preservation.

The Difference Between yield and return

It's important to distinguish between yield and return. While return is used to exit a function and return a value, yield is used to pause the function, save its state, and return a value. The function can then be resumed right after the yield statement.

Performance Implications

The use of yield can have significant performance implications. Since it allows for generating values on-the-fly, it reduces memory consumption, especially when dealing with large datasets. Generators are thus more memory-efficient than returning lists or other sequences, as they produce one item at a time.

The yield statement is a powerful feature in Python, enabling the creation of generators which are efficient in both memory and execution. By understanding how yield works and how it can be used in various scenarios, Python programmers can write more efficient and elegant code, especially when dealing with large or complex data structures. As we move forward, we will explore how to iterate through sequences using generators and iterators, further demonstrating the utility of the yield.

Iterating through Sequences

Iterating through sequences is a fundamental aspect of programming in Python, especially when dealing with collections like lists, tuples, or even more complex data structures. While Python provides several built-in methods and functions to iterate, using generators and iterators offers a more efficient and elegant approach, particularly for large datasets. This chapter will explore various methods of iterating through sequences, highlighting the advantages of using generators and iterators.

Traditional Iteration Methods

Before delving into generators and iterators, it's important to understand traditional iteration methods in Python. The most common method is the for loop, which is used to iterate over items in any sequence (such as a list or string), in the order that they appear.

Here's a basic example of using a for loop to iterate over a list:

```
numbers=[1,2,3,4,5]

for number in numbers:

  print number
```

While this method is straightforward, it is not always the most efficient, especially for very large sequences.

Figure 7.9: *output of usage of for loop*

The preceding **Figure 7.9** displays the output of usage of for loop.

Iterating with Generators

Generators provide an alternative method for iterating through sequences, especially when dealing with large data sets. They allow you to declare a function that behaves like an iterator, i.e., it can be used in a for loop.

Here's an example of iterating through a large range of numbers using a generator:

```
def iterate_large_sequence(upper_limit):

    """Generator function that yields numbers from 0 up to, but not
including, the specified upper limit."""

    current = 0

    while current < upper_limit:

        yield current

        current += 1

# Example of how to use the generator

for num in iterate_large_sequence(1000000):

    # Handle each number, placeholder for actual processing

    pass
```

In this example, `iterate_large_sequence` is a generator function that yields numbers from 0 to `upper_limit`. This is much more memory-efficient than creating a list of a million numbers and then iterating over it.

Iterating with Iterators

Iterators are also an efficient way to iterate through sequences, particularly when using built-in functions like `iter()` and `next()`. An iterator can be created from any `iterable` object in Python, such as lists, tuples, or strings.

Here's an example of manually iterating over a list using an iterator:

```
numbers = [1, 2, 3, 4, 5]

it = iter(numbers)

try:

    while True:

        print(next(it))

except StopIteration:

    pass
```

In this code, iter(numbers) returns an iterator object for the list numbers, and next(it) is used to get the next item from the iterator. The StopIteration exception signals the end of the sequence.

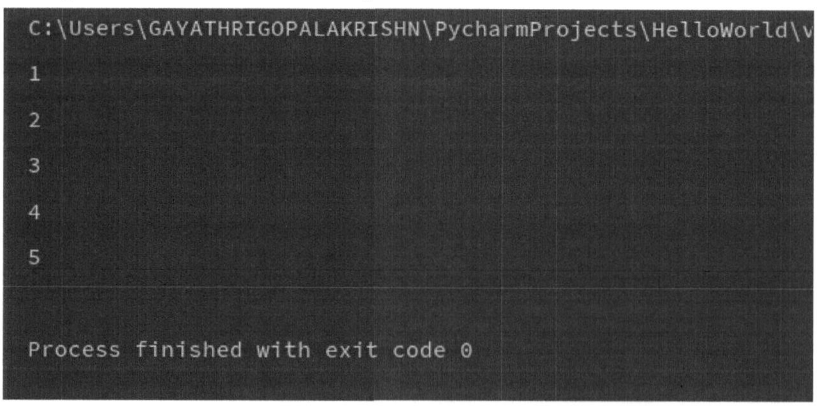

Figure 7.10: *output of iterating with iterators*

The preceding `Figure 7.10` displays the output of iterating with iterators.

Generator Expressions

A generator expression is a more concise way to create generators. It looks like a list comprehension but uses parentheses instead of square brackets.

Here's an example:

```
squares = (a*a for a in range(10))

for val in squares:

    print(val)
```

This generator expression generates squares of numbers from `0` to `9`. It's a compact and memory-efficient way to generate values.

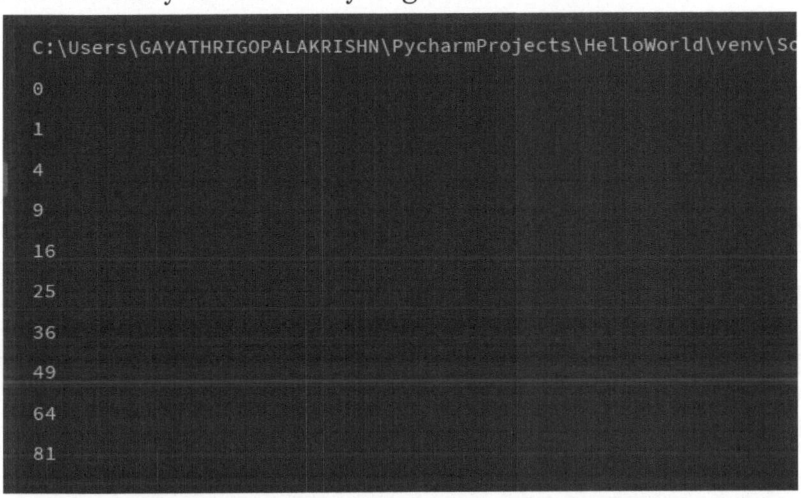

`Figure 7.11`: *output of generator expressions*

The preceding `Figure 7.11` displays the output of generator expressions.

Use Cases for Iterating with Generators and Iterators

Generators and iterators are particularly useful in scenarios involving large datasets or streams of data. They are also handy when the complete dataset is not available at the start, such as data read from a file, a database, or a network.

For example, consider a scenario where you need to read lines from a large file and process them:

```
def stream_large_file(path):

    """Generator function that streams lines from a specified file, removing any leading or trailing whitespace."""

    with open(path, 'r') as file_handle:

        for content in file_handle:

            yield content.strip()


# Demonstrating how to use the generator

for content in stream_large_file('massive_document.txt'):

pass
```

This function efficiently reads a large file line by line without loading the entire file into memory.

Iterating through sequences is a key part of Python programming, and understanding how to do this efficiently is crucial. Generators and iterators offer powerful and memory-efficient methods for iteration, especially useful in handling large datasets or data streams. By employing these techniques, Python programmers can write more efficient, readable, and elegant code. In the next chapter, we will explore practical applications of these concepts, demonstrating their utility in real-world scenarios.

Practical Applications

The true power of generators and iterators is best appreciated when applied to real-world scenarios. Their ability to handle large datasets efficiently, process streams of data on-the-fly, and simplify complex data processing tasks makes them invaluable in various practical applications. This chapter will explore several scenarios where generators and iterators can be effectively utilized, with examples demonstrating their implementation and benefits.

Application 1: Working with Large Data Files

One of the most common applications of generators is in processing large data files. Unlike traditional methods that require loading the entire file into memory, generators allow for processing the file line by line, thus conserving memory.

Here's an example of using a generator to process a large log file:

```
def stream_log_entries(log_path):

    """Generator function that iteratively reads each line from a log file, stripping unnecessary whitespace."""

    with open(log_path, 'r') as log_file:

        for entry in log_file:

            yield entry.strip()


# Demonstrating how to utilize the generator

for entry in stream_log_entries('server.log'):

    # Placeholder for specific log line processing

    pass
```

In this example, stream_log_entries is a generator that yields one line of the log file at a time. This approach is particularly useful for very large files, where loading the entire file into memory would be impractical.

Application 2: Data Stream Processing

Generators are ideally suited for processing data streams, such as real-time data from sensors, stock market feeds, or social media streams. They can process and yield data as it arrives, making them perfect for such applications.

Consider an example where we process data from a sensor:

```
def process_sensor_data(sensor):

    while True:

        data = sensor.get_data()
```

```
        if data:

            yield data


# Example usage

sensor = Sensor()

for data in process_sensor_data(sensor):

    # Analyze sensor data

    pass
```

Here, process_sensor_data is a generator that continuously yields data from a sensor. This setup is useful for real-time data processing applications.

Application 3: Pagination and Lazy Evaluation

Generators are excellent for implementing pagination or lazy evaluation, where you retrieve and process a part of a dataset at a time. This is particularly useful in web development, database queries, or working with APIs.

Here's an example of using a generator for paginated API requests:

```
def process_sensor_data(sensor):

    while True:

        data = sensor.get_data()

        if data:

            yield data


# Example usage

sensor = Sensor()

for data in process_sensor_data(sensor):

    # Analyze sensor data
```

```
    pass
```

This function fetches data from a paginated API, yielding items page by page.

Application 4: Infinite Sequences

Generators are useful for generating infinite sequences, which would be impossible to store in memory. This can be applied in simulations, gaming, or generating a sequence of values.

Example: Generating an infinite sequence of Fibonacci numbers:

```
def fibonacci():
    x, y = 0, 1
    while True:
        yield x
        x, y = y, x + y
# Example usage
for num in fibonacci():
    if num > 10000: break
    print(num)
```

This generator produces an infinite Fibonacci sequence, only limited by the break condition in the `for` loop.

Figure 7.12: output of Fibonacci series

The preceding `Figure 7.12` displays the output of Fibonacci series.

Application 5: Coroutine-Based Programming

Generators can be used to implement coroutines in Python, which allow for cooperative multitasking and asynchronous programming. This is particularly useful in scenarios like networked applications, where tasks can be paused and resumed as data becomes available.

Here's a basic example of a coroutine:

```
def coroutine():

    while True:

        value = yield

        # Process the value

# Example usage

co = coroutine()

next(co)  # Prime the coroutine
```

```
co.send(10)  # Send a value to the coroutine
```

In this example, `coroutine` is a generator used as a coroutine. It processes values sent to it asynchronously.

In this example, coroutine is a generator used as a coroutine. It processes values sent to it asynchronously.

Generators and iterators have diverse applications in real-world scenarios. Their ability to handle large datasets efficiently, process streams of data, manage pagination and lazy evaluation, generate infinite sequences, and enable coroutine-based programming makes them indispensable tools in Python programming. Understanding and leveraging these concepts can significantly enhance the efficiency and effectiveness of Python applications in various domains. As we have seen, the practical applications of generators and iterators are as vast as they are vital.

Conclusion

In conclusion, generators and iterators are powerful tools in Python that enable efficient data handling and processing. Generators are particularly useful for creating sequences of data that do not need to be stored in memory all at once, making them ideal for large data sets and stream-like data processing. Iterators allow Python programmers to traverse through these and other data types in a consistent manner. By mastering these concepts, you can enhance your programming skills and prepare yourself for more complex data manipulations.

Looking ahead, the next chapter will delve into Data Structures. This will cover essential ways to organize, manage, and store data efficiently, which is crucial for developing effective algorithms and improving performance in Python applications. Stay tuned to explore more on how various data structures can be implemented and utilized in Python.

Exercise: Test Your Understanding

Answer the following questions and test your understanding of learning from `Chapter 7`:

`Q. 1.` What is an iterator in Python?

`Q. 2.` How do generators differ from regular functions?

`Q. 3.` Can you name two methods that are mandatory for an iterator?

`Q. 4.` What happens when a generator function calls yield?

`Q. 5.` Why are generators and iterators preferred for large datasets?

`Q. 6.` How is a generator function defined in Python?

`Q. 7.` What makes generator functions more memory-efficient?

`Q. 8.` Can generator functions maintain their internal state between calls?

`Q. 9.` Give an example of a simple generator function?

`Q. 10.` Are generator functions capable of handling complex logic?

`Q. 11.` What is the role of the yield statement in a generator function?

`Q. 12.` How does yield differ from return in Python functions?

`Q. 13.` Can a generator function have multiple yield statements?

`Q. 14.` What happens when a generator function resumes execution?

`Q. 15.` Is it possible to send data back into a generator function?

`Q. 16.` What is a common method used to iterate over items in a sequence in Python?

`Q. 17.` Why are generators preferable for iterating over large sequences?

`Q. 18.` Can iterators be created for built-in data types in Python?

`Q. 19.` What is a generator expression?

`Q. 20.` Give an example where iterators are particularly useful?

Q. 21. How can generators be used in file processing?

Q. 22. In what scenarios are generators ideal for data stream processing?

Q. 23. How can generators facilitate pagination in web applications?

Q. 24. What is an example of using generators to create infinite sequences?

Q. 25. Can generators be used for asynchronous programming?

Notes

Date:

Keep an Open Mind

Programming is an art; like any artist, you need to keep an open mind and be willing to experiment. Don't be afraid to make mistakes – they are part of learning. Every error message is a step closer to your goal. Happy coding!

Chapter 8

Data Structures

Data structures are fundamental concepts in programming that enable the organization, management, and storage of data in a computer. They are critical for efficient data handling and can significantly impact the performance of software applications. In programming, a well-chosen data structure can improve the efficiency of data access and manipulation, leading to more efficient algorithms and more responsive software.

At their core, data structures are about organizing data in a way that aligns with the operations to be performed on them. This organization can take many forms, from simple arrays and lists to more complex structures like trees and graphs. The choice of data structure affects how quickly and efficiently these operations can be executed. For instance, searching for an item in a well-organized data structure can be much faster than searching through an unstructured collection of data.

In this chapter, we will cover:

- Overview of Data Structures
- Lists: Creation and Manipulation
- Tuples: Immutable Data Structures
- Dictionaries: Key-Value Pairs
- Common Data Structure Operations

Overview of Data Structures

Python, known for its simplicity and readability, offers a variety of built-in data structures that are flexible and easy to use.

These include:

- Lists: Python lists are dynamic arrays that can store elements of different types. They are ordered, mutable, and allow duplicate elements. Lists are ideal for situations where the data collection might grow or shrink, and where the order of elements matters.
- Tuples: Tuples are similar to lists but are immutable. Once a tuple is created, its elements cannot be changed. Tuples are faster than lists and are used to write-protect data.
- Sets: Sets are unordered collections of unique elements. They are mutable and are especially useful for membership testing, removing duplicates from a sequence, and mathematical operations like union, intersection, difference, and symmetric difference.
- Dictionaries: Dictionaries in Python are unordered collections of key-value pairs. They are mutable and indexed by keys, which can be any immutable type. Dictionaries are optimized for retrieving data when the key is known.

In addition to these, Python also supports more specialized data structures such as heaps, queues, and stacks through its standard libraries.

Dynamic Typing and its Effect on Data Structures

One of the key features of Python is its dynamic typing system. This means that the type of variable is determined at runtime, not in advance. This flexibility greatly influences how data structures are used and manipulated in Python.

- Flexibility in Data Types: In Python, data structures can hold different types of data. For example, a list can contain integers, strings, and even other lists. This flexibility is a direct result of Python's dynamic typing.
- Ease of Use: Dynamic typing makes Python data structures easy to use and flexible. You don't need to declare the type of data a structure will hold in advance, making the code more concise and readable.
- Performance Considerations: While dynamic typing offers flexibility, it can sometimes lead to less efficient memory usage and slower processing times compared to statically typed languages. This is because the interpreter needs to store type information for each element and perform type checking at runtime.

- Error Checking: Dynamic typing means that some errors that could be caught at compile time in statically typed languages are only found at runtime in Python. This aspect requires developers to be more vigilant with testing and debugging when working with complex data structures.

Understanding data structures and their implementation in Python is crucial for any programmer working in the language. The choice of the right data structure can greatly impact the efficiency and performance of a program. Python's dynamic typing adds a layer of flexibility to these data structures, making them more versatile but also requiring careful consideration regarding performance and error handling. As one delves deeper into Python programming, mastering these data structures and understanding their interaction with Python's dynamic typing system becomes essential for writing efficient, effective code.

Lists: Creation and Manipulation

In Python, a list is a versatile, ordered collection of items, where each item can be of a different type. Lists are one of the most commonly used data structures in Python due to their flexibility and ease of use. They can hold a mix of integers, floats, strings, other lists, and more, making them extremely useful for various programming tasks.

Creating Lists

To create a list in Python, you simply enclose items in square brackets `[ ]`, separated by commas. For example:

```
my_list = [1, 2, 3, 'Python', [4, 5]]
```

Here, `my_list` is a list containing three integers, a string, and another list.

Accessing List Elements

List elements are accessed using their index, with the first element at index `0`. For instance:

```
print(my_list[0])  # Outputs 1
```

```
print(my_list[3])  # Outputs 'Python'
```

Figure 8.1: Output of list

Python also supports negative indexing, where -1 refers to the last item, -2 to the second last, and so on:

```
print(my_list[-1])  # Outputs [4, 5]
```

Figure 8.2: Output of accessing list

Manipulating Lists

Lists are mutable, meaning you can add, remove, or change their elements.

Adding Elements

Using **append()**: Adds an item to the end of the list.

```
my_list.append('new item')

print(my_list)  # Outputs [1, 2, 3, 'Python', [4, 5], 'new item']
```

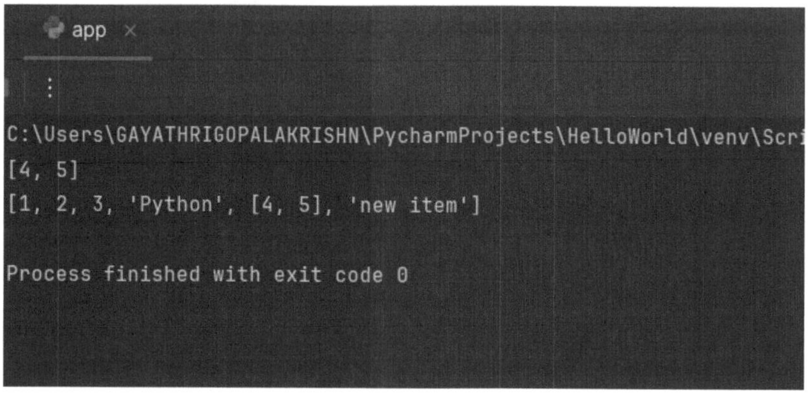

Figure 8.3: *Output of appending list elements*

The preceding `Figure 8.2` shows the output of Appending List Elements.

Using `insert()`: Inserts an item to a specified index.

```
my_list.append('new item')
print(my_list)  # Outputs [1, 2, 3, 'Python', [4, 5], 'new item']
my_list.insert(2, 'inserted item')
print(my_list)  # Outputs [1, 2, 'inserted item', 3, 'Python', [4, 5],
'new item']
```

Figure 8.4: *Adding list Elements*

The preceding `Figure 8.4` shows the output of Adding List Elements.

This code inserts 'inserted item' at index `2`.

Removing Elements

Using `remove()`: Removes the first occurrence of an item.

```
my_list = [1, 2, 3, 'Python', [4, 5]]
```

```
print(my_list[0])  # Outputs 1

print(my_list[3])  # Outputs 'Python'

print(my_list[-1])  # Outputs [4, 5]

my_list.append('new item')

print(my_list)  # Outputs [1, 2, 3, 'Python', [4, 5], 'new item']

my_list.insert(2, 'inserted item')

print(my_list)  # Outputs [1, 2, 'inserted item', 3, 'Python', [4, 5],
'new item']

my_list.remove('Python')

print(my_list)  # Outputs [1, 2, 'inserted item', 3, [4, 5], 'new item']
```

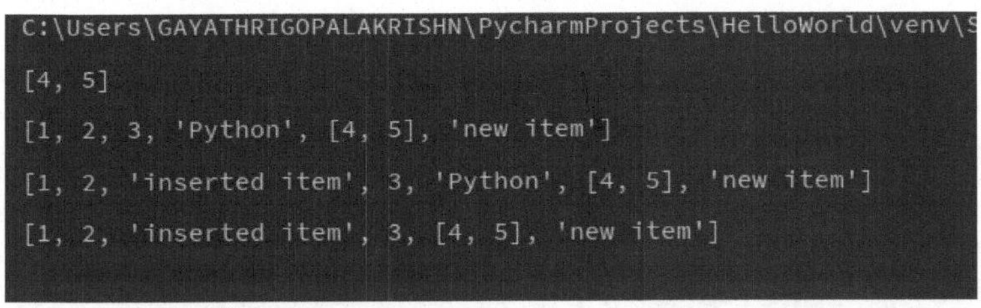

Figure 8.5: *Output of elements after removing from list*

This removes 'Python' from the list.

Using **pop()**: Removes the item at the specified index (or the last item if no index is provided).

```
popped_item = my_list.pop()

print(popped_item)  # Outputs 'new item'

print(my_list)       # Outputs [1, 2, 'inserted item', 3, [4, 5]]
```

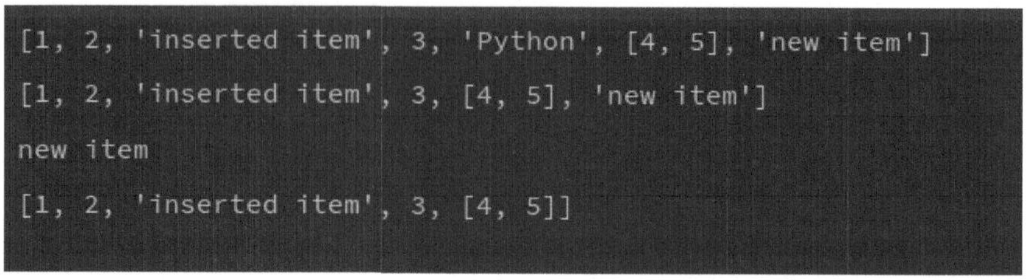

Figure 8.6: *Output of elements*

Modifying Elements

You can change the value of a list item by accessing it by its index:

```
my_list[1] = 'modified item'

print(my_list)  # Outputs [1, 'modified item', 'inserted item', 3, [4, 5]]
```

This code modifies the second element of **`my_list`**.

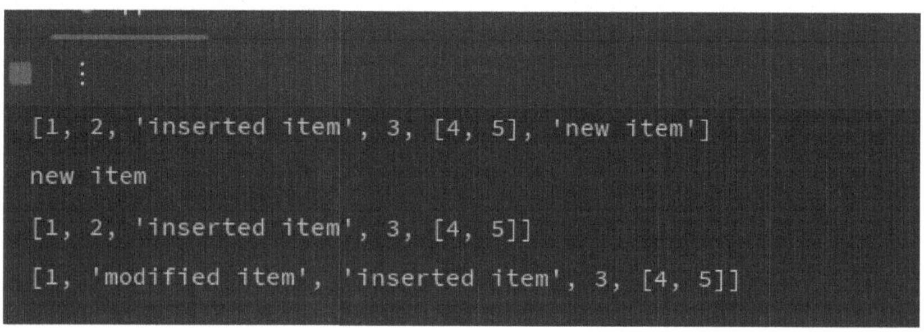

Figure 8.7: *modified list*

Additional List Operations

Lists in Python come with many more methods for different purposes.

Extending a List

Use **`extend()`** to add multiple elements from another **`iterable`** (like another list) to the end of the list.

```
another_list = [6, 7, 8]

my_list.extend(another_list)
```

```
print(my_list)  # Outputs [1, 'modified item', 'inserted item', 3, [4, 5], 6, 7, 8]
```

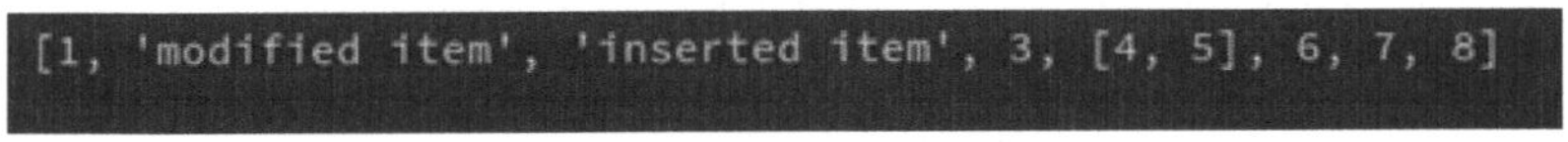

Figure 8.8: modified list

Finding an Element's Index

The **index()** method returns the first index of a specified value.

```
index_of_item = my_list.index('modified item')

print(index_of_item)  # Outputs 1
```

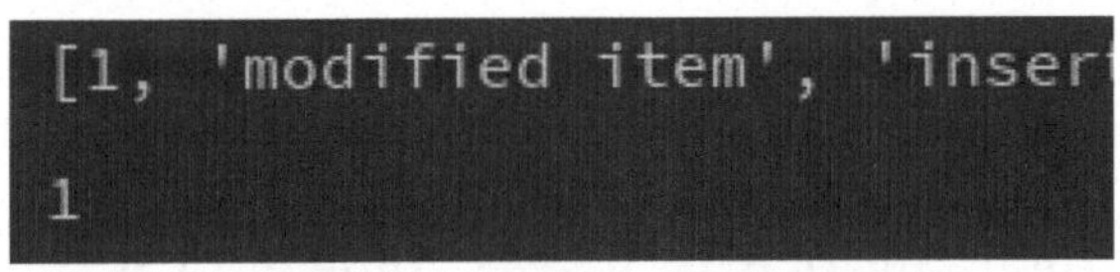

Figure 8.9: *finding element*

Counting Occurrences

Use **count()** to count how many times an item appears in a list.

```
my_list.append(8)

count_of_8 = my_list.count(8)

print(count_of_8)  # Outputs 2, assuming 8 appears twice in the list
```

Figure 8.10: occurrences

Reversing a List

Use `reverse()` to reverse the items of the list in place.

```
my_list.reverse()

print(my_list)  # Outputs a reversed list
```

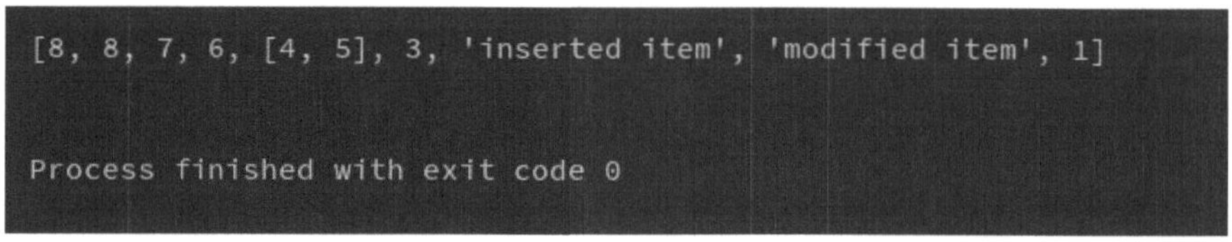

Figure 8.11: Reversed list

Sorting a List

Use `sort()` to sort the items of a list in ascending or descending order.

```
numbers = [3, 1, 4, 1, 5, 9, 2]

numbers.sort()

print(numbers)  # Outputs [1, 1, 2, 3, 4, 5, 9]
```

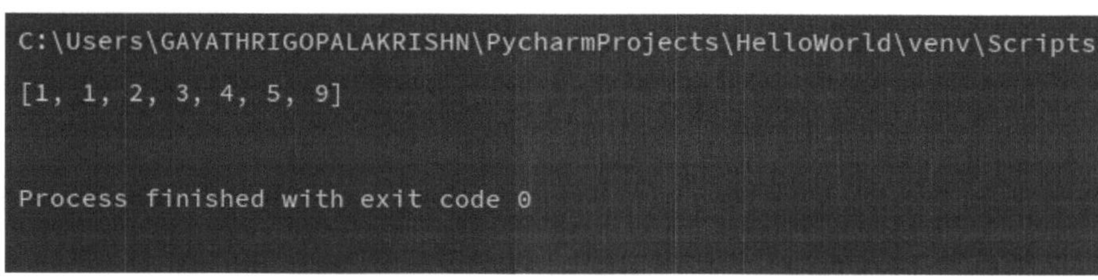

Figure 8.12: Sorted list

Clearing a List

Use `clear()` to remove all items from the list.

```
my_list.clear()

print(my_list)  # Outputs []
```

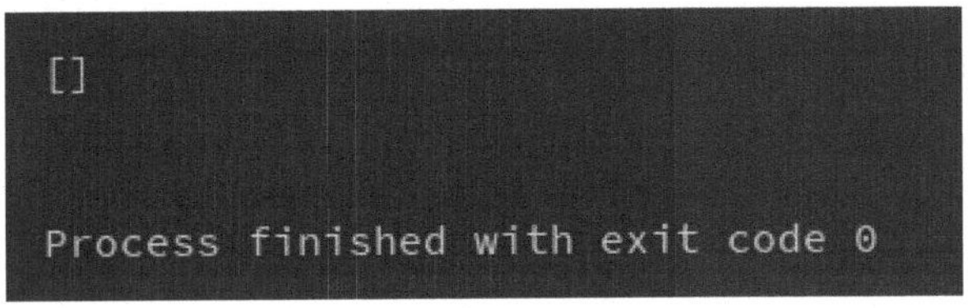

Figure 8.13: Empty list

Understanding how to create, access, and manipulate lists is fundamental in Python programming. Lists are incredibly versatile and can be used in a wide range of applications, from simple data storage to complex data processing tasks. The ability to hold different types of data and the numerous built-in methods for list manipulation make them an invaluable tool in a Python programmer's toolkit. The examples provided give a glimpse into the practical use of lists, demonstrating their flexibility and ease of use in various scenarios.

Tuples: Immutable Data Structures

Tuples in Python are quite like lists in terms of storing a collection of items. However, they have some key differences that make them unique and valuable in certain situations. A tuple is a collection which is ordered and immutable. This means that once a tuple is created, its contents cannot be modified, added to, or removed.

Differences Between Tuples and Lists

In this section we will discuss key differences

Immutability vs. Mutability

Tuples: Immutable, meaning once a tuple is created, you cannot change its contents.

Lists: Mutable, allowing for changes, additions, or deletions of their elements.

Tuples: Defined by enclosing elements in parentheses (), but can also be created without them, simply by separating items with commas.

Lists: Defined by square brackets `[ ]`.

Performance

Tuples: Generally faster than lists due to their immutability.

Lists: Slightly slower, as they need additional memory for dynamic memory allocation.

Use Cases

Tuples: Used for data that should not change throughout the course of a program.

Lists: Used when you need a collection that is changeable and needs to be modified.

Concept of Immutability

Immutability in programming refers to objects whose state cannot be modified after they are created. This feature is critical in situations where data integrity is essential, as it prevents accidental changes. In Python, tuples are the standard way to store immutable sequences of objects.

When to Use Tuples Over Lists

- Data Integrity: Use a tuple when you want to ensure the data cannot be changed accidentally.
- Performance: Tuples can be a more performant choice when dealing with large datasets, as they have a smaller memory footprint and faster processing.
- Hashable Objects: Since tuples are immutable, they can be used as keys in dictionaries, unlike lists.

Let's consider the example:

```
# Creating a tuple

my_tuple = (1, 'a', 3.14)

# Accessing elements

print(my_tuple[1])  # Outputs 'a'
```

Creating a Tuple

```
my_tuple = (1, 'a', 3.14)
```

This line creates a tuple **my_tuple** containing three elements: an integer 1, a string 'a', and a float 3.14. The elements are enclosed in parentheses.

Accessing Elements

```
print(my_tuple[1])  # Outputs 'a'
```

Tuples, like lists, are ordered, and their elements can be accessed via indexing. Here, **my_tuple[1]** accesses the second element (since indexing starts at 0), which is the string 'a'.

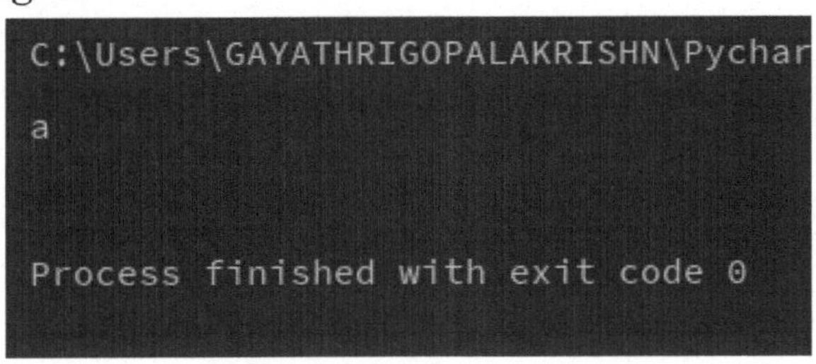

Figure 8.14: *Output of Tuple*

Tuple Without Parentheses

Tuples can also be created without explicit parentheses, using just commas.

```
my_tuple = (1, 'a', 3.14)

# Accessing elements

print(my_tuple[1])  # Outputs 'a'

another_tuple = 'Python', 42

print(another_tuple)  # Outputs ('Python', 42)
```

This creates a tuple **another_tuple** with two elements: **'Python'** and **42**.

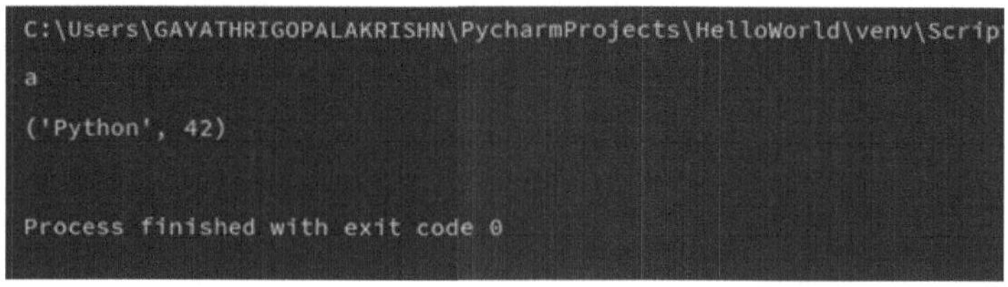

***Figure 8.15**: Output of another_tuple*

Single Element Tuple

Creating a single-element tuple requires a trailing comma.

```
# Creating a tuple

my_tuple = (1, ‘a’, 3.14)

# Accessing elements

print(my_tuple[1])  # Outputs ‘a’

another_tuple = ‘Python’, 42

print(another_tuple)  # Outputs (‘Python’, 42)

single_element_tuple = (5,)

print(single_element_tuple)  # Outputs (5,)
```

Without the comma, Python would not recognize it as a tuple.

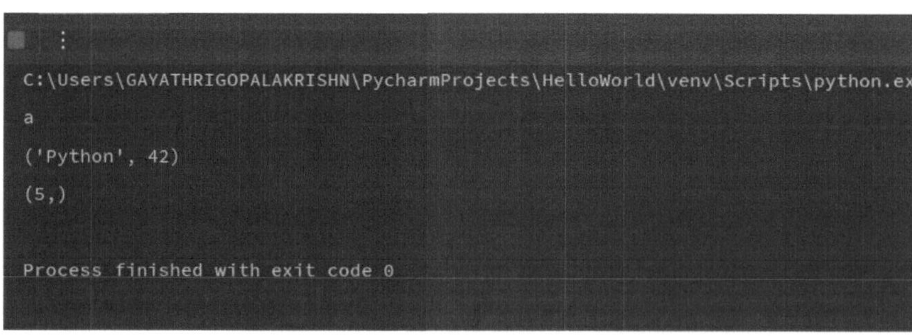

***Figure 8.16**: Output of single element*

Tuple Unpacking

Tuples allow an elegant way to unpack values.

```
# Creating a tuple

my_tuple = (1, 'a', 3.14)

# Accessing elements

print(my_tuple[1])  # Outputs 'a'

another_tuple = 'Python', 42

print(another_tuple)  # Outputs ('Python', 42)

single_element_tuple = (5,)

print(single_element_tuple)  # Outputs (5,)

name, age = another_tuple

print(name)  # Outputs 'Python'

print(age)  # Outputs 42
```

This unpacks the values of **another_tuple** into variables name and age.

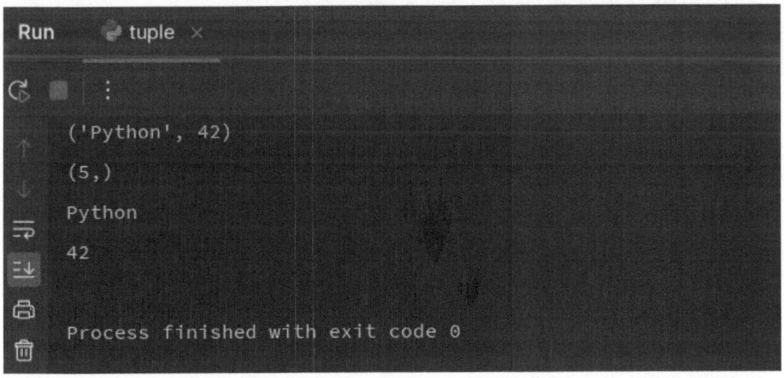

Figure 8.17: *Tuple unpacking*

Immutability in Action

Attempting to change a tuple's contents results in an error.

```
my_tuple[1] = 'b'  # Uncommenting this would raise a TypeError

print(my_tuple)
```

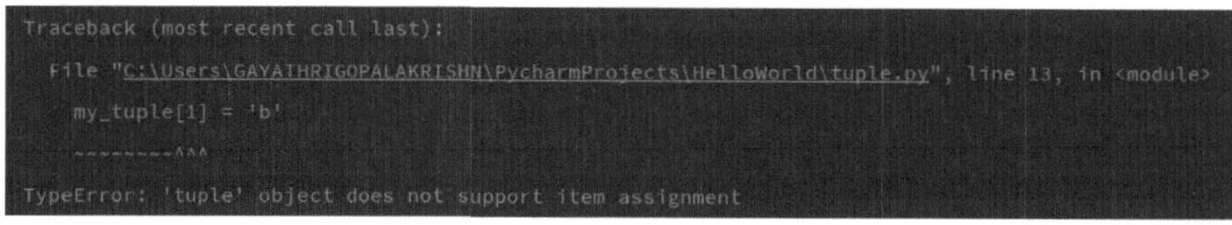

Figure 8.18: *Assignment error*

This line, if executed, would attempt to change the second element of my_tuple, resulting in a TypeError because tuples are immutable.

Iterating Over a Tuple

Like lists, tuples can be iterated over in a loop.

```
for item in my_tuple:

    print(item)
```

This loop prints each item in my_tuple, demonstrating that tuples, while immutable, are still iterable.

Figure 8.19: *Iterating tuple*

Using Tuples as Dictionary Keys

Tuples can be used as keys in dictionaries, which is not possible with lists.

```
tuple_as_key = {(1, 2): "tuple key"}
```

```
print(tuple_as_key[(1, 2)])  # Outputs 'tuple key'
```

This creates a dictionary with a tuple `(1, 2)` as a key.

```
tuple key


Process finished with exit code 0
```

Figure 8.20: *tuple key*

So, tuples are a fundamental data structure in Python, offering immutability and hence a way to ensure data integrity. They are particularly useful in situations where a collection of items is needed, but those items should not be modified. Understanding when and how to use tuples, in contrast to lists, is a key skill in Python programming. The examples provided highlight the practicality and functionality of tuples, demonstrating their immutable nature and how they can be used in various scenarios.

Dictionaries: Key-Value Pairs

In Python, dictionaries are versatile and powerful data structures that store data in key-value pairs. Each key-value pair in a dictionary is an item, with the key acting as a unique identifier for its corresponding value. Dictionaries are unordered collections (as of Python 3.7, they are considered ordered), meaning the items do not have a defined order.

Use Cases of Dictionaries

Dictionaries are widely used in various applications due to their efficiency in data retrieval. They are ideal for cases where data needs to be associated in a way that allows quick look-ups, updates, and deletions, such as:

- Storing Data with Unique Identifiers: Such as storing user information with usernames as keys.
- Implementing Mappings: Like word to definition mappings in a dictionary.
- Database-like Storage: For lightweight, in-memory databases.
- Data Caching: Storing precomputed values for quick access.

Creating Dictionaries

To create a dictionary, you enclose key-value pairs in curly braces {}, with a colon : separating each key from its value.

For example:

```
my_dict = {'name': 'Alice', 'age': 25}
```

Here, my_dict is a dictionary with two key-value pairs: 'name': 'Alice' and 'age': 25.

Accessing Dictionary Elements

Dictionary elements are accessed using their keys:

```
print(my_dict['name'])  # Outputs 'Alice'
```

This line prints the value associated with the key 'name' in my_dict, which is 'Alice'.

```
my_dict = {'name': 'Alice', 'age': 25}

print(my_dict['name'])  # Outputs 'Alice'
```

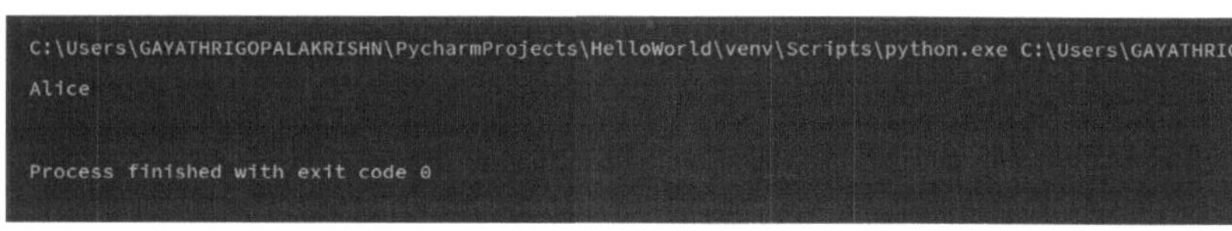

Figure 8.21: *Dictionary elements*

Manipulating Dictionaries

Dictionaries are mutable, and their elements can be added, removed, or modified.

Adding Elements

```
my_dict['location'] = 'New York'
```

This adds a new key-value pair 'location': 'New York' to my_dict.

```
my_dict['location'] = 'New York'
```

This adds a new key-value pair 'location': 'New York' to my_dict.

```
my_dict = {'name': 'Alice', 'age': 25}

print(my_dict['name'])  # Outputs 'Alice'

my_dict['location'] = 'New York'

age = my_dict.pop('age')

my_dict['name'] = 'Bob'
```

Figure 8.22: *Dictionary elements*

Removing Elements

Using **pop()**: This removes the key 'age' and its associated value from **my_dict** and returns the value.

```
my_dict = {'name': 'Alice', 'age': 25}

print(my_dict['name'])  # Outputs 'Alice'

my_dict['location'] = 'New York'

age = my_dict.pop('age')

print(my_dict)

print(age)
```

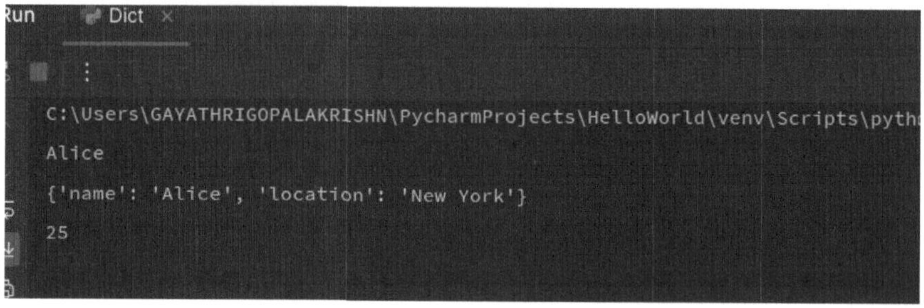

Figure 8.23: *Removing element*

Modifying Elements

```
my_dict[‘name’] = ‘Bob’
```

This modifies the value associated with the key ‘name’ to ‘Bob’.

Iterating Over a Dictionary

You can iterate over the keys, values, or key-value pairs in a dictionary:

```
my_dict = {‘name’: ‘Alice’, ‘age’: 25}

print(my_dict[‘name’])  # Outputs ‘Alice’

my_dict[‘location’] = ‘New York’

age = my_dict.pop(‘age’)

my_dict[‘name’] = ‘Bob’

for key, value in my_dict.items():

    print(f”{key}: {value}”)
```

This loop iterates over each key-value pair in **my_dict**, printing both the key and the value.

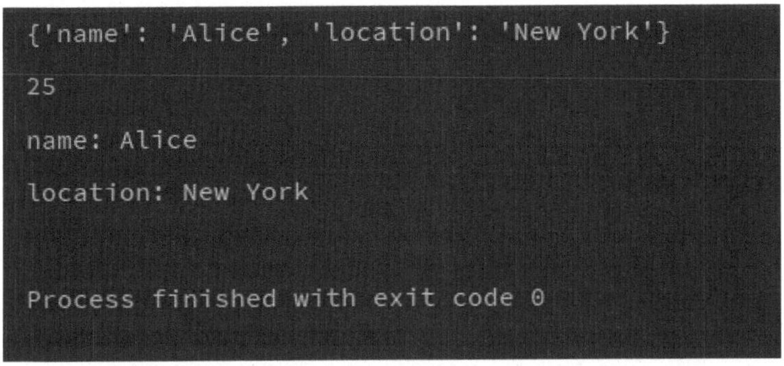

Figure 8.24: *Iterating over a Dictionary*

Creating a Nested Dictionary

Dictionaries can contain other dictionaries, allowing for nested data structures.

```
nested_dict = {'employee1': {'name': 'Alice', 'age': 25}, 'employee2': {'name': 'Bob', 'age': 30}}
```

Here, `nested_dict` contains two key-value pairs, each with a dictionary as a value.

Accessing Elements in a Nested Dictionary

To access elements in a nested dictionary, chain the keys.

```
print(nested_dict['employee1']['name'])  # Outputs 'Alice'
```

This retrieves the name of `'employee1'` from `nested_dict`.

```
nested_dict = {'employee1': {'name': 'Alice', 'age': 25}, 'employee2': {'name': 'Bob', 'age': 30}}
```

Figure 8.25: *Accessing element in nested dictionary*

Default Values with get()

The **get()** method returns the value for a key, or a default if the key is not found.

```
nested_dict = {'employee1': {'name': 'Alice', 'age': 25}, 'employee2': {'name': 'Bob', 'age': 30}}

print(nested_dict['employee1']['name'])  # Outputs 'Alice'

print(my_dict.get('age', 'Not available'))  # Outputs 'Not available'Since 'age' has been removed from my_dict, this returns the default value 'Not available'.
```

Since 'age' has been removed from **my_dict**, this returns the default value 'Not available'.

Figure 8.26: Not available

Iterating Over Keys and Values

You can also iterate over just keys or just values.

```
for key in my_dict.keys():

    print(key)

for value in my_dict.values():

    print(value)
```

The first loop prints all the keys, and the second loop prints all the values in my_dict.

```
name
location
Alice
New York
```

***Figure 8.27**: Iterating over Key and value*

Updating a Dictionary

The `update()` method can add multiple key-value pairs to a dictionary.

my_dict.update({'age': 26, 'email': 'bob@example.com'})

This adds 'age': 26 and 'email': 'bob@example.com' to my_dict.

```
{'name': 'Alice', 'location': 'New York', 'age': 26, 'email': 'bob@example.com'}
```

***Figure 8.28**: Update dictionary*

Removing All Items

The `clear()` method removes all items from the dictionary.

my_dict.clear()

This empties my_dict.

Dictionaries in Python are a fundamental and highly efficient data structure for managing key-value pairs. Their versatility in handling complex and nested data, combined with the speed of accessing elements, makes them indispensable in many programming scenarios. The mutability of dictionaries allows for dynamic and flexible data manipulation, and Python provides a variety of methods to work with dictionaries effectively. The examples provided showcase the practical applications and operations that can be performed with dictionaries, demonstrating their power and flexibility in Python programming.

Common Data Structure Operations

Python's data structures, such as lists, tuples, dictionaries, and sets, share a set of common operations. Understanding these operations is crucial for efficient data manipulation and analysis. These operations include iteration, length checking, membership testing, and more. Each operation has its performance implications, which vary depending on the data structure used.

Overview of Common Operations

Iteration: Iterating over data structures is a fundamental operation. It allows you to access each element in a structure, typically using a loop.

- Length Checking: This operation involves determining the number of elements in a data structure.
- Membership Testing: It checks whether an element is present in a data structure.
- Indexing and Slicing: Accessing elements by their position (indexing) or accessing a subset of elements (slicing).
- Adding/Removing Elements: Operations for modifying data structures by adding or removing elements.

Performance Implications

The performance of these operations can vary significantly:

- Lists and Tuples: Fast iteration and indexing but slow membership tests (especially for large lists) and adding/removing elements (except at the end of lists).
- Dictionaries and Sets: Extremely fast membership tests and adding/removing elements, but they do not support indexing and slicing.
- Tuples: Being immutable, they cannot add or remove elements after creation.

```
# Common operation on a list

my_list = [1,2,3]

print(len(my_list)) # Length of the list

print(2 in my_list) # Membership test


# Common operation on a dictionary
```

```
my_dict = {'name': 'Alice', 'age': 25}

print(len(my_dict)) # length of the dictionary

print('name' in my_dict) # membership test (key)
```

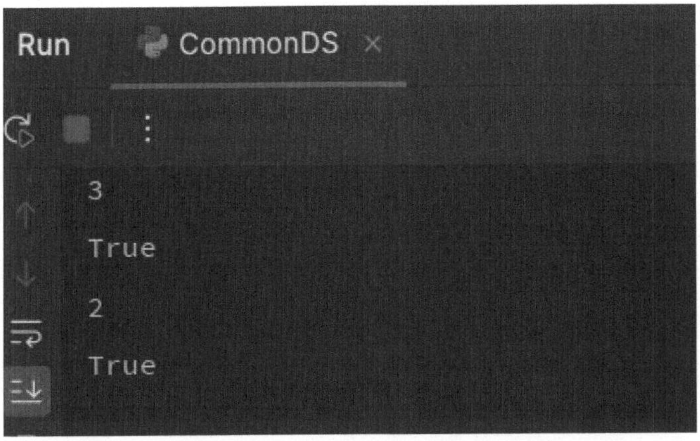

Figure 8.29: Common operations

Length of a List

```
print(len(my_list))
```

This line prints the length (number of elements) of `my_list`, which is `3`.

Membership Test in a List

```
print(2 in my_list)
```

This line checks if the number `2` is an element of `my_list`. It prints True as `2` is present in the list.

Length of a Dictionary

```
print(len(my_dict))
```

This prints the number of key-value pairs in my_dict, which is 2 ('name' and 'age').

Membership Test in a Dictionary

```
print('name' in my_dict)
```

This checks if 'name' is a key in `my_dict`. It prints True since `'name'` is indeed a key in the dictionary.

Iterating Over a List

Iterating over each element in a list can be done with a for loop.

```
for item in my_list:

    print(item)
```

This loop prints each element in `my_list`.

Indexing in Lists

Accessing an element by its position.

```
print(my_list[0])  # Outputs the first element
```

This line prints the first element of `my_list`, which is `1`.

Slicing Lists

Getting a subset of a list.

```
print(my_list[1:3])  # Outputs [2, 3]
```

This line prints a slice of `my_list` from index `1` to `2` (excluding index `3`).

Adding Elements to a Set

Sets allow adding unique elements.

```
my_set = {1, 2}

my_set.add(3)

print(my_set)  # Outputs {1, 2, 3}
```

This adds the number `3` to `my_set`.

Removing Elements from a Dictionary

Using pop() to remove a key-value pair.

```
age = my_dict.pop('age')

print(age)  # Outputs 25
```

This removes the key **'age'** from **my_dict** and prints its value.

In Python, different data structures support a variety of common operations, each with its performance characteristics. Understanding these operations and their implications on performance is essential for writing efficient Python code. The examples provided illustrate how these operations are implemented across different data structures, highlighting the versatility and power of Python's data structures in various programming scenarios.

Conclusion

In this chapter, we have discussed the fundamental data structures in Python. We started with an overview and discussed their importance in organizing and managing data efficiently. We also explored lists, learning to create and manipulate these universal and dynamic sequences. Following this, we examined tuples, appreciating their immutability and how they can be used to store data collections that should stay the same.

Next, we delved into dictionaries, discovering the power of key-value pairs and how they provide a flexible way to map and retrieve data. Understanding the operations that can be performed on these data structures is crucial for efficient data management. Lastly, we covered common data structure operations, equipping ourselves with essential techniques to manipulate and access data efficiently.

By learning these core data structures, we have built a solid foundation for handling data effectively in Python.

In the next chapter, we will focus on understanding file handling, how to read from and write files, and how to expand our programming capabilities further.

Exercise: Test Your Understanding

Answer the following questions and test your understanding of learning from `Chapter 8`:

`Q. 1.` What is a data structure in programming?

`Q. 2.` Why are data structures important in programming?

`Q. 3.` Name two commonly used data structures in Python?

`Q. 4.` How does a data structure impact the performance of a program?

`Q. 5.` What is the difference between primitive and composite data structures?

Notes

Date:

Chapter 9
Collections

In the realm of Python programming, the collections module stands as a cornerstone for advanced data manipulation and efficient data structure utilization. This module extends Python's built-in container types, offering specialized alternatives like deque, Counter, NamedTuple, and OrderedDict. Each of these structures is designed for specific scenarios, significantly enhancing the capability to handle data effectively. From managing ordered dictionaries to counting items with ease, and from structuring data with named tuples to efficient insertions and deletions with deques, this guide delves into the practical applications and advantages of these powerful tools, elevating your Python coding prowess to new heights.

In this chapter we will cover:

- Overview of the Collections Module
- Why Collections?
- Components of the Collections Module
- Working with Deque and Counter
- NamedTuple in Python
- Use Cases and Scenarios
- Enhanced Data Manipulation

Overview of the Collections Module

The Collections Module in Python is a built-in module that implements specialized container data types, providing alternatives to Python's general-purpose built-in containers. The primary focus of the collection module is to offer additional functionality beyond the standard data structures like lists, sets, tuples, and dictionaries. In this overview, we will delve into the intricacies of this module, understanding its components and how they enhance Python's data handling capabilities.

Why Collections?

Before diving into the specifics, it's crucial to understand why Python offers the collections module. Standard data structures are versatile, but they often don't provide the most efficient solution for all data management scenarios. Collections module fills this gap with optimized structures for specific tasks, leading to more readable, maintainable, and efficient code.

Components of the Collections Module

The Collections Module contains several data structures, each designed to solve different problems:

- Counter: A dictionary subclass for counting hashable objects.
- Deque: A list-like container with fast appends and pops on either end.
- NamedTuple: A function for creating tuple subclasses with named fields.
- OrderedDict: A dictionary subclass that remembers the order entries were added.
- DefaultDict: A dictionary subclass that calls a factory function to supply missing values.
- ChainMap: A class for creating a single view of multiple mappings.
- UserDict, UserList, UserString: Wrapper classes around dictionary, list, and string objects for easier subclassing.

Understanding the Use of Collections

The collections module provides these data structures as tools to deal with various common data manipulation tasks in a more optimized way. For instance, Counter is tailor-made for counting occurrences, which would otherwise require manual dictionary manipulation. Similarly, `OrderedDict` maintains the order of elements, which is not a feature in the standard dictionary prior to `Python 3.7`.

Let's illustrate the use of one of these structures, `namedtuple`, with an example:

```
import collections

# Sample code showing basic usage of a namedtuple

Point = collections.namedtuple('Point', 'x y')

pt = Point(1, 2)

print(pt.x, pt.y)
```

- import collections: This line imports the collections module, which contains the namedtuple function along with other specialized data structures.
- Point = collections.namedtuple('Point', 'x y'): Here, we are using the namedtuple function to create a new subclass of tuple called Point. The second argument 'x y' defines the field names, which means each Point object will have an x and y attribute.
- pt = Point(1, 2): We create an instance of the Point named tuple and pass values for x and y. It's similar to creating a tuple, but with named fields for readability and convenience.
- print(pt.x, pt.y): Finally, we access the fields x and y of the Point object and print them. Named tuples allow you to access values by name instead of index, which makes the code more readable and maintainable.

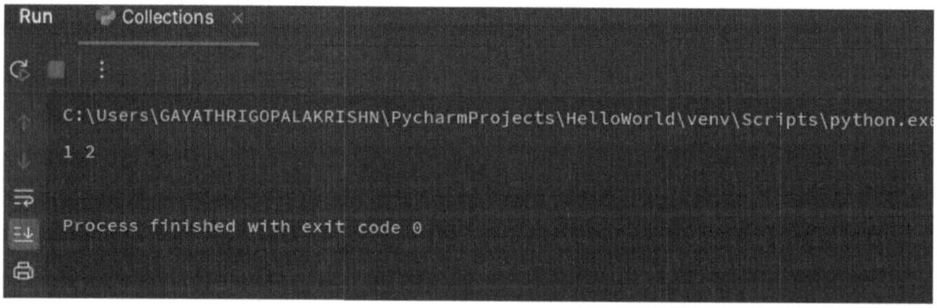

Figure 9.1: *output of a namedtuple*

The preceding **Figure 9.1** shows the output of a named tuple.

The Power of Collections

The collections module is a powerful toolkit in Python's standard library. It provides data structures that are both high-performance and user-friendly. The specialized nature of these structures means they can greatly simplify certain coding tasks and enhance performance.

For example, Counter can be used for quick tallies, which are common in data analysis. Deque, with its fast appends and pops from both ends, is ideal for queue-like data structures. `NamedTuple` makes code involving tuples more readable, and `OrderedDict` is perfect when the order of elements is critical.

Python's collections module is an essential part of the Python standard library, especially for developers looking to write more efficient, readable, and maintainable code. By providing specialized data structures, it caters to a variety of needs, from simple counting to complex data manipulations. Understanding and utilizing these tools can significantly improve the functionality and performance of Python programs. The collections module, therefore, is not just a supplement to Python's built-in data structures; it's a powerful toolkit, capable of handling a wide range of programming tasks more effectively.

Working with Deque and Counter

A deque (double-ended queue) is a generalization of stacks and queues. It supports thread-safe, memory-efficient appends and pops from either side of the deque.

A Counter is a `dict` subclass for counting `hashable` objects. It's a collection where elements are stored as dictionary keys and counts as dictionary values.

Deque in Python

A deque, pronounced as "deck", stands for "double-ended queue". It's part of the collections module in Python and is an enhanced version of a queue that allows adding and removing elements from both ends with equal ease and efficiency. Unlike lists in Python, deques are optimized for these operations, providing faster append and pop operations from both ends.

Why Use Deque?

Deques are particularly useful when you need a queue-like data structure that allows for fast adding and removing of elements from both ends. They are ideal for problems where elements need to be processed in both first-in-first-out (FIFO) and last-in-first-out (LIFO) orders.

```
from collections import deque
dq = deque([1, 2, 3])
dq.appendleft(0)
dq.append(4)
print(dq)
```

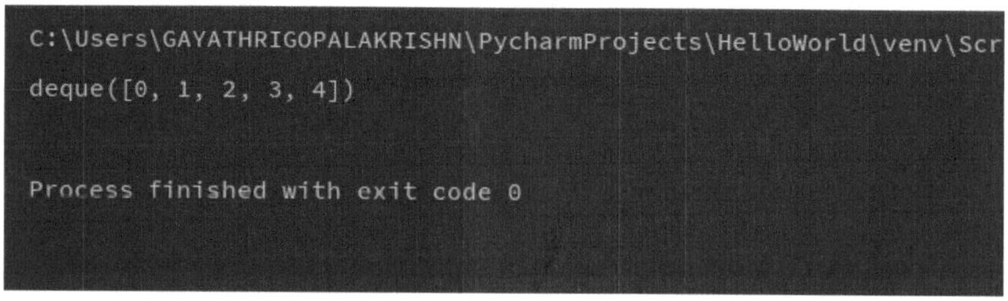

Figure 9.2: *output of a dequeue*

The preceding `Figure 9.2` shows the output of a dequeue.

Common Use Cases

Followings are common use cases:

- Implementing Queues and Stacks: Deque can be used to implement both queue and stack data structures efficiently.
- Handling Sliding Window Problems: In algorithmic problems that involve sliding windows (like moving averages), deques provide an efficient way of adding and removing elements from the window.
- Undo Features in Applications: They are great for creating an 'undo' feature in applications, where operations can be added and removed from both ends as needed.

```
from collections import deque
# Create a deque with some initial items
dq = deque(['a', 'b', 'c'])
```

```
# Add elements to the end
dq.append('d')
dq.append('e')

# Add elements to the beginning
dq.appendleft('z')

# Remove and return the rightmost item
right = dq.pop()

# Remove and return the leftmost item
left = dq.popleft()

print("Deque:", dq)
print("Rightmost removed:", right)
print("Leftmost removed:", left)
```

Let's understand the code-snippet:

- from collections import deque: This line imports the deque class from the collections module.
- dq = deque(['a', 'b', 'c']): Here, we initialize a deque with elements 'a', 'b', and 'c'.
- dq.append('d'): Adds 'd' to the right end of the deque.
- dq.append('e'): Adds 'e' to the right end, demonstrating how elements can be added to the end.
- dq.appendleft('z'): Adds 'z' to the left end, showcasing the ability to add elements to the start.
- right = dq.pop(): Removes and returns the rightmost item from the deque.
- left = dq.popleft(): Similarly, this removes and returns the leftmost item.

The print statements display the current state of the **deque** and the elements removed from both ends.

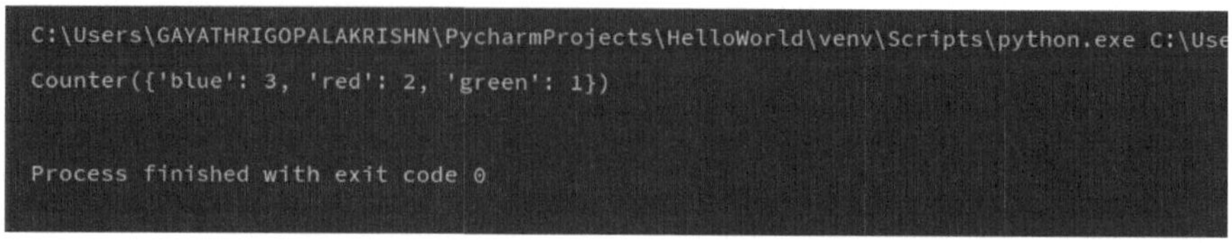

Figure 9.3: *output of implementation of data structures using dequeue*

The preceding **Figure 9.3** shows the output of implementation of data structures using dequeue.

Counter in Python

Counter is a subclass of dictionary provided by the collections module in Python. It's designed to count **hashable** objects. Essentially, it's a mapping where elements are stored as dictionary keys and their counts are stored as dictionary values.

Why Use Counter?

Counters are incredibly useful for counting occurrences of elements in an **iterable**, which is a common requirement in data analysis and processing tasks. They simplify the process of tallying up items, which otherwise requires manually managing a dictionary and handling missing keys.

```
from collections import Counter

cnt = Counter()

for word in ['red', 'blue', 'red', 'green', 'blue', 'blue']:

    cnt[word] += 1

print(cnt)
```

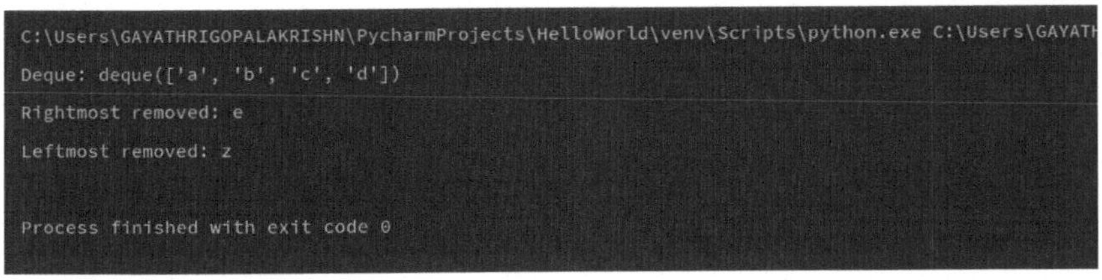

Figure 9.4: *output of implementation of counter*

The preceding **Figure 9.4** shows the output of implementation of counter.

Common Use Cases

Followings are the common use cases:

- Counting Items: Counters are ideal for counting the occurrences of items in a list or elements in an iterable.
- Data Analysis: In data science, Counters can be used to analyze frequencies of elements.
- Validation of Requirements: Counters can be used to validate if certain requirements are met in a dataset, like if a certain number of specific elements are present.

```
from collections import Counter


# Creating a Counter from a list

item_counts = Counter([‘apple’, ‘orange’, ‘apple’, ‘pear’, ‘orange’,
‘banana’])


# Update the count for ‘apple’

item_counts.update([‘apple’])


# Get the count of ‘orange’

orange_count = item_counts[‘orange’]
```

```
# Display the most common items

common_items = item_counts.most_common(2)


print("Item Counts:", item_counts)

print("Orange Count:", orange_count)

print("Most Common Items:", common_items)
```

Code-snippet explanation:

- from collections import Counter: This imports the Counter class.
- item_counts = Counter([...]): We create a Counter object, which automatically counts the elements in the provided list.
- item_counts.update(['apple']): Updates the count of 'apple' in the Counter.
- orange_count = item_counts['orange']: Retrieves the count of 'orange'.
- common_items = item_counts.most_common(2): Finds the two most common items.
- The print statements display the overall counts, the count of oranges, and the most common items.

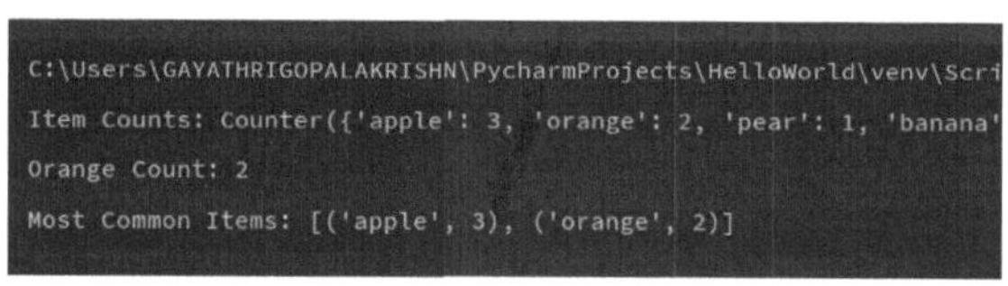

Figure 9.5: *output of implementation of counter with an example*

The preceding **Figure 9.5** shows the output of implementation of counter with an example.

Deque and Counter are two incredibly powerful tools in Python's collections module that offer specialized functionalities for specific use cases. Deque provides a more efficient way to handle double-ended queue operations, while Counter simplifies counting and tallying tasks. Understanding these tools and incorporating them into Python code can lead to more efficient, readable, and maintainable solutions, particularly in data processing and algorithmic problem-solving contexts.

NamedTuple in Python

`namedtuple`, part of Python's collections module, offers a convenient way to create lightweight, immutable, and readable tuple-like objects. Unlike regular tuples, where you access elements using integer indexes, `namedtuple` allows you to access elements by names, which makes your code more readable and self-documenting.

Why Use NamedTuple?

`NamedTuples` are useful for a variety of reasons:

- Readability: Accessing elements by name rather than index makes the code clearer.
- Immutability: Like tuples, NamedTuples are immutable, making them suitable for constant data storage.
- Lightweight: They use less memory than regular objects.

Common Use Cases

Followings are the common use cases:

- Data Representation: Representing complex data structures in a simple, readable form.
- CSV Parsing: Ideal for handling rows of CSV files, allowing access by field names.
- Function Return Values: Great for returning multiple values from a function in a named and organized way.

```
from collections import namedtuple

# Define a namedtuple type called 'Car'

Car = namedtuple('Car', 'color mileage')

# Create an instance of Car

my_car = Car('red', 3812.4)

# Accessing fields

print(my_car.color)
```

Code-snippet explanation:

- from collections import namedtuple: This imports the namedtuple factory function from the collections module.
- Car = namedtuple('Car', 'color mileage'): Creates a new namedtuple type named Car with fields color and mileage.
- my_car = Car('red', 3812.4): Creates an instance of Car. The arguments 'red' and 3812.4 are assigned to color and mileage, respectively.
- print(my_car.color): Accesses the color field of my_car. Named fields make it clear what each field represents.

Figure 9.6: *output of implementation of named tuple*

The preceding `Figure 9.6` shows the output of implementation of named tuple with an example.

Additional Examples

In this section we will delve into more examples to understand the topic:

Example 1: Employee Record

```
from collections import namedtuple

Employee = namedtuple('Employee', 'name id position')

emp = Employee('Alice', 'E123', 'Engineer')

print(emp)
```

- Import Statement:

from collections import namedtuple. This line imports the namedtuple factory function from the collections module. namedtuple is a utility that helps in creating tuple-like objects with named fields. It's a way to create lightweight, immutable objects.

- Creating a NamedTuple:

Employee = namedtuple('Employee', 'name id position')

Here, a new namedtuple type called Employee is being defined. The namedtuple function takes two arguments: the name of the new type ('Employee') and a string with space-separated field names ('name id position'). This line creates a new class Employee with the fields name, id, and position.

- Creating an Instance of the NamedTuple:

emp = Employee('Alice', 'E123', 'Engineer')

This line creates an instance of the Employee namedtuple. The arguments 'Alice', 'E123', and 'Engineer' are assigned to the fields name, id, and position, respectively. Now emp is an Employee object with these attributes.

- Printing the NamedTuple Object:

print(emp)

This line prints the emp object. When a namedtuple instance is printed, it displays in a readable, tuple-like format, showing the field names and their corresponding values. For emp, it will print something like Employee(name='Alice', id='E123', position='Engineer'), clearly indicating each field and its value.

Overall, this code snippet is a simple demonstration of defining and using a namedtuple in Python, making it possible to create readable, structured, and immutable objects.

Figure 9.7: *output of creating an employee record using a named tuple*

The preceding **Figure 9.7** shows the output of creating an employee record using a named tuple.

Example 2: Coordinates

```
from collections import namedtuple

Point = namedtuple('Point', 'x y')

p1 = Point(10, y=20)

print(p1)
```

- Import Statement:
  from collections import namedtuple
  This line imports the namedtuple function from the collections module. namedtuple is a utility in Python that enables the creation of tuple-like objects that are accessible via both index and named attributes.
- Defining a NamedTuple:
  Point = namedtuple('Point', 'x y')
  A new namedtuple type called Point is being defined here. The namedtuple function takes two arguments: the typename ('Point') and a space-separated string of field names ('x y'). This line creates a class Point with two fields: x and y. These fields will represent coordinates in a 2D space.
- Creating an Instance of the NamedTuple:
  p1 = Point(10, y=20)
  This line creates an instance of the Point namedtuple. The value 10 is assigned to the first field x, and the named argument y=20 explicitly assigns the value 20 to the second field y. This way of initializing allows for clear and readable assignment of values to the namedtuple's fields.
- Printing the NamedTuple Object:
  print(p1)
  This line prints the p1 namedtuple object. When a namedtuple is printed, it is displayed in a readable format showing the field names and their corresponding values. The output for this line will be Point(x=10, y=20), indicating the values of the x and y coordinates of the point.

Overall, this code snippet showcases how to define, instantiate, and use a namedtuple in Python for managing simple data structures like a 2D point in this case. The use of namedtuple makes the code more readable and structured compared to using regular tuples.

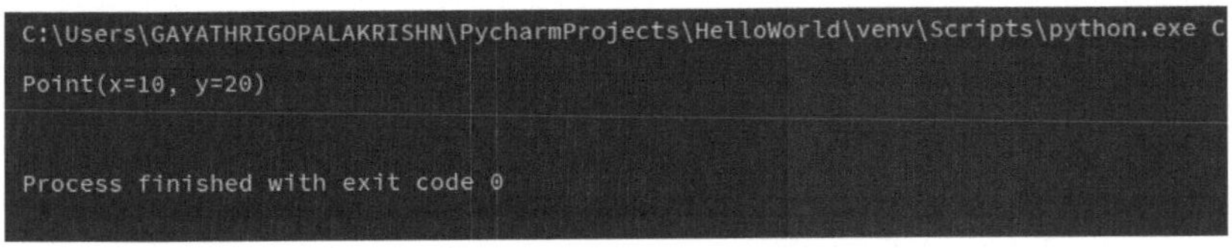

`Figure 9.8`: output of creating a coordinate using a named tuple

The preceding **`Figure 9.8`** shows the output of creating a coordinate using a named tuple.

OrderedDict in Python

`OrderedDict` is a subclass of the built-in **`dict`** class. It maintains the order in which the elements were added, unlike a standard dictionary (*prior to Python 3.7*) which doesn't track insertion order. This feature makes **`OrderedDict`** particularly useful when the order of elements is crucial, such as in an ordered list of key-value pairs.

Why Use OrderedDict?

Despite regular dictionaries in Python 3.7 and later maintaining insertion order, OrderedDict still has its unique uses:

- Equality Testing: Two OrderedDict objects are equal if their order of insertion and contents are the same.
- Reordering: OrderedDict allows reordering of the dictionary, which is not possible with regular dictionaries.
- Common Use Cases
- Maintaining Insertion Order: Preserving the order in which keys are added to the dictionary.
- Data Serialization: Useful in JSON serialization where the order of elements is significant.

```
from collections import OrderedDict

# Creating an OrderedDict

od = OrderedDict()

# Adding items to the OrderedDict

od['a'] = 1
```

```
od['b'] = 2

od['c'] = 3

# Printing keys in the order they were added

print(list(od.keys()))
```

Explanation of the code-snippet:

- **from collections import OrderedDict:** Imports OrderedDict from the collections module.
- **od = OrderedDict():** Creates an instance of OrderedDict.
- **od['a'] = 1:** Adds a key-value pair ('a', 1) to the ordered dictionary.
- **od['b'] = 2 and od['c'] = 3:** Adds more key-value pairs in order.
- **print(list(od.keys())):** Prints the keys of od. Unlike a regular dict, OrderedDict maintains the order of keys as they were added.

Figure 9.9: *output of creating an ordered dictionary*

The preceding `Figure 9.9` shows the output of creating an ordered dictionary.

Additional Examples

In this section we will discuss more examples:

Example 1: Reordering an OrderedDict

```
from collections import OrderedDict

od = OrderedDict([('a', 1), ('b', 2), ('c', 3)])

od.move_to_end('b', last=False)

print(od)
```

Import Statement: from collections import OrderedDict

This line imports the OrderedDict class from the collections module. OrderedDict is a subclass of the standard Python dictionary (dict) which maintains the order in which the elements (key-value pairs) are added.

Creating an OrderedDict:od = OrderedDict([('a', 1), ('b', 2), ('c', 3)])

OrderedDict([('a', 1), ('b', 2), ('c', 3)]): This initializes an OrderedDict object named od. The OrderedDict is constructed with a list of tuples, where each tuple represents a key-value pair.

The key-value pairs ('a', 1), ('b', 2), and ('c', 3) are added to od in that specific order. This means that 'a' is the first key, 'b' the second, and 'c' the third.

Reordering an Item in OrderedDict:

od.move_to_end('b', last=False)

The move_to_end() method is used to move a specified key ('b' in this case) to either end of the OrderedDict.

The key 'b' is the one being moved, and the parameter last=False indicates that 'b' should be moved to the beginning (front) of the OrderedDict.

After this operation, the order of the elements in od will be 'b', 'a', 'c'.

Printing the OrderedDict:

print(od)

This line prints the current state of the OrderedDict od.

Given the previous operations, the output will reflect the new order of the elements in od, which, after moving 'b' to the beginning, should be OrderedDict([('b', 2), ('a', 1), ('c', 3)]).

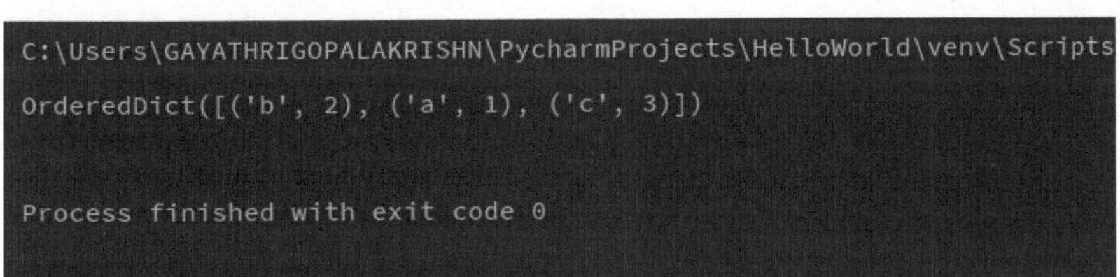

Figure 9.10: *output of reordering an ordered dictionary*

The preceding **Figure 9.10** shows the output of reordering an ordered dictionary.

Example 2: Comparing Two OrderedDicts

```
from collections import OrderedDict

ordered_dict_1 = OrderedDict([(‘a’, 1), (‘b’, 2)])

ordered_dict_2 = OrderedDict([(‘b’, 2), (‘a’, 1)])

print(ordered_dict_1 == ordered_dict_2)  # False, because the order is different
```

Importing OrderedDict: You start by importing OrderedDict from the collections module.

Creating OrderedDict Instances:

ordered_dict_1 = OrderedDict([(‘a’, 1), (‘b’, 2)]): Creates an ordered dictionary, od1, with two key-value pairs, (‘a’, 1) and (‘b’, 2), in this specific order.

Ordered_dict_2 = OrdcrcdDict([(‘b’, 2), (‘a’, 1)]): Creates another ordered dictionary, od2, but this time the order of key-value pairs is reversed: (‘b’, 2) comes before (‘a’, 1).

Comparison:

print(ordered_dict_1 == ordered_dict_2): This line compares the two OrderedDict instances. In regular dictionaries, the order of key-value pairs doesn’t impact equality - dictionaries are considered equal if they contain the same keys and values, regardless of the order. However, OrderedDict takes the order of the elements into account. Although od1 and od2 have the same keys and values, they are in a different order. Therefore, the comparison od1 == od2 results in False.

This behavior of OrderedDict is particularly useful in scenarios where the order of elements is as important as the elements themselves, such as in certain data processing tasks or when maintaining a record of events in the order they occurred.

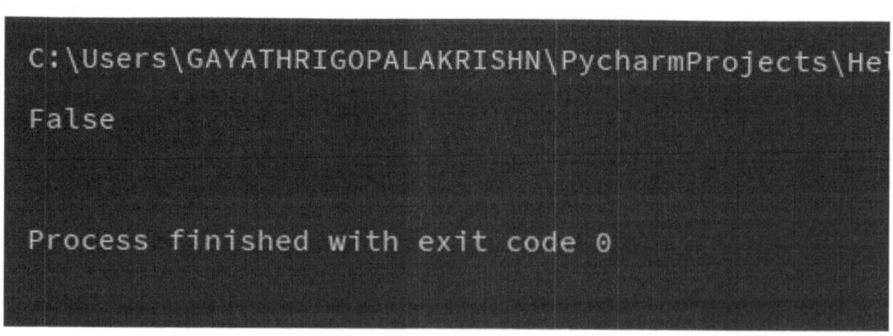

Figure 9.11: *output of comparing two ordered dictionaries*

The preceding `Figure 9.11` shows the output of comparing two ordered dictionaries.

NamedTuple and OrderedDict are two powerful tools in Python's collections module. namedtuple provides an efficient way to create lightweight, immutable objects with named fields, enhancing code readability and maintainability. OrderedDict, on the other hand, is essential for scenarios where the order of elements matters and offers features like equality testing based on order, which regular dictionaries lack. Understanding and utilizing these structures can significantly improve the organization, readability, and performance of Python code, especially in scenarios where data structure and order are paramount.

Use Cases and Scenarios

The real power of Python's collections module shines through in its practical applications.

Here are some scenarios where these structures prove invaluable:

- Order Management with OrderedDict: In an e-commerce platform, maintaining the order of customer purchases is crucial. An OrderedDict can be used to store orders in the sequence they were made, facilitating chronological processing or display.
- Word Frequency Analysis with Counter: Analyzing text data, such as calculating the frequency of words in a document, can be efficiently performed using Counter. This structure automates the process of counting occurrences, making the code more concise and readable.
- Data Structuring with NamedTuple: In data analysis, representing rows of a dataset as namedtuple objects can make the analysis more intuitive, as fields can be accessed by names, enhancing code clarity.
- Task Scheduling with Deque: In systems design, managing tasks in a queue where tasks can be added or removed from both ends (like in CPU scheduling algorithms) can be efficiently implemented using a deque.

These examples illustrate just a few of the many situations where the specialized data structures of the collections module can be effectively employed to write clean, efficient, and maintainable Python code. Understanding and leveraging these tools can greatly enhance a developer's ability to handle complex data manipulation tasks.

Let's delve into practical applications for each of these structures, providing detailed explanations and sample code.

Order Management with OrderedDict

Scenario: Maintaining the order of customer purchases in an e-commerce platform is crucial for chronological processing and display.

Application: OrderedDict is ideal for this task as it preserves the order of entries, which is essential for tracking order histories or displaying items in the order they were added.

```
from collections import OrderedDict

# Simulating an order management system

orders = OrderedDict()

orders['20201201'] = 'Electronics'

orders['20201202'] = 'Books'

orders['20201203'] = 'Home Appliances'

# Iterating over the orders to process them in the order they were made

for order_date, order_item in orders.items():

    print(f"Processing order from {order_date}: {order_item}")
```

Explanation of code-example:

- from collections import OrderedDict: Imports the OrderedDict class from the collections module.
- orders = OrderedDict(): Initializes an empty OrderedDict called orders.
- orders['20201201'] = 'Electronics': Adds an item with key '20201201' and value 'Electronics' to orders.
- orders['20201202'] = 'Books': Adds another item with key '20201202' and value 'Books'.
- orders['20201203'] = 'Home Appliances': Adds a third item with key '20201203' and value 'Home Appliances'.
- The for loop iterates over the OrderedDict. order_date and order_item receive the key and value from each item in orders.
- print(f"Processing order from {order_date}: {order_item}"): Prints the order date and item, preserving the order in which they were added.

Figure 9.12: *output of Order Management with OrderedDict*

The preceding **Figure 9.12** shows the output of Order Management with **OrderedDict.**

Word Frequency Analysis with Counter

Scenario: Analyzing text data, such as calculating the frequency of words in a document.

Application: Counter simplifies the process of counting occurrences of each word, making the code concise and readable.

```
from collections import Counter

# Example text

text = "a quick brown fox jumps over the lazy dog a quick brown dog"


# Counting the frequency of each word in the text

word_counts = Counter(text.split())


# Displaying the most common words

for word, count in word_counts.most_common(3):

    print(f"Word: '{word}', Frequency: {count}")
```

Code-example explanation:

- from collections import Counter: Imports Counter from the collections module.
- text = "a quick brown fox jumps over the lazy dog a quick brown dog": A string containing a sample text.
- word_counts = Counter(text.split()): Splits the text into words and counts the occurrences of each word.
- for word, count in word_counts.most_common(3): Iterates over the three most common words and their counts.
- print(f"Word: '{word}', Frequency: {count}"): Prints each word and its frequency.

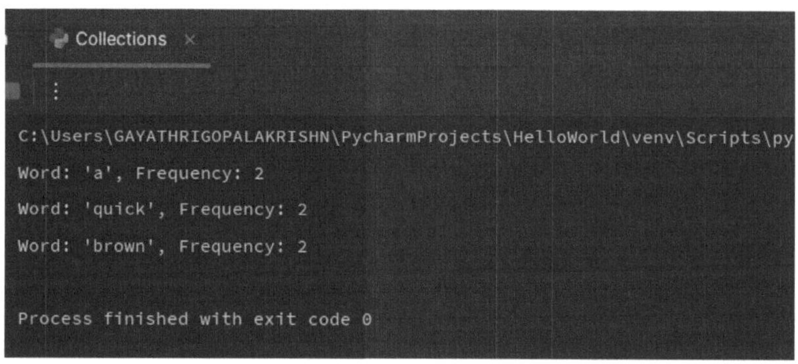

Figure 9.13: *output of Word Frequency Analyzer*

The preceding **`Figure 9.13`** shows the output of Word Frequency Analyzer.

Data Structuring with NamedTuple

Scenario: Representing rows of a dataset in a more structured and readable format.

Application: **`namedtuple`** provides a way to access data fields by names, enhancing code clarity, especially in data analysis.

```
from collections import namedtuple

# Define a namedtuple for a customer

Customer = namedtuple('Customer', 'name age purchases')
```

```
# Example customers

customer1 = Customer('Alice', 30, 3)

customer2 = Customer('Bob', 22, 1)


# Accessing and using namedtuple fields

print(f"{customer1.name} (Age: {customer1.age}) - Purchases: {customer1.
purchases}")

print(f"{customer2.name} (Age: {customer2.age}) - Purchases: {customer2.
purchases}")
```

Code-example explanation:

- from collections import namedtuple: Imports namedtuple from the collections module.
- Customer = namedtuple('Customer', 'name age purchases'): Creates a namedtuple type Customer with fields name, age, and purchases.
- customer1 = Customer('Alice', 30, 3): Instantiates a Customer named Alice, aged 30, with 3 purchases.
- customer2 = Customer('Bob', 22, 1): Instantiates another Customer named Bob, aged 22, with 1 purchase.
- The print statements output the details of each customer in a readable format.

Figure 9.14: *output of Data Structuring with NamedTuple*

The preceding **Figure 9.14** shows the output of Data Structuring with **NamedTuple**.

Task Scheduling with Deque

Scenario: Managing tasks in a queue where tasks can be added or removed from both ends, such as in CPU scheduling algorithms.

Application: A deque is highly efficient for this purpose, allowing quick additions and removals from either end.

```
from collections import deque

# Creating a deque for task scheduling

tasks = deque([‘Task1’, ‘Task2’, ‘Task3’])

# Adding a high-priority task

tasks.appendleft(‘Urgent Task’)

# Processing tasks

while tasks:

    current_task = tasks.popleft()

    print(f”Processing {current_task}”)


# Adding a new task to be processed last

tasks.append(‘End-of-day Task’)
```

Code example explanation:

- from collections import deque: Imports deque from the collections module.
- tasks = deque([‘Task1’, ‘Task2’, ‘Task3’]): Initializes a deque with three tasks.
- tasks.appendleft(‘Urgent Task’): Adds an ‘Urgent Task’ to the beginning of the deque.
- The while loop continues as long as tasks is not empty.
- current_task = tasks.popleft(): Removes and returns the leftmost task (the next task to process).
- print(f”Processing {current_task}”): Prints the task being processed.
- tasks.append(‘End-of-day Task’): Adds a new task at the end of the deque, to be processed last.

```
C:\Users\GAYATHRIGOPALAKRISHN\PycharmProjects\HelloWorld\venv\S
Processing Urgent Task
Processing Task1
Processing Task2
Processing Task3

Process finished with exit code 0
```

***Figure 9.15**: output of Task Scheduling with Deque*

The preceding **Figure 9.15** shows the output of Task Scheduling with Deque.

Each of these examples illustrates the practical application of Python's collections module, demonstrating the module's flexibility and efficiency in handling various data structures.

Enhanced Data Manipulation

The Collections module in Python not only introduces a variety of specialized data structures but also significantly simplifies and enhances complex data manipulation tasks. This advanced capability allows developers to handle data with more sophistication, efficiency, and clarity.

Reordering with OrderedDict

Scenario: Often, the requirement arises to rearrange the items in a dictionary based on specific criteria, such as moving certain items to the end or beginning based on their keys or values.

Application: OrderedDict from the collections module is perfect for this task, as it maintains the order of insertion and allows changes to the order.

```
from collections import OrderedDict

# Creating an OrderedDict with initial items

inventory = OrderedDict([('apple', 50), ('banana', 25), ('orange', 75)])
```

```
# Move 'banana' to the end

inventory.move_to_end('banana')

# Move 'apple' to the beginning

inventory.move_to_end('apple', last=False)

print("Reordered Inventory:", inventory)
```

Code example explanation:

- The OrderedDict is initialized with a set of items.
- move_to_end('banana') moves 'banana' to the end of the OrderedDict.
- move_to_end('apple', last=False) moves 'apple' to the beginning.
- The final print statement displays the reordered inventory, showcasing the flexibility of OrderedDict in reordering items.

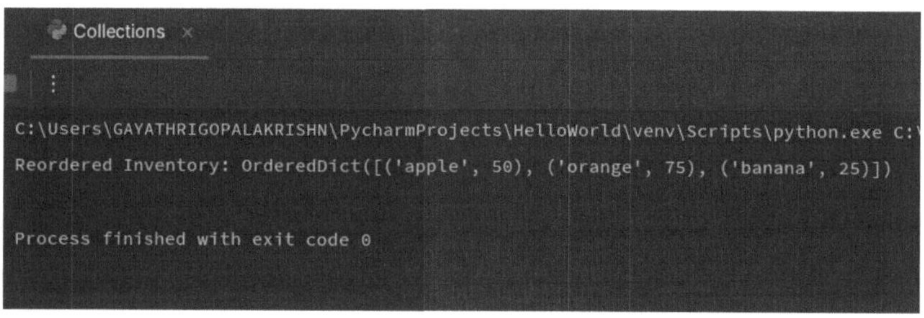

Figure 9.16: *output of Reordering with OrderedDict*

The preceding **Figure 9.16** shows the output of Reordering with **OrderedDict**.

Statistics with Counter

Scenario: Analyzing data to extract statistics such as the most common elements or the total count of specific items is a common task in data analysis.

Application: The Counter class is ideal for these purposes, as it simplifies counting and analyzing frequencies of elements in an iterable.

```
from collections import Counter

# Sample data: List of responses in a survey
```

```
responses = ['Yes', 'No', 'Yes', 'No', 'Yes', 'Maybe', 'Yes', 'No',
'Maybe', 'Maybe']

# Creating a Counter for the responses

response_counter = Counter(responses)

# Most common response

most_common_response = response_counter.most_common(1)[0]

print("Most common response:", most_common_response)

# Total count of 'Maybe' responses

maybe_count = response_counter['Maybe']

print("Total 'Maybe' responses:", maybe_count)
```

Code example explanation:

- Counter(responses) creates a Counter object that counts the frequency of each item in responses.
- most_common(1) retrieves the most common response along with its count.
- response_counter['Maybe'] directly accesses the count of 'Maybe' responses.
- The print statements then display the most common response and the total count of 'Maybe', exemplifying how Counter can be used for statistical analysis.

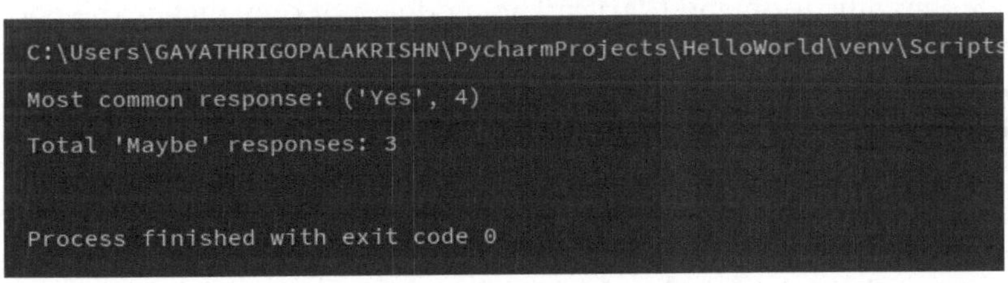

Figure 9.17: *output of Statistics with Counter*

The preceding **Figure 9.17** shows the output of Statistics with Counter.

These examples illustrate the power of Python's collections module in enhancing data manipulation tasks. By providing specialized data structures like **OrderedDict** and Counter, Python allows developers to perform complex data manipulations in a more intuitive and efficient manner. These structures reduce the need for manual data handling and complex logic, thereby simplifying the code and making it more readable and maintainable. Whether it's reordering items in a dictionary or performing statistical analysis on data, the collections module provides robust tools to handle such tasks with ease.

Conclusion

Python's Collections module is an invaluable asset in the toolbox of any Python programmer. It extends the capabilities of Python's built-in data structures, offering specialized alternatives like deque, Counter, `NamedTuple`, `OrderedDict`, and others. These structures are not just enhancements of the basic types but are pivotal in addressing specific problems more efficiently and effectively.

- Specialized Data Structures: The Collections module provides data structures that are tailored for specific tasks, such as counting items (Counter), managing ordered data (OrderedDict), efficiently handling double-ended queues (deque), and creating structured, readable objects (NamedTuple).
- Enhanced Efficiency and Readability: By offering tools that are optimized for particular tasks, the Collections module allows for more efficient data processing and manipulation. This efficiency, coupled with the increased readability and maintainability of the code, makes the module a go-to solution for complex data handling.
- Practical Applications: The use cases covered demonstrate the practicality of these data structures in real-world scenarios. From managing order sequences in e-commerce systems to statistical analysis in data science, the Collections module has wide-ranging applications.
- Code Simplification and Clarity: The module not only makes the code more efficient but also more intuitive and clearer. Structures like NamedTuple enhance code readability, and Counter simplifies tasks that would otherwise require verbose and complex coding.
- Versatility in Python Programming: The Collections module exemplifies the versatility and power of Python as a programming language. It underscores Python's philosophy of simplicity and elegance, providing powerful tools that can be easily understood and implemented.

The Collections module is a testament to Python's capability to handle data in a sophisticated manner. Understanding and utilizing these tools can significantly elevate a programmer's ability to tackle various programming challenges. Whether for data analysis, system design, or algorithm development, the Collections module offers robust, efficient, and elegant solutions, making it an essential part of any Python programmer's knowledge base.

Exercise: Test Your Understanding

Answer the following questions and test your understanding of learning from **Chapter 9**:

Q. 1. What is the purpose of Python's collections module?

Q. 2. Name two data structures provided by the collections module.

Q. 3. Are the data structures in the collections module more efficient than Python's general-purpose data structures?

Q. 4. Can **namedtuple** be found in the collections module?

Q. 5. Is **OrderedDict** still useful in Python versions where dictionaries maintain insertion order?

Q. 6. How is a generator function defined in Python?

Notes

Date:

JOIN US ON THE ARCCHIE PUBLICATIONS DISCORD SERVER

Connect with fellow readers, authors, and enthusiasts to discuss all things related to our publications and the exciting world of AI, programming, and learning. Share your insights, ask questions, and engage in vibrant discussions to expand your knowledge and inspire creativity. Take advantage of this opportunity to be part of a dynamic community dedicated to exploring the frontiers of technology and innovation. Join our Discord Server today and be part of the ARCCHIE Publications community!

https://discord.gg/z26SenmpEt

Chapter 10

GUI Development Using Python

In the realm of software development, the Graphical User Interface (GUI) stands as a pivotal element that bridges the gap between the user and the backend processing of applications. GUIs are designed to provide a visually interactive and intuitive experience, enabling users to engage with software through graphical elements like windows, buttons, and text fields, rather than through text-based interfaces. This introduction aims to shed light on GUI development, particularly focusing on its implementation using Python, a versatile and widely used programming language.

In this chapter, we will cover:

- Introduction to GUI Development
- GUI Components and Layouts
- Building a Simple GUI Application
- Interactivity and User Experience
- Creating a Practical Project

Introduction to GUI Development

The objective of this section is to provide a foundational understanding of Graphical User Interface (GUI) development, focusing on its components, their interactions, and the underlying principles that guide effective GUI design. This exploration is critical for anyone looking to create intuitive, user-friendly applications.

Definition of GUI

GUI, an acronym for Graphical User Interface, refers to the graphical elements through which users interact with electronic devices. This concept revolutionized the way humans interact with computers, transitioning from the era of command-line interfaces (CLI) to a more user-friendly, visually oriented mode of interaction. A GUI typically includes elements such as windows, icons, buttons, and menus that respond to user actions like clicks, drags, and keyboard inputs, making digital interactions more natural and intuitive.

History and Evolution of GUI

The concept of a GUI has its roots in the 1970s when Xerox PARC developed the first GUI. This innovation marked a significant shift from text-based interfaces to graphical ones, enabling users to interact with computers more intuitively. Over the years, GUIs have evolved tremendously, with major contributions from companies like Apple and Microsoft, leading to the modern, sophisticated interfaces we see today. These interfaces have transitioned from simple 2D graphics to complex 3D and touch-based systems, making technology more accessible and user-friendly.

Basic Principles of GUI Design

Before we delve into other topics related to GUI, lets discuss the basic principles of GUI design.

- Consistency: A consistent interface allows users to apply prior knowledge from one part of the application to another. Consistent use of elements, colors, and fonts makes an application more intuitive.
- Feedback: The system should always inform users about what is happening through appropriate feedback within a reasonable time.
- Efficiency: GUIs should streamline user tasks, minimizing the steps required to perform actions, and providing shortcuts for experienced users.

- Aesthetics: A well-designed GUI should not only be functional but also pleasing to the eye. This includes thoughtful use of colors, typography, and spacing.
- User Control: Users should feel in control of the interactions, with the ability to undo actions and navigate the application freely.

The Role of Python in GUI Development

Python, known for its simplicity and readability, has become a popular choice for developing GUI applications. Its simplicity allows developers, from beginners to experts, to create functional and attractive interfaces. Python's role in GUI development is significant due to several factors:

- Wide Range of Libraries and Frameworks: Python offers a variety of libraries and frameworks that simplify the GUI development process. These tools provide pre-built components and functionalities, reducing the amount of code developers need to write from scratch.
- Cross-Platform Compatibility: Python-based GUI applications can run on various operating systems, including Windows, macOS, and Linux, without significant alterations. This cross-platform nature makes Python a versatile choice for GUI development.
- Community and Support: Python has a large and active community. This means abundant resources, tutorials, and forums are available, making it easier for developers to learn and troubleshoot GUI development.
- Integration with Other Technologies: Python's ability to integrate with other technologies and its support for various data formats make it an excellent choice for developing complex applications that require backend processing, data visualization, and other advanced functionalities.

Overview of Popular Python GUI Frameworks

Python's versatility in GUI development is largely due to its rich set of frameworks. Each framework has its unique features and use cases. Some of the most popular ones include `Tkinter`, `PyQt`, and `Kivy`.

- Tkinter: Tkinter is the standard GUI toolkit for Python. It is included with Python, making it easily accessible for beginners. Tkinter is suitable for small to medium-sized applications and is known for its simplicity. It provides a straightforward way to create windows, dialogs, buttons, and other GUI elements. However, it may not be the best choice for highly complex or modern-looking applications.
- PyQt: PyQt is a set of Python bindings for the Qt application framework. It is powerful and versatile, suitable for creating both simple and complex

applications. PyQt provides a wide range of tools and functionalities, including advanced features like 2D and 3D graphics, networking, and database handling. Its capability to create visually appealing and modern GUIs makes it a popular choice for professional-grade software development.

- Kivy: Kivy is an open-source Python library for developing multitouch applications. It is particularly well-suited for applications that require gestures or touch input. Kivy is known for its ability to run on multiple platforms, including mobile devices, and for its rich set of widgets. It is an excellent choice for developers looking to create applications with a sophisticated and modern touch interface.

GUI development in Python offers an accessible yet powerful avenue for creating interactive applications. The language's simplicity, combined with the robust frameworks available, makes it an excellent choice for both newcomers and experienced developers. Whether it's creating a simple desktop tool or a complex cross-platform application, Python's capabilities in GUI development are vast and versatile, catering to a wide range of project requirements. As technology continues to evolve, Python's role in GUI development is likely to grow, adapting to new trends and user needs in the ever-changing landscape of software development.

Introduction to Event-Driven Programming

Event-driven programming is a fundamental concept in GUI development. In this paradigm, the flow of the program is determined by events—user actions like mouse clicks, key presses, or system-generated events. This approach contrasts with traditional linear programming, where the flow is predetermined. In event-driven programming, the application responds to various events, making it interactive and responsive to user inputs.

Example Code: Basic Window Creation Using `Tkinter`

`Tkinter` is the standard GUI toolkit in Python. Here is a simple example of how to create a basic window:

```
import tkinter as tk


# Create the main window
```

```
root = tk.Tk()


# Set the title of the window

root.title("My First GUI")


# Set the size of the window

root.geometry("300x200")


# Start the GUI event loop

root.mainloop()
```

Explanation of the Code

`import tkinter as tk`: This line imports the `Tkinter` module, making its functions and classes available for use.

`root = tk.Tk()`: Here, we create the main window. `Tk()` is a class in `Tkinter` which is used to create the main window of an application.

`root.title("My First GUI")`: This sets the title of the window to "`My First GUI`". The title is displayed in the title bar of the window.

`root.geometry("300x200")`: This line sets the size of the window to 300 pixels wide and 200 pixels tall.

`root.mainloop()`: The `mainloop()` is an infinite loop used to run the application, wait for an event to occur, and process the event till the window is not closed. This is essential for any `Tkinter` application, as it keeps the window open and responsive.

Figure 10.1: *output of Basic window creation*

The preceding `Figure 10.1` shows the output of a basic window creation.

So, GUI development is an essential skill in modern software development, requiring an understanding of both design principles and technical implementation. The evolution of GUIs reflects a broader trend towards more user-friendly, intuitive interfaces, and learning to create these using tools like Tkinter is a valuable skill for any aspiring developer.

GUI Components and Layouts

This section aims to delve into the various components commonly used in Graphical User Interfaces (GUIs) and explore the concept of layout managers, which are crucial for arranging these components in a coherent and visually appealing manner. The understanding of these elements is fundamental to crafting user-friendly interfaces.

Overview of Common GUI Components

GUI components, often referred to as widgets, are the building blocks of a graphical user interface. Some of the most used components in GUI development include:

- `Buttons`: Used for initiating actions. They are typically labeled with text or icons to indicate their function.

- `Labels`: Display non-editable text or images, usually for descriptive purposes.
- `Text Fields`: Allow users to input and edit text.
- `Checkboxes` and `Radio Buttons`: Provide options for users to select, with checkboxes allowing multiple selections and radio buttons allowing only one.
- `Menus` and `Toolbars`: Offer various commands and options in a structured format.
- `Sliders` and `Progress Bars`: Sliders allow for adjustable inputs, while progress bars show the progress of a task.
- Understanding Layout Managers
- Layout managers are used to control the placement and sizing of GUI components within a container.

In `Tkinter`, the primary layout managers are:

- `Pack`: Arranges widgets in a block, allowing for vertical or horizontal placement.
- `Grid`: Places widgets in a grid format, offering precise control over row and column placement.
- `Place`: Allows explicit positioning of widgets by specifying coordinates.

Understanding these layout managers is crucial for creating an organized and responsive GUI.

Best Practices for Designing User-Friendly Interfaces

Designing a user-friendly interface involves more than just understanding the tools; it requires an emphasis on user experience. Some best practices include:

- `Clarity`: Ensure that the purpose of each component is clear to the user.
- `Consistency`: Keep the styling and behavior of similar elements consistent throughout the application.
- `Responsiveness`: Design interfaces that adapt to different screen sizes and resolutions.
- `Accessibility`: Consider the needs of users with disabilities, such as providing keyboard navigation and screen reader compatibility.
- `Simplicity`: Avoid clutter and focus on the essential elements to provide a straightforward user experience.

In the proceeding code example of Tkinter application which demonstrate the various components and layout strategies:

```
import tkinter as tk
from tkinter import ttk
# Create the main window
root = tk.Tk()
root.title("Component Showcase")

# Create and place a label
label = ttk.Label(root, text="Enter your name:")
label.grid(row=0, column=0, padx=10, pady=10)

# Create and place a text field
entry = ttk.Entry(root)
entry.grid(row=0, column=1, padx=10, pady=10)

# Create and place a button
button = ttk.Button(root, text="Submit")
button.grid(row=1, column=0, columnspan=2, pady=10)

# Create and place a checkbox
checkbox = ttk.Checkbutton(root, text="Remember me")
checkbox.grid(row=2, column=0, columnspan=2)

# Start the GUI event loop
root.mainloop()
```

Explanation of the Code

- Window Setup: `root = tk.Tk()` creates the main window, and `root.title("Component Showcase")` sets its title.
- `Label`: `ttk.Label(root, text="Enter your name:")` creates a label widget, and `label.grid(row=0, column=0, padx=10, pady=10)` places it in the grid layout.
- Text Field: `ttk.Entry(root)` creates a text entry field. The grid method is used again to position it next to the label.
- Button: `ttk.Button(root, text="Submit")` creates a button. It spans two columns for better visual appeal.
- Checkbox: `ttk.Checkbutton(root, text="Remember me")` adds a checkbox for additional interaction.

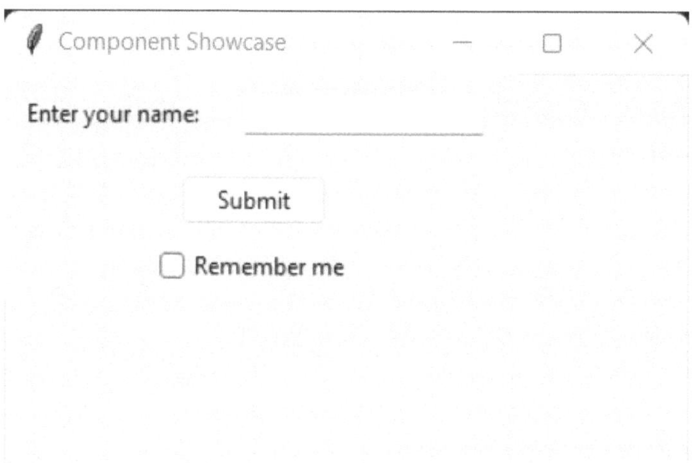

Figure 10.2: *output of demonstrating various components and layout strategies*

The preceding `Figure 10.2` shows the output of demonstrating various components and layout strategies.

This code demonstrates a simple layout where components are arranged using the grid layout manager. Each widget serves a specific purpose, contributing to a user-friendly experience. The use of padding (`padx` and `pady`) ensures that the components are not cramped, enhancing the overall aesthetics. Understanding and utilizing these components and layout strategies are key steps in creating effective and appealing GUI applications.

Building a Simple GUI Application

The aim of this section is to guide the reader through the development of a basic yet functional GUI application. By creating a simple project, such as a calculator or a to-do list, the reader will learn how to integrate various GUI components, organize their layout, and understand the importance of debugging and testing in application development.

Step-by-Step Guide to Building a Simple Application – A calculator

Let us take the example of creating a simple calculator using Python and `Tkinter`. This project will demonstrate the integration of various components like buttons, labels, and text fields.

- **Planning the Layout and Functionality**
    - Define what operations the calculator will perform (e.g., addition, subtraction, multiplication, division).
    - Sketch a layout that includes a display area for the input/output and buttons for the digits and operations.
- **Setting Up the GUI**
    - Create the main window.
    - Add a text field for the display area.
    - Arrange buttons in a grid layout.
- **Programming the Logic**
    - Write functions to handle button clicks.
    - Implement the calculations.
- **Testing and Debugging**
    - Test each functionality.
    - Debug any issues that arise.

Consider following code example of Simple Calculator

```
import tkinter as tk


def on_button_click(character):

    if character == 'C':
```

```
        display.delete(0, tk.END)
    elif character == '=':
        try:
            result = eval(display.get())
            display.delete(0, tk.END)
            display.insert(0, str(result))
        except Exception as e:
            display.delete(0, tk.END)
            display.insert(0, "Error")
    else:
        display.insert(tk.END, character)

# Create the main window
root = tk.Tk()
root.title("Simple Calculator")

# Create the display field
display = tk.Entry(root, justify='right')
display.grid(row=0, column=0, columnspan=4, sticky='nsew')

# List of button labels
buttons = [
    '7', '8', '9', '+',
    '4', '5', '6', '-',
```

```
    '1', '2', '3', '*',

    'C', '0', '=', '/'

]


# Create and place buttons

for i, button in enumerate(buttons):

    tk.Button(root, text=button, command=lambda b=button: on_button_
click(b)).grid(row=i//4 + 1, column=i%4)


# Start the GUI event loop

root.mainloop()
```

Explanation of the Code

Function `on_button_click`: This function handles button clicks. It performs calculations or updates the display based on the button clicked.

Setting Up the GUI

- root = tk.Tk() creates the main window.
- display = tk.Entry(root, justify='right') adds a text field for input and output, aligned to the right.
- display.grid(row=0, column=0, columnspan=4, sticky='nsew') positions the display at the top, spanning four columns.

Creating Buttons

- A list of button labels is defined.
- A loop creates buttons for each label and places them in a grid layout.
- **command=lambda b=button: on_button_click(b)** assigns a function to each button, passing the button label to the function.

Main Loop

- root.mainloop() starts the GUI event loop.

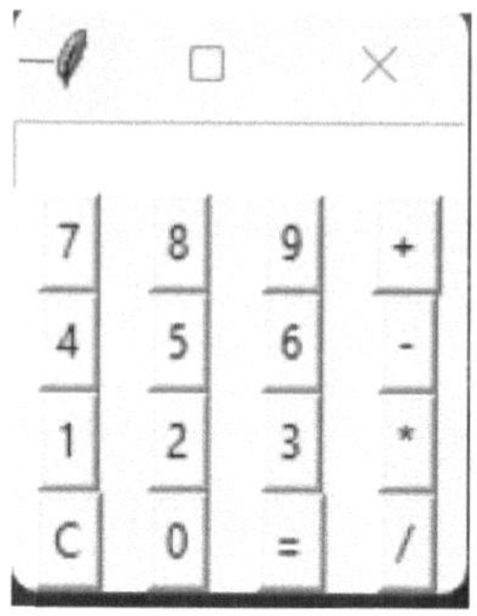

Figure 10.3: output of a simple calculator

The preceding `Figure 10.3` shows the output of a simple calculator.

Debugging and Testing

- Test Each Functionality: Click each button and ensure it performs the expected operation.
- Handle Exceptions: The try-except block in the calculation function prevents the application from crashing due to errors like division by zero.
- Validate User Inputs: Ensure the calculator handles non-numeric inputs gracefully.

Simple To-Do List Application

This example provides a complete code for a basic `To-Do List` application using Python and `Tkinter`. It demonstrates the creation of a GUI application where users can add, view, and delete tasks.

```
import tkinter as tk

from tkinter import messagebox


def add_task():

    task = task_entry.get()

    if task:

        listbox_tasks.insert(tk.END, task)
```

```
        task_entry.delete(0, tk.END)

    else:

        messagebox.showwarning("Warning", "You must enter a task.")


def delete_task():

    try:

        task_index = listbox_tasks.curselection()[0]

        listbox_tasks.delete(task_index)

    except IndexError:

        messagebox.showwarning("Warning", "You must select a task to
delete.")


# Create the main window

root = tk.Tk()

root.title("To-Do List")


# Create a frame for the Entry and Add button

frame_tasks = tk.Frame(root)

frame_tasks.pack()


# Create the entry widget

task_entry = tk.Entry(frame_tasks, width=50)

task_entry.pack(side=tk.LEFT)


# Create the add task button
```

```
button_add_task = tk.Button(frame_tasks, text="Add task", command=add_
task)

button_add_task.pack(side=tk.LEFT)

# Create the listbox to display tasks

listbox_tasks = tk.Listbox(root, height=10, width=50)

listbox_tasks.pack()

# Create the delete task button

button_delete_task = tk.Button(root, text="Delete task", command=delete_
task)

button_delete_task.pack()

# Start the main event loop

root.mainloop()
```

Let's understand the preceding code example:

Import Statements

- import tkinter as tk: Imports the Tkinter module.
- from tkinter import messagebox: Imports the messagebox submodule for displaying warning dialogs.

Function add_task

- Adds a new task to the listbox.
- Retrieves the task from the entry widget and checks if it's not empty.
- Inserts the task into the listbox and clears the entry widget.
- Displays a warning if no task is entered.

Function delete_task

- Deletes the selected task from the listbox.
- Retrieves the index of the currently selected task and removes it.
- Catches an IndexError to handle cases where no task is selected and shows a warning.

Creating the Main Window

- root = tk.Tk() initializes the main application window.
- root.title("To-Do List") sets the title of the window.
- Creating Widgets:
- frame_tasks is a frame widget that groups the entry and add button together.
- task_entry is an entry widget allowing users to type in tasks.
- button_add_task is a button that triggers the add_task function.
- listbox_tasks is a listbox that displays the list of tasks.
- button_delete_task is a button that triggers the delete_task function.

Layout Management

- pack() is used to place widgets in the window. The side parameter is used with the entry and button widgets to arrange them horizontally.
- Starting the Application:
- root.mainloop() starts the main event loop of the application, which waits for user interaction.
- This code provides a functional To-Do List application where users can add tasks, view them in a list, and delete them as needed. It showcases the use of various Tkinter widgets and layout management, as well as basic event handling and user interaction through the GUI.

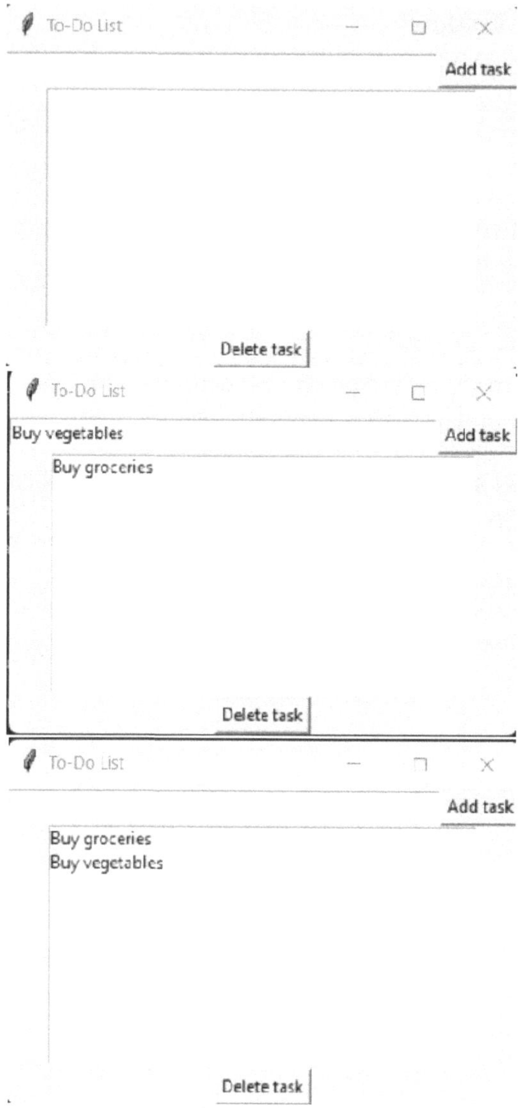

`Figure 10.4`: *output of a to-do list*

The preceding `Figure 10.4` shows the output of a to-do list.

By following these steps and examining the provided code, the reader can gain a practical understanding of building a simple yet functional GUI application in Python. This project integrates various components, demonstrating how they work together to create a cohesive application. Debugging and testing are integral to this process, ensuring that the application not only functions correctly but also handle errors and unexpected inputs effectively.

Interactivity and User Experience

This section aims to enhance the interaction between the user and the application, focusing on handling user inputs and events, providing feedback, and improving accessibility and usability. These aspects are crucial for creating applications that are not only functional but also engaging and easy to use.

Handling User Inputs and Events

Handling user inputs and events is about making the application responsive to the actions of the user. This includes clicking buttons, entering text, selecting menu items, and more. Effective handling ensures the application responds appropriately to each action.

Providing Feedback to User Actions

Feedback is essential for a good user experience. It can be in the form of visual cues, messages, or sounds that inform the user about the result of their actions. This helps in making the application more intuitive.

Improving Accessibility and Usability

Accessibility involves designing applications that can be used by people with various disabilities, while usability focuses on making the application easy and efficient to use for everyone. This includes clear navigation, readable text, and logical layout.

Enhanced To-Do List Application

Let's enhance the simple To-Do List application with additional features like a menu bar and dialog boxes.

```
import tkinter as tk

from tkinter import messagebox, simpledialog
```

```
def add_task():
    task = simpledialog.askstring("Add Task", "Enter a task:")
    if task:
        listbox_tasks.insert(tk.END, task)

def delete_task():
    try:
        task_index = listbox_tasks.curselection()[0]
        listbox_tasks.delete(task_index)
    except IndexError:
        messagebox.showwarning("Warning", "Select a task to delete.")

def about():
    messagebox.showinfo("About", "To-Do List Application\nVersion 1.0")

# Create the main window
root = tk.Tk()
root.title("Enhanced To-Do List")

# Create a menu bar
menu_bar = tk.Menu(root)
root.config(menu=menu_bar)

# Add menu items
```

```
file_menu = tk.Menu(menu_bar, tearoff=0)
menu_bar.add_cascade(label="File", menu=file_menu)
file_menu.add_command(label="Add Task", command=add_task)
file_menu.add_command(label="Delete Task", command=delete_task)
file_menu.add_separator()
file_menu.add_command(label="Exit", command=root.quit)

help_menu = tk.Menu(menu_bar, tearoff=0)
menu_bar.add_cascade(label="Help", menu=help_menu)
help_menu.add_command(label="About", command=about)

# Create the listbox to display tasks
listbox_tasks = tk.Listbox(root, height=10, width=50)
listbox_tasks.pack()

# Start the main event loop
root.mainloop()
```

Let us understand the preceding code:

Import Statements

Additional simpledialog module for input dialogs.

Function add_task:

Updated to use simpledialog.askstring for input, providing a dialog box for task entry.

Function delete_task

Unchanged, but now works in conjunction with the menu.

Function about

New function to show an informational dialog about the application.

Creating the Main Window and Menu Bar

- root = tk.Tk() and root.title("Enhanced To-Do List") create and title the main window.
- menu_bar = tk.Menu(root) creates a menu bar.
- root.config(menu=menu_bar) attaches the menu bar to the main window.

Setting Up Menus:

- file_menu and help_menu are created as drop-down menus.
- Menu items are added with add_command, linked to respective functions like add_task, delete_task, and about.
- add_cascade attaches these menus to the menu bar.

Creating the Listbox

- listbox_tasks is the same as in the previous example.

Starting the Application

- root.mainloop() starts the main event loop.

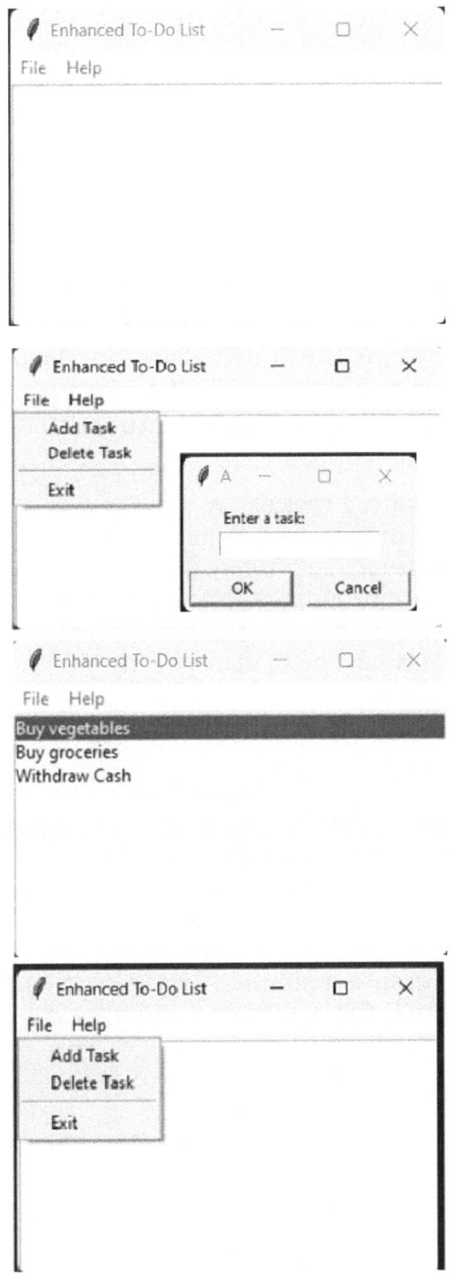

***Figure 10.5**: output of a to-do list(enhanced)*

The preceding `Figure 10.5` show the output of a to-do list (enhanced)

This enhanced version of the To-Do List application demonstrates improved interactivity and user experience. The addition of menu bars and dialog boxes makes the application more functional and user-friendly, while also introducing elements of standard application design. These improvements showcase the importance of considering user interaction and feedback in GUI development.

Creating a Practical Project

The objective here is to apply the knowledge gained from previous sections to develop a more complex and practical GUI application. This process involves careful planning, incorporating advanced features, and understanding how to package and distribute the application.

- Planning and Designing a Project
    - Identify the purpose and target audience.
    - Sketch the layout and decide on the functionalities.
    - Choose the appropriate tools and libraries.
- Advanced Features like Threading for Background Tasks
    - Implement threading to manage long-running processes without freezing the GUI.
    - Ensure thread safety and proper communication between threads and the GUI.
- Packaging and Distributing the Application
    - Convert the Python script into a standalone application.
    - Use tools like PyInstaller for packaging.
    - Distribute the application for various operating systems.

For this example, we'll create a simple file explorer application using Python and `Tkinter`, demonstrating file navigation and basic file operations.

```
import tkinter as tk

from tkinter import filedialog, messagebox

import os



def open_directory():
```

```
    path = filedialog.askdirectory()

    if path:

        list_files(path)


def list_files(path):

    listbox_files.delete(0, tk.END)

    try:

        for file in os.listdir(path):

            listbox_files.insert(tk.END, file)

    except PermissionError:

        messagebox.showerror("Error", "Permission Denied")


def on_file_select(event):

    index = listbox_files.curselection()[0]

    selected_file = listbox_files.get(index)

    label_file_info.config(text=f"Selected File: {selected_file}")


# Create the main window

root = tk.Tk()

root.title("Simple File Explorer")


# Create a button to open directory

button_open_directory = tk.Button(root, text="Open Directory",
command=open_directory)

button_open_directory.pack()
```

```
# Create a listbox to display files

listbox_files = tk.Listbox(root, height=15, width=50)

listbox_files.bind('<<ListboxSelect>>', on_file_select)

listbox_files.pack()


# Create a label to show selected file info

label_file_info = tk.Label(root, text="Selected File: None")

label_file_info.pack()


# Start the main event loop

root.mainloop()
```

Let us understand the code example:

Import Statements

- import os to handle file system operations.
- Tkinter modules for GUI components and file dialogs.

Function open_directory

- Opens a dialog to select a directory.
- Calls list_files function to display the files in the selected directory.

Function list_files

- Clears the listbox and populates it with files from the selected directory.
- Handles PermissionError if access to a file is denied.

Function on_file_select

- Called when a file is selected in the listbox.
- Updates a label with information about the selected file.

Setting Up the GUI

- Creates the main window, a button for opening directories, a listbox for displaying files, and a label for showing selected file information.

Event Binding

- listbox_files.bind connects an event (selection of a listbox item) to the on_file_select function.

Starting the Application

- root.mainloop() runs the main event loop of the GUI.

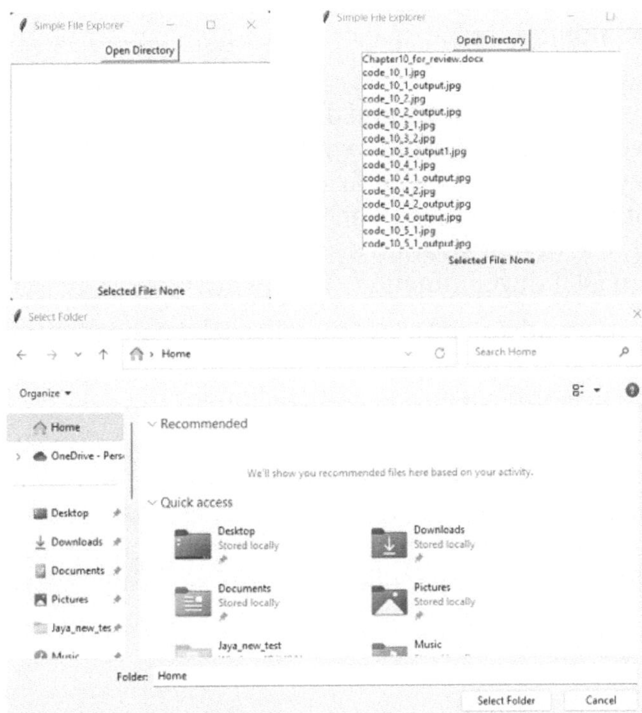

Figure 10.6: output of a file explorer

The preceding **Figure 10.6** shows the output of a file explorer.

This file explorer is a practical example of a more complex application that incorporates file system navigation and event handling. It demonstrates how to plan, design, and implement an application with a specific purpose, incorporating user interactions and feedback. The skills acquired from building this project lay a solid foundation for tackling even more advanced applications, including those that require threading and packaging for distribution.

Conclusion

In this chapter, we embarked on a comprehensive journey through the world of GUI development in Python. Starting from the basics, we explored the fundamental concepts, tools, and best practices essential for crafting intuitive and responsive graphical user interfaces. By delving into topics such as the history and evolution of GUIs, the intricacies of various components and layouts, and the nuances of user interaction and experience, we gained a holistic understanding of what makes a GUI application both functional and engaging.

Through the step-by-step guides and detailed examples, ranging from a simple calculator to a more complex file explorer application, we not only learned how to utilize Python's powerful libraries like Tkinter but also how to integrate various elements to create cohesive and practical applications. These examples served as a practical demonstration of the concepts discussed, offering hands-on experience in GUI development.

We also tackled more advanced aspects such as threading for background tasks and the steps involved in packaging and distributing an application, preparing you to handle real-world scenarios and challenges in GUI development.

As we conclude this chapter, it's important to remember that GUI development is an ever-evolving field, with new technologies and design paradigms emerging regularly. The foundation laid in this chapter provides a solid base for further exploration and learning. Whether your goal is to develop simple tools or complex, feature-rich applications, the skills and knowledge acquired here will serve as valuable assets in your programming toolkit.

Exercise: Test Your Understanding

Answer the following questions and test your understanding of learning from **Chapter 10**:

Q. 1. What does GUI stand for and what is its primary purpose in software development?

Q. 2. Name two popular Python libraries for GUI development.

Q. 3. How does GUI development differ from command-line interface development?

Q. 4. Why is Python a popular choice for developing GUI applications?

Q. 5. What is event-driven programming in the context of GUIs?

Notes

Date:

Python in Action

From web development to data analysis, from artificial intelligence to automation, Python is used in countless fields and industries. As you work through the exercises and projects in this book, think about how you can apply your new skills to real-world problems and create impactful solutions.

Chapter 11

Basics of Database with Python

In this chapter, we will dive into the world of databases and explore how Python can be used to interact with them effectively. Databases play a crucial role in many real-world applications, from managing stock inventory for a fruit vendor, as we'll see in our use-case, to powering complex data-driven web applications. Python is very useful, which makes it a skill for programmer and data enthusiast.

The entire chapter is based on the use case revolves around a fictional fruit vendor, "`The Fruit Wala`" who has recently expanded their business from a shop to a factory. This expansion comes with the challenge of efficiently managing stock inventory. The Fruit Wala recognizes the need to transition from manual record-keeping to a more robust and automated system. To achieve this, they intend to use an SQL database as the backbone of their stock management system, with Python as the primary programming language for developing the backend.

The vendor's staff, while experienced in inventory management, may not have a background in Python programming. Therefore, this chapter aims to serve as a quick reference guide, enabling The Fruit Wala's team to swiftly learn how to write Python code to interact with an SQL database. The aim of this chapter is to provide a basic and hands-on concept so that the vendor's staff will have the knowledge and confidence needed to establish database connections, execute

SQL queries, and effectively manage their stock data using Python.

In this chapter we will discuss:

- An overview to Database
- Database operations using Python
- Managing Database Data
- Error handling in Database Operations

An overview to Database

In this section, we will learn basic concepts and hands-on examples to connect SQL database using Python. We will explain these concepts with the help of our use case:

A database is a structured collection of data that plays a crucial role in various aspects of modern life, from business and technology to research and everyday applications. It serves as a central repository for storing, managing, and retrieving information. This section will delve into the core components of a database, using a SQL database named `FWMaster` as an example to illustrate these concepts.

Key Components of a Database

There are several key components of a database, each serving a specific purpose. All these components combine and represent a database.

Key components are discussed as below:

Table

Tables are the fundamental structure in a relational database. They consist of rows and columns, with each column representing a specific attribute or field, and each row representing a unique record or entry. Tables store the actual data in a structured format.

In `Master` SQL database, the collection of data is organized into tables, with each table representing a specific type of information. For instance, we have two tables, `Fruitmaster` and `Suppliermaster`, each designed for a different purpose. The data within databases is fundamental and can be of various types, such as text, numbers, dates, or even complex objects.

Let's consider the `Fruitmaster` table as an example.

```
CREATE TABLE Fruitmaster (

    id INT PRIMARY KEY,

    code VARCHAR(10),

    shortname VARCHAR(20),

    name VARCHAR(50),

    description TEXT,

    type VARCHAR(20)

);
```

It stores information about different types of fruits, with columns: **`id`**, **`code`**, **`shortname`**, **`name`**, **`description`**, and **`type`**. This structure allows us to efficiently store and retrieve data about various fruits.

Schema

The schema defines the structure of the database, including the tables, their relationships, and the constraints applied to the data. It serves as a blueprint for the database and enforces data integrity. It specifies which tables exist, what columns they have, and how they are related. In our Master database, the schema defines the structure of **`Fruitmaster`** and **`Suppliermaster`**.

Data types

Data types specify the kind of data that can be stored in each column of a table. Common data types include integers, strings, dates, and booleans. Data types help ensure data consistency and accuracy.

Here's a chart with some common data types and their descriptions:

Data Type	Description	Example
`Integer`	Whole numbers (integers)	*type_id INT*
`Decimal`	Fixed-point numbers with decimal places	*price DECIMAL(10, 2)*
`VARCHAR`	Variable-length character strings	*name VARCHAR(50)*
`CHAR`	Fixed-length character strings	*Type CHAR(4)*
`DATE`	Date values	*pur_date DATE*
`TIME`	Time values	*checkin_time TIME*
`DATETIME`	Date and Time values	*timestamp DATETIME*
`BOOLEAN`	True/False values	*is_active BOOLEAN*
`BLOB`	Binary Large Objects (used for binary data)	*image BLOB*

Table 11.1: SQL Data Type

Now, consider below code example for `Fruitmaster`:

```
-- Creating the Fruitmaster table

CREATE TABLE Fruitmaster (

    id INTEGER PRIMARY KEY,

    code CHAR(4),

    shortname VARCHAR(10),

    name VARCHAR(50),

    description VARCHAR(255),

    type VARCHAR(20)

);
```

```
-- Inserting a sample fruit record

INSERT INTO Fruitmaster (id, code, shortname, name, description, type)

VALUES (1, 'APPL', 'Apple', 'Red Delicious Apple', 'Sweet and crisp ap-
ple variety.', 'Fruit');

-- Querying data from the Fruitmaster table

SELECT * FROM Fruitmaster;
```

With the help of above code, we created a table `Fruitmaster` and then insert a record, finally we used a SELECT query to retrieve the data from the `Fruitmaster` table. As per our use-case, this table is suitable for storing information about different types of fruits, and you can add more records for various fruits by following the same structure. The id column serves as a unique identifier for each fruit, and the other columns provide details about each fruit, such as its code, name, description, and type.

Normalization

Normalization is a process to eliminate data redundancy and maintain data integrity. It involves breaking down large tables into smaller, related tables to reduce redundancy and improve data quality.

```
CREATE TABLE Fruits (

    id INT PRIMARY KEY,

    name VARCHAR(50),

    type_id INT,

    description TEXT

);


CREATE TABLE FruitTypes (

    id INT PRIMARY KEY,

    name VARCHAR(20)

);
```

By using above code, we are normalization our **Fruitmaster** by segregating its type column into a new table called **FruitTypes** and our main table becomes Fruits which stores detail of fruits with **type_id** of **FruitTypes** table.

Based on the explanation provided above, normalization refers to the procedure of structuring data in a database with the aim of reducing redundancy and upholding data integrity. Various normalization forms, such as 1NF, 2NF, 3NF, and so on, serve as guidelines for this process. However, delving into these intricacies is beyond the scope of this book.

Primary Key

A primary key is a unique identifier for each record in a table. It enforces data integrity by ensuring that each row has a unique key, and it is used for linking tables through foreign keys.

For instance, you can use primary keys to ensure unique values in the **id** column of **Fruitmaster**.

```
ALTER TABLE Fruitmaster ADD PRIMARY KEY (id);
```

Foreign Key

A foreign key is a column or set of columns in one table that refers to the primary key in another table. This establishes relationships between tables and allows for the creation of complex data structures.

```
CREATE TABLE Fruits (

    id INT PRIMARY KEY,

    name VARCHAR(50),

    type_id INT,

    description TEXT,

    FOREIGN KEY (type_id) REFERENCES FruitTypes(id)

);
```

The **Fruits** table has a foreign key named **type_id** that references the **id** field of the **FruitTypes** table. This relationship ensures that the **type_id** values in the **Fruits** table must match with existing id values in the **FruitTypes** table.

Indexes

Indexes are data structures that improve the speed of data retrieval operations by providing a fast way to look up rows in a table based on the values in one or more columns. Indexes are particularly useful for large databases.

For example, if you frequently search for fruits by their code, you can create an index on the code column in the `Fruitmaster` table:

```
CREATE INDEX idx_code ON Fruitmaster (code).
```

Queries

Queries are used to retrievc, update, and manipulate data in the database. SQL (Structured Query Language) is a common language for interacting with relational databases.

For instance, to retrieve all fruits of a particular type from `Fruitmaster`, you might use the following query:

```
SELECT * FROM Fruitmaster WHERE type = 'Citrus'
```

In another example, when you insert a new fruit into the `Fruits` table, you can specify its type by using an existing `id` value from the `FruitTypes` table. This ensures data consistency and prevents the insertion of invalid fruit types.

```
-- Insert a fruit type into the FruitTypes table

INSERT INTO FruitTypes (id, name) VALUES (1, 'Citrus');

-- Insert a fruit into the Fruits table and link it to a fruit type

INSERT INTO Fruits (id, name, type_id, description) VALUES (1, 'Orange',
1, 'Sweet and tangy citrus fruit');
```

Stored procedures and Functions

These are pre-defined sets of SQL statements that can be executed as a single unit. They are often used for data manipulation, validation, and automation.

Views

Views are virtual tables that present data from one or more tables in a specific way, allowing for easier data access and simplifying complex queries.

Triggers

Triggers are special types of stored procedures that are automatically executed in response to specific data events, such as insertions, updates, or deletions. They are used for enforcing business rules and data integrity.

Security and Access Control

Database systems have mechanisms for controlling who can access the database, what actions they can perform, and which data they can access. This includes user roles, permissions, and authentication.

Concurrency Control

To manage multiple users or processes accessing the database simultaneously, databases employ concurrency control mechanisms to ensure data consistency and prevent conflicts.

Backup and Recovery

Regular backups of the database are essential to safeguard against data loss due to hardware failures, software errors, or other issues. Recovery procedures ensure that data can be restored in case of a failure.

Transaction Management

Databases support the concept of transactions, which are sequences of one or more SQL operations treated as a single unit of work. Transactions ensure data consistency and atomicity (all-or-nothing) of changes.

Technical Pre-requisites to start working with Database using Python

To start working with an SQL database using Python, you'll need to have Python installed, as well as the necessary libraries for interacting with databases.

Followings are the step-by-step instructions to install the required pre-requisite tools:

1. **Install Python**: If you don't already have Python installed, you can download it from the official website: *https://www.python.org/downloads/*

Install pip: pip is a package manager for Python that will help you install necessary libraries. You might already have it installed with Python. If you don't have it, you can install it by following the instructions here: *https://pip.pypa.io/en/stable/installation/* to check pip, open your command prompt or terminal and run:

```
pip --version
```

2. **Install a Code Editor or Integrated Development Environment (IDE)**: Though this step is not mandatory, it is advisable to install a code editor or IDE of your choice. Doing so will facilitate the creation and execution of your Python code. While I personally like Visual Studio Code, you have various options to choose from a variety of code editors and tools such as PyCharm or Jupyter Notebook.
3. **Open a Terminal or Command Prompt**: You'll need a command-line interface to install Python packages and create your database. You'll need two main libraries for working with SQL databases in Python
    - **pyodbc** this library is used to connect SQL server from Python. To Do so, run following command:

```
pip install pyodbc
```

- **SQLAlchemy** This is an Object-Relational Mapping (ORM) library that can be used to work with various SQL databases, including MS SQL Server. To install, run following command:

```
pip install sqlalchemy
```

4. **SQL Server Driver** You'll need a SQL Server ODBC driver to connect to SQL Server. If you're working with an on-premise SQL Server, you might need to download and install the driver specific to your SQL Server version.
5. **Connection Details** Make sure you have the necessary connection details, such as the server address, database name, username, and password. If you're working with Azure SQL, you'll also need the Azure SQL server name and the authentication method (usually SQL Server Authentication).

Once you have these prerequisites in place, you can start working with SQL databases using Python. Here's a simple example of how to connect to a SQL Server database using pyodbc and SQLAlchemy:

```
import pyodbc

from sqlalchemy import create_engine


# Define connection parameters

server = 'your_server_name'

database = 'your_database_name'

username = 'your_username'

password = 'your_password'


# Create a pyodbc connection

conn = pyodbc.connect('DRIVER={SQL Server Native Client 11.0};SERVER=' +
server + ';DATABASE=' + database + ';UID=' + username + ';PWD=' + pass-
word)
```

```
# Create a SQLAlchemy engine

engine = create_engine(f"mssql+pyodbc://{username}:{password}@{server}/{database}?driver=SQL Server Native Client 11.0")
```

In the above code confirm you replace all the required values for **'your_server_name'**, **'your_database_name'**, **'your_username'**, and **'your_password'** with your specific connection details before you execute the code.

The following code will print the top **5** records from **fruitMaster** table having type **citrus**:

```
# Use SQLAlchemy to execute a SQL query

query = text("SELECT TOP 5 * FROM fruitMaster WHERE type = 'citrus'")

result = conn.execute(query)


# Fetch and print the results

for row in result:

    print(row)


# Close the database connection

conn.close()
```

The above code can throw an error related to unknown table or database which is obvious and completely expected at this stage.

Use case: Prepare database

As per our use case, let us first prepare our database **FWmaster** with tables **FruitMaster** and **SupplierMaster**.

Create Fruitmaster table

```
cursor.execute('''

    CREATE TABLE Fruitmaster (
```

```
        id INT PRIMARY KEY,

        code VARCHAR(10),

        name VARCHAR(255),

        type VARCHAR(50)

    )

''')
```

With the help of above, we created a new table `FruitMaster` with columns:

- id (INT)
- code (VARCHAR)
- name (VARCHAR)
- type (VARCHAR)

```
# Create Suppliermaster table

cursor.execute('''

    CREATE TABLE Suppliermaster (

        id INT PRIMARY KEY,

        code VARCHAR(10),

        name VARCHAR(255)

    )

''')
```

With the help of above, we created a new table `SupplierMaster` with columns:

- id (INT)
- code (VARCHAR)
- name (VARCHAR)

Database operations using Python

Until this point, we have covered our use-case, environment installation, and setup. We've also delved into the fundamental concepts of databases and their components. We are now fully equipped to commence our database operations. In the upcoming section, we will execute and comprehend various database operations using Python code.

Executing SQL Queries (CRUD operations)

CRUD, which stands for Create, Read, Update, and Delete, represents the fundamental database operations that remain consistent across various programming languages, albeit with potential syntax variations. These operations serve as the core building blocks for executing SQL queries. In this section, we'll explore how to perform these operations using Python code.

Create (C)

The Create operation involves inserting new records into a database. In SQL, this is typically done with the **INSERT** statement. For Python, consider the following code:

```
import pyodbc


# Establish a database connection

connection = pyodbc.connect('DRIVER={SQL Server};SERVER=fruitwaladb-server;DATABASE=FWMaster;UID=fwAdmin;PWD=ThisIsaTempPass')

cursor = connection.cursor()

# Inserting new data

cursor.execute('INSERT INTO Fruitmaster (name, description, type) VALUES (?, ?, ?);', ('Banana', 'Yellow and sweet', 'fruit'))

connection.commit()
```

Read (R)

The Read operation is used to retrieve data from a database. In SQL, the **SELECT** statement is employed to fetch records.

```
# Retrieving data

cursor.execute('SELECT name, description FROM Fruitmaster WHERE type = ?;', ('banana',))

rows = cursor.fetchall()

for row in rows:

    print(f'Name: {row.name}, Description: {row.description}')
```

Alternatively, you can use SQLAlchemy to create an ORM (Object-Relational Mapping) that simplifies database interaction:

```
from sqlalchemy import create_engine, Column, Integer, String

from sqlalchemy.orm import sessionmaker

from sqlalchemy.ext.declarative import declarative_base


# Define the SQLAlchemy model

Base = declarative_base()


class FruitMaster(Base):

    __tablename__ = 'FruitMaster'

    id = Column(Integer, primary_key=True)

    Name = Column(String)

    Quantity = Column(Integer)


# Establish a SQLAlchemy database connection
```

```
engine = create_engine('mssql+pyodbc://fwAdmin:ThisIsaTempPass@fruit-waladbserver/FWMaster')

Session = sessionmaker(bind=engine)

session = Session()

# Fetch all records from the FruitMaster table

fruits = session.query(FruitMaster).all()

for fruit in fruits:

    print(fruit.Name, fruit.Quantity)
```

Update (U)

The Update operation modifies existing records in the database. In SQL, this is done using the **UPDATE** statement.

```
# Updating data

cursor.execute('UPDATE Fruitmaster SET description = ? WHERE name = ?;', ('Sweet and tropical', 'Banana'))

connection.commit()
```

With SQLAlchemy, updating records is more intuitive:

```
# Update the quantity of Apples using SQLAlchemy
apple = session.query(FruitMaster).filter_by(Name='Banana').first()
apple.Quantity = 150
session.commit()
```

Delete (D)

The Delete operation removes records from the database. SQL employs the **DELETE** statement for this purpose.

```
# Deleting data

cursor.execute('DELETE FROM Fruitmaster WHERE name = ?;', ('Banana',))

connection.commit()
```

In SQLAlchemy, deleting records is straightforward:

```
# Delete records of a certain fruit using SQLAlchemy

session.query(FruitMaster).filter_by(Name='Apple').delete()

session.commit()
```

Discussing SQL Injections

SQL injection is a type of cyber-attack in which an attacker manipulates an SQL query to execute unintended actions on a database. It occurs when an application fails to properly validate and sanitize user inputs before using them in SQL queries. In simple words, SQL injection is a technique where an attacker inserts malicious SQL code into user inputs to manipulate the database query executed by an application. If the application does not properly validate or sanitize user inputs, it can allow attackers to gain unauthorized access to a database, steal, modify, or delete data, and potentially take control of the application itself.

The SQL injections are dangerous for any affected application:

- **Data Leakage**: Attackers can use SQL injections to extract sensitive data from the database, such as user credentials, personal information, or financial data.

- **Data Modification**: Attackers can alter the data in the database, leading to data corruption or fraudulent transactions. For example, changing the balance of a bank account.

- **Unauthorized Access**: SQL injection can enable attackers to bypass authentication mechanisms and gain unauthorized access to the application, possibly leading to further exploitation.

- **Application Takeover**: In some cases, SQL injection can be used to gain control over the application's server, potentially allowing for full compromise of the system.

- **Loss of Reputation**: Successful SQL injections can damage an organization's reputation and erode user trust, which can be difficult to regain.

Look at the code below; it appears straightforward and ready to proceed. It establishes a connection to the **FruitMaster** table and retrieves records based on user input:

```
import pyodbc

conn = pyodbc.connect('DRIVER={SQL Server};SERVER=fruitwaladbserver;DATABASE=FWMaster;UID=fwAdmin;PWD=ThisIsaTempPass')

cursor = conn.cursor()


user_input = input("Enter a fruit name: ")

query = f"SELECT * FROM FruitMaster WHERE name = '{user_input}'"

cursor.execute(query)


for row in cursor.fetchall():

    print(row)
```

Let's examine this code: the user's input for the fruit name is directly incorporated into the SQL query. An attacker could potentially exploit this vulnerability by inserting malicious input, such as **'; DROP TABLE FruitMaster--**, effectively deleting the "**FruitMaster**" table. It's important to be aware that the code provided is susceptible to SQL injection, highlighting the significant dangers associated with this type of attack. Even a seemingly simple piece of code like this has the potential to wreak havoc on an entire database if not handled with proper caution.

We have a solution to address the issue and safeguard against SQL injection. The initial code utilizes a standard SQL query, and the recommended remedy involves the utilization of parameterized queries or prepared statements.

Please review the following code, which has been corrected to enhance security:

```
import pyodbc

conn = pyodbc.connect('DRIVER={SQL Server};SERVER=fruitwaladbserver;DA-
TABASE=FWMaster;UID=fwAdmin;PWD=ThisIsaTempPass')

cursor = conn.cursor()


user_input = input("Enter a fruit name: ")

query = "SELECT * FROM FruitMaster WHERE name = ?"

cursor.execute(query, user_input)


for row in cursor.fetchall():

    print(row)
```

Finally, we fixed the infected code. By using a parameterized query, the user input is treated as a parameter rather than being directly embedded in the SQL statement, making it immune to SQL injection attacks.

Exploring Concepts: Joins, Clauses, Aggregation, and Sorting

Joins, Clauses, Aggregation, and Sorting are the core concepts of SQL and one should understand while working with databases. In this section, we will understand the basics of these concepts with code examples using Python.

Joins

Joins are used to combine data from multiple tables based on a related column between them. Common types of joins are **`INNER JOIN`**, **`LEFT JOIN`**, **`RIGHT JOIN`**, and **`FULL JOIN`**.

Consider the following code with **INNER JOIN**:

```
import pyodbc


# Define connection parameters

server = 'fruitwaladbserver'

database = 'FWMaster'

username = 'fwAdmin'

password = 'ThisIsaTempPass'

connection_string = f"DRIVER={{SQL Server}};SERVER={server};DATABASE={-
database};UID={username};PWD={password}"


# Create a connection

conn = pyodbc.connect(connection_string)

cursor = conn.cursor()


# Perform an INNER JOIN

sql_query = """

SELECT FruitMaster.name, SupplierMaster.name

FROM FruitMaster

INNER JOIN SupplierMaster ON FruitMaster.id = SupplierMaster.id

"""

cursor.execute(sql_query)

result = cursor.fetchall()
```

```
for row in result:
    print(row)

conn.close()
```

Another version of the code using `SQLAlchemy`

```
from sqlalchemy import create_engine, Column, Integer, String, select, and_
from sqlalchemy.orm import sessionmaker
from sqlalchemy.ext.declarative import declarative_base

# Define connection parameters
server = 'fruitwaladbserver'
database = 'FWMaster'
username = 'fwAdmin'
password = 'ThisIsaTempPass'
connection_string = f"mssql+pyodbc://{username}:{password}@{server}/{database}?driver=ODBC+Driver+17+for+SQL+Server"

# Create an SQLAlchemy engine
engine = create_engine(connection_string, echo=True)

# Create a session
Session = sessionmaker(bind=engine)
session = Session()
```

```
# Define SQLAlchemy ORM classes for the tables
Base = declarative_base()


class FruitMaster(Base):
    __tablename__ = 'FruitMaster'
    id = Column(Integer, primary_key=True)
    code = Column(String)
    name = Column(String)
    type = Column(String)


class SupplierMaster(Base):
    __tablename__ = 'SupplierMaster'
    id = Column(Integer, primary_key=True)
    code = Column(String)
    name = Column(String)
# Perform an INNER JOIN using SQLAlchemy
join_query = select([FruitMaster.name, SupplierMaster.name]).where(-
FruitMaster.id == SupplierMaster.id)
result = session.execute(join_query).fetchall()


for row in result:
    print(row)


session.close()
```

Clauses

Clauses in SQL are used to filter, group, or manipulate data. Common clauses include **WHERE GROUP BY**, **HAVING**, and more. We will not delve into all the clauses as these are beyond the scope of this chapter.

WHERE Clause: The **WHERE** clause is used to filter rows from a table based on a specified condition. It allows you to retrieve only the rows that meet the specified criteria.

```
import pyodbc


# Define connection parameters

server = 'fruitwaladbserver'

database = 'FWMaster'

username = 'fwAdmin'

password = 'ThisIsaTempPass'


# Create a connection

connection_string = f"DRIVER={{SQL Server}};SERVER={server};DATABASE={-
database};UID={username};PWD={password}"

conn = pyodbc.connect(connection_string)

cursor = conn.cursor()


# WHERE clause example

sql_query = """

SELECT name, type

FROM FruitMaster

WHERE type = 'Apple'
```

```
"""

cursor.execute(sql_query)

result = cursor.fetchall()


for row in result:

    print(row)

conn.close()
```

GROUP BY Clause: The **GROUP BY** clause is used to group rows that have the same values into summary rows, often used with aggregation functions like **COUNT**, **SUM**, **AVG**, etc.

```
# GROUP BY clause example

conn = pyodbc.connect(connection_string)

cursor = conn.cursor()


sql_query = """

SELECT type, COUNT(id) AS count

FROM FruitMaster

GROUP BY type

"""

cursor.execute(sql_query)

result = cursor.fetchall()

for row in result:

    print(row)

conn.close()
```

HAVING Clause: The **HAVING** clause is used in combination with **GROUP BY** and allows you to filter the results of an aggregation. It is applied after the **GROUP BY** clause.

```
# HAVING clause example

conn = pyodbc.connect(connection_string)

cursor = conn.cursor()


sql_query = """

SELECT type, COUNT(id) AS count

FROM FruitMaster

GROUP BY type

HAVING COUNT(id) > 2

"""

cursor.execute(sql_query)

result = cursor.fetchall()


for row in result:

    print(row)

conn.close()
```

Aggregation

Aggregations are used to perform operations on a set of values, such as calculating the sum, average, count, etc. Common aggregation functions include **SUM**, **AVG**, **COUNT**, **MAX**, and **MIN**. We will not delve into all the aggregation functions as these are beyond the scope of this chapter.

COUNT: The **COUNT** function is used to count the number of rows in a table or the number of rows that satisfy a specific condition.

```
import pyodbc

# Define connection parameters
server = 'fruitwaladbserver'
database = 'FWMaster'
username = 'fwAdmin'
password = 'ThisIsaTempPass'

# Create a connection
connection_string = f"DRIVER={{SQL Server}};SERVER={server};DATABASE={-
database};UID={username};PWD={password}"
conn = pyodbc.connect(connection_string)
cursor = conn.cursor()

# Count the number of rows in the FruitMaster table
sql_query = "SELECT COUNT(*) FROM FruitMaster"
cursor.execute(sql_query)
result = cursor.fetchone()

print("Total number of rows in FruitMaster:", result[0])

# Count the number of apples in the FruitMaster table
sql_query = "SELECT COUNT(*) FROM FruitMaster WHERE type = 'Apple'"
cursor.execute(sql_query)
```

```
result = cursor.fetchone()

print("Number of apples in FruitMaster:", result[0])

conn.close()
```

SUM: The **SUM** function is used to calculate the sum of a numeric column.

```
import pyodbc

# Define connection parameters
# (Same as above)

# Create a connection
# (Same as above)

# Calculate the total number of apples in the FruitMaster table
sql_query = "SELECT SUM(id) FROM FruitMaster WHERE type = 'Apple'"
cursor.execute(sql_query)
result = cursor.fetchone()

print("Total number of apples in FruitMaster:", result[0])

conn.close()
```

AVG: The **AVG** function is used to calculate the average of numeric values in a column.

```
import pyodbc


# Define connection parameters
# (Same as above)


# Create a connection
# (Same as above)


# Calculate the average ID of fruits in the FruitMaster table
sql_query = "SELECT AVG(id) FROM FruitMaster"
cursor.execute(sql_query)
result = cursor.fetchone()


print("Average ID of fruits in FruitMaster:", result[0])


conn.close()
```

MAX: The **MAX** function is used to find the maximum value in a column.

```
import pyodbc


# Define connection parameters
# (Same as above)
```

```
# Create a connection
# (Same as above)

# Find the fruit with the highest ID in the FruitMaster table
sql_query = "SELECT MAX(id) FROM FruitMaster"
cursor.execute(sql_query)
result = cursor.fetchone()

print("Fruit with the highest ID in FruitMaster:", result[0])

conn.close()
```

MIN: The **MIN** function is used to find the minimum value in a column.

```
import pyodbc

# Define connection parameters
# (Same as above)

# Create a connection
# (Same as above)

# Find the fruit with the lowest ID in the FruitMaster table
sql_query = "SELECT MIN(id) FROM FruitMaster"
cursor.execute(sql_query)
```

```
result = cursor.fetchone()

print("Fruit with the lowest ID in FruitMaster:", result[0])

conn.close()
```

Sorting

Sorting is used to arrange the result set in a specific order, typically in ascending or descending order. The **ORDER BY** clause is used for sorting. The **ORDER BY** clause is used to sort the result set in ascending (**ASC**) or descending (**DESC**) order based on one or more columns.

```
# ORDER BY clause example

conn = pyodbc.connect(connection_string)

cursor = conn.cursor()

sql_query = """

SELECT name

FROM FruitMaster

ORDER BY name DESC

"""

cursor.execute(sql_query)

result = cursor.fetchall()


for row in result:

    print(row)


conn.close()
```

Let's demonstrate **Clauses Aggregations**, and **Sorting** together using code examples:

Using **pyodbc** for **Clauses**, **Aggregations**, and **Sorting**:

```
# Example: Selecting and sorting fruits of a specific type

sql_query = """

SELECT name

FROM FruitMaster

WHERE type = 'Apple'

ORDER BY name

"""

cursor.execute(sql_query)

result = cursor.fetchall()


for row in result:

    print(row)


# Example: Counting the number of suppliers for each fruit type

sql_query = """

SELECT type, COUNT(id) AS supplier_count

FROM FruitMaster

GROUP BY type

HAVING COUNT(id) > 2

ORDER BY type
```

```
""""

cursor.execute(sql_query)

result = cursor.fetchall()


for row in result:

    print(row)


conn.close()
```

Using **SQLAlchemy** for **Clauses**, **Aggregations**, and **Sorting**:

```
# Example: Selecting and sorting fruits of a specific type

select_query = select([FruitMaster.name]).where(FruitMaster.type == 'Ap-
ple').order_by(FruitMaster.name)

result = session.execute(select_query).fetchall()


for row in result:

    print(row)


# Example: Counting the number of suppliers for each fruit type

count_query = select([FruitMaster.type, func.count(FruitMaster.id).la-
bel('supplier_count')]) \

    .group_by(FruitMaster.type) \

    .having(func.count(FruitMaster.id) > 2) \

    .order_by(FruitMaster.type)

result = session.execute(count_query).fetchall()
```

```
for row in result:
    print(row)

session.close()
```

Discussing Stored Procedures and Functions

Stored procedures and functions are reusable pieces of code in SQL. We'll show you how to execute them using Python.

Consider following code for Stored procedure:

```
# Calling a stored procedure
cursor.execute('EXEC sp_GetFruitByName ?', ('apple',))
result = cursor.fetchone()
print(f'Fruit Description: {result.description}')
```

Consider following code for Function:

```
# Calling a user-defined function
cursor.execute('SELECT dbo.CalculatePrice(3.0, 4.5) AS TotalPrice;')
result = cursor.fetchone()
print(f'Total Price: ${result.TotalPrice:.2f}')
```

Managing Database data

Databases often have multiple users accessing data concurrently. Managing database data involves ensuring that multiple users can work with the data efficiently and consistently. This is typically achieved using transactions and various isolation levels. In the context of SQL databases, transactions are used to group one or more SQL statements into a single unit of work that is either fully completed or fully rolled back if an error occurs.

Let's elaborate on this concept with code examples:

Transactions

In SQL databases, transactions are used to ensure the consistency and integrity of data. A transaction groups one or more SQL statements into a single unit of work. If any statement within a transaction fails, the entire transaction can be rolled back to maintain data consistency.

```
from sqlalchemy import create_engine, text


# Create a database engine

engine = create_engine('mssql+pyodbc://fwAdmin:ThisIsaTempPass@fruit-waladbserver/FWMaster')


# Start a transaction

with engine.begin() as conn:

    try:

        conn.execute(text("INSERT INTO FruitMaster (code, name, type) VALUES (:code, :name, :type)"), code='F1', name='Apple', type='Fruit')

        conn.execute(text("INSERT INTO SupplierMaster (code, name) VALUES (:code, :name)"), code='S1', name='Supplier A')

    except Exception as e:

        conn.rollback()
```

```
        print(f"Transaction failed: {e}")
    else:
        conn.commit()
        print("Transaction successful")
```

Isolation Levels

Isolation levels define how transactions interact with each other. They control the level of visibility that one transaction has to the changes made by another. Common isolation levels include **READ UNCOMMITTED**, **READ COMMITTED**, **REPEATABLE READ**, and **SERIALIZABLE**.

```
from sqlalchemy import create_engine, text

engine = create_engine('mssql+pyodbc://fwAdmin:ThisIsaTempPass@fruit-waladbserver/FWMaster')

# Set isolation level to SERIALIZABLE
connection = engine.connect()
connection.execution_options(isolation_level="SERIALIZABLE")

# Perform SQL operations
# ...

connection.close()
```

Disaster Recovery

Disaster recovery is a crucial aspect of database management that involves planning and implementing strategies to ensure data and system availability in the event of unforeseen disasters or failures.

Followings are the key points highlighting the importance of disaster recovery:

- `Data Protection`: Disaster recovery measures, such as regular backups, protect against data loss due to hardware failures, corruption, or accidental deletion. In Python, you can schedule backups using libraries like **`apscheduler`**.
- `Business Continuity`: Disaster recovery ensures that business operations can continue even in the face of catastrophic events, such as server crashes or natural disasters.
- `Reduced Downtime`: Quick recovery minimizes downtime, reducing the impact on business operations. Python can be used to automate the recovery process, ensuring faster restoration.
- `Compliance and Legal Requirements`: Many industries and regions have legal requirements for data retention and recovery. Disaster recovery helps organizations meet compliance standards.
- `Data Integrity`: Ensuring that the recovered data is consistent and reliable is vital. Consistency checks and data validation processes in Python can be part of the recovery process.

While specific disaster recovery strategies may vary, it is essential to implement a combination of regular backups, failover systems, and a well-documented recovery plan.

Error handling in Database operations

Error handling is a fundamental concept in programming, and it is essential for robust and reliable code. In Python, error handling is achieved using exceptions. An exception is an event that occurs during the execution of a program and disrupts the normal flow of instructions. When an exception occurs, Python raises an exception object to handle the error gracefully and provide information about what went wrong.

In Python, error handling involves the use of try, except, finally, and optionally, else blocks. Here are the basic concepts:

- **try**: The **try** block contains the code that might raise an exception.
- **except**: The **except** block is executed when an exception is raised within the try block. You can specify which exception(s) to catch or use a generic **except** block to catch all exceptions.
- **finally**: The **finally** block is always executed, whether an exception occurs or not. It's typically used for cleanup operations.
- **else**: The **else** block is executed if no exception is raised in the **try** block.

Custom Exceptions in Python

Custom exceptions are user-defined exceptions that allow you to create specific error classes tailored to your application's needs. To create a custom exception, you typically define a new class that is inherited from the base Exception class or one of its subclasses.

Here's an example of creating a custom exception:

```
class MyCustomException(Exception):

    def __init__(self, message):

        super().__init__(message)
```

The above code is simply defined as **MyCustomException.**

Consider following code to handle exceptions in database operations:

```
import pyodbc


# Define connection parameters
```

```
server = 'fruitwaladbserver'

database = 'FWMaster'

username = 'fwAdmin'

password = 'ThisIsaTempPass'


try:

    conn = pyodbc.connect(f"DRIVER={{SQL Server}};SERVER={server};DATA-
BASE={database};UID={username};PWD={password}")

    cursor = conn.cursor()


    # Perform database operations here


except pyodbc.Error as e:

    # Handle database-specific exceptions

    print("Database Error:", str(e))


except Exception as e:

    # Handle other exceptions

    print("Error:", str(e))


finally:

    if 'cursor' in locals():

        cursor.close()

    if 'conn' in locals():

        conn.close()
```

Another code examples:

```
from sqlalchemy import create_engine

from sqlalchemy.exc import SQLAlchemyError


# Define the database URL (use your database configuration)

db_url = f"mssql+pyodbc://{username}:{password}@{server}/{data-
base}?driver=SQL Server Native Client 11.0"


try:

    engine = create_engine(db_url)

    connection = engine.connect()


    # Perform database operations using SQLAlchemy ORM or Core


except SQLAlchemyError as e:

    # Handle SQLAlchemy-specific exceptions

    print("SQLAlchemy Error:", str(e))


except Exception as e:

    # Handle other exceptions

    print("Error:", str(e))


finally:
```

```
    if 'connection' in locals():
        connection.close()
```

Consider following code for Custom database exception:

```
import pyodbc

class DatabaseConnectionError(Exception):
    pass

# Define connection parameters
server = 'fruitwaladbserver'
database = 'FWMaster'
username = 'fwAdmin'
password = 'ThisIsaTempPass'

try:
    conn = pyodbc.connect(f"DRIVER={{SQL Server}};SERVER={server};DATA-
BASE={database};UID={username};PWD={password}")
    cursor = conn.cursor()

    # Perform database operations here

except pyodbc.Error as e:
    # Handle database-specific exceptions
    print("Database Error:", str(e))
```

```
    raise DatabaseConnectionError("Error connecting to the database")
from e


except Exception as e:

    # Handle other exceptions

    print("Error:", str(e))


finally:

    if 'cursor' in locals():

        cursor.close()

    if 'conn' in locals():

        conn.close()
```

In this example, we've defined a custom exception `DatabaseConnectionError` that's raised when there's an issue with the database connection. You can raise this custom exception in specific situations and handle it as needed.

Consider following code for Database custom exception using `SQLAlchemy`:

```
from sqlalchemy import create_engine

from sqlalchemy.exc import SQLAlchemyError


class DatabaseOperationError(Exception):

    pass


# Define the database URL (use your database configuration)

db_url = f"mssql+pyodbc://{username}:{password}@{server}/{data-
base}?driver=SQL Server Native Client 11.0"
```

```
try:

    engine = create_engine(db_url)

    connection = engine.connect()


    # Perform database operations using SQLAlchemy ORM or Core


except SQLAlchemyError as e:

    # Handle SQLAlchemy-specific exceptions

    print("SQLAlchemy Error:", str(e))

    raise DatabaseOperationError("Error performing database operation") from e


except Exception as e:

    # Handle other exceptions

    print("Error:", str(e))


finally:

    if 'connection' in locals():

        connection.close()
```

In this example, we've defined a custom exception `DatabaseOperationError` that's raised when there's an issue with a specific database operation. You can raise this custom exception for any operation-specific errors and handle it accordingly.

Custom exceptions help you make your code more readable and maintainable by clearly indicating the type of error that occurred during database operations.

Conclusion

In this chapter, we've explored the basics of working with databases in Python. We covered database connections, executing SQL queries, CRUD operations, data management, and error handling, all within a real-world use case context.

In the next chapter, we will explore concepts of threading.

Exercise: Test Your Understanding

Answer the following questions and test your understanding of learning from `Chapter 11`:

`Q. 1.` What is the purpose of SQL in database management, and how does Python facilitate its use?

`Q. 2.` How to prevent SQL injections in Python?

`Q. 3.` Why is error handling required in database operations? Explain the use of a custom exception in Python.

`Q. 4.` Explain JOIN in SQL and how to use JOIN in Python?

`Q. 5.` What are transactions in database management? Explain the implementation of transactions in Python.

Notes

Date:

Chapter 12
Introduction to Python Threading

Threads are known as a fundamental concept of any programming language. In this chapter we will learn concepts and practical scenarios of threading in Python programming. Moreover, Threading allows multiple tasks to be executed concurrently within a single Python process, unlocking the potential for improved performance and responsiveness in applications. In this chapter we will cover an overview of threading concepts, including thread creation, synchronization, communication, and thread management. With the help of this chapter, we will learn how to leverage Python's threading module to create and manage threads, synchronize access to shared resources, and coordinate the execution of concurrent tasks. Through practical examples and explanations.

In this chapter, we will cover:

- Introduction to Multithreading
- Creating Threads in Python
- Thread Synchronization
- Concurrent Programming Concepts
- Practical Multithreading Examples

Understanding the concept

In Python, a process refers to an instance of a running program. It is an independent entity that can execute code and has its own memory space, system resources, and execution environment.

Here are some key points about Python processes:

- **Independence**: Each Python process runs independently of other processes. It has its own memory space, which means variables and data structures defined within one process are not accessible to another process unless shared explicitly.
- **Resource Allocation**: Python processes are allocated resources by the operating system, such as CPU time, memory, and file descriptors. Each process operates in its own memory space, preventing interference and ensuring isolation.
- **Parallelism**: Multiple Python processes can run concurrently on multi-core systems, taking advantage of parallelism to improve performance. Processes can communicate with each other through inter-process communication (IPC) mechanisms such as pipes, sockets, and shared memory.
- **Process Creation**: In Python, processes can be created using the multiprocessing module, which provides a high-level interface for spawning new processes, managing communication between processes, and synchronizing their execution.
- **Isolation**: Python processes are isolated from each other, meaning that they do not share global state by default. This isolation helps prevent unintended side effects and makes it easier to reason about the behavior of individual processes.

Overall, Python processes provide a powerful mechanism for achieving concurrency and parallelism, enabling developers to create responsive, scalable, and efficient applications.

In general, a thread is the smallest unit of execution within a process. We can explore by breaking down the key aspects of threads as below:

- **Execution Flow**: A thread represents a sequence of instructions that can be executed independently within a process. Each thread has its own program counter, stack, and set of registers, allowing it to execute code independently of other threads.
- **Concurrency**: Threads allow multiple tasks to be executed concurrently within a single process. This means that multiple threads can execute code simultaneously, potentially speeding up the overall execution of a program by taking advantage of the parallelism offered by modern multi-core processors.

- **Shared Resources**: Since threads within a process share the same address space, they can access and modify shared resources such as variables, data structures, and I/O devices. However, this shared access can lead to synchronization issues, such as race conditions and data corruption, which need to be carefully managed using synchronization mechanisms like locks, semaphores, and mutexes.
- **Lightweight**: Threads are typically lightweight compared to processes, as they share resources such as memory and file descriptors with other threads within the same process. Creating and switching between threads is generally faster and more efficient than creating and switching between processes.
- **Multithreading**: Multithreading refers to the use of multiple threads within a single process to perform concurrent tasks. Multithreading can improve the responsiveness and performance of applications, particularly in scenarios where tasks can be executed independently and in parallel.
- **Thread States**: Threads can be in various states during their lifecycle, including running, ready, blocked, and terminated. The operating system scheduler is responsible for managing thc execution of threads and transitioning them between different states based on factors such as thread priorities, I/O operations, and synchronization events.

To understand and explore the threading in Python let's explore it in coming sections with code examples:

Multithreading at a glance

Multithreading in Python refers to the capability of a Python program to execute multiple threads concurrently within a single process. Threads are lightweight subprocesses that share the same memory space and resources, allowing for parallel task execution.

In Python, multithreading is achieved using the threading module, which provides a high-level interface for creating and managing threads. Each thread represents an independent sequence of instructions that can run concurrently with other threads.

Multithreading in Python offers significant benefits, enhancing application responsiveness and performance. It is particularly effective in scenarios where tasks can be executed independently and in parallel. For instance, a web server application can use multithreading to handle multiple client requests simultaneously, thereby improving its scalability and throughput.

Developers need to be aware of Python's Global Interpreter Lock (GIL) and its impact on multithreading. The GIL ensures that only one thread executes Python bytecode at a time, which can affect the performance of multithreaded Python programs, especially on multi-core systems.

Despite the limitations imposed by the GIL, multithreading can still be beneficial in certain situations, such as I/O-bound tasks where threads spend most of their time waiting for external resources like network requests or disk I/O.

Overall, multithreading in Python provides developers with a flexible and powerful mechanism for achieving concurrency and parallelism in their applications, enabling them to create responsive, efficient, and scalable software solutions.

To understand more, let's write a simple multithreading program in Python. This program will explain multithreading; in this small program, we will create multiple threads to perform CPU-bound tasks concurrently.

Note: *Please refer to Chapter 1 in case you missed to install Python and code editor.*

Open your favorite editor and write following Python Code:

```
import threading

# This function calculates square of numbers

def cal_num_square(number):

    square = number * number

    print(f"The square of {number} is {square}")

# Numbers in a List

# This can be more dynamica by taking input from user

numbers = [2, 4, 8, 32, 256]

# Here, create threads for each and individual numbers

threads = []

for number in numbers:
```

```
    thread = threading.Thread(target=cal_num_square, args=(number,))

    threads.append(thread)

    thread.start()


# Wait until all threads finished

for thread in threads:

    thread.join()


print(“All threads have finished execution”)
```

In the preceding code, our function **cal_num_square** which takes number list as an input and then calculates the squares of the number. To make code quicker we take a list of number in **numbers** and provides this list as an input to the function. The list iterates using **threading.Thread** class. Here, we start the thread using **start()** and wait for all threads to finish execution **join()** method.

After execution of this code, you'll see that each thread calculates the square of a number concurrently. The use of multithreading allows the program to perform these calculations more quickly by leveraging the available CPU resources. The final output would be like the proceeding image (**Figure 12.1**)

Figure 12.1: *output of firstcode-threading.py*

In the above program, all threads wait till completion due to the use of the **join()** method. After creating and starting all the threads, the main program enters a loop where it iterates over each thread in the threads list and calls **the join()** method on each thread.

The **join()** method blocks the main program's execution until the thread it is called on has finished executing. Therefore, by calling **join()** on each thread in the loop, the main program waits for all threads to finish executing before proceeding to the next line of code, which prints the message "**`All threads have finished execution`**". This ensures that all threads have completed their tasks before the main program finishes.

In the above program, it is not determined how much CPU utilization is happened for this program. Regarding CPU utilization, the system monitoring tools such as top (on Linux) or Task Manager (on Windows) to view CPU utilization. When multithreaded Python program executes, it may observe an increase in CPU utilization as multiple threads are executing concurrently and utilizing CPU resources. However, due to Python's Global Interpreter Lock (GIL), the actual CPU utilization may not reach the maximum potential, especially for CPU-bound tasks.

Now, let's try to see the CPU utilization within the Python code itself, the platform-specific libraries, or tools such as **`psutil`** for Python. This library allows to retrieve system information, including CPU utilization, directly from the Python code.

To achieve so let's install `psutil` using pip:

```
pip install psutil
```

After execution of above pip from command prompt (Windows); it will install the utility as visualized in the proceeding **`Figure 12.2`**

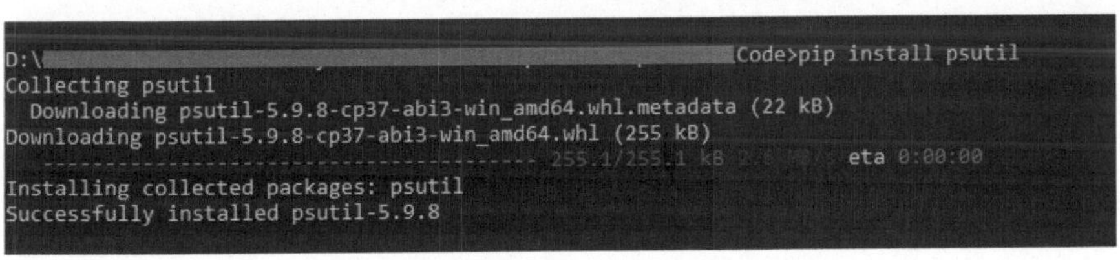

`Figure 12.2`: *Execution of pip*

The following code snippet consists of CPU utilization:

```
import threading

import psutil


# This function calculates square of numbers

def cal_num_square(number):

    # Get CPU utilization before calculation

    cpu_before = psutil.cpu_percent(interval=None)


    # Calculate square

    square = number * number

    print(f"Thread {threading.current_thread().name}: The square of {number} is {square}")


    # Get CPU utilization after calculation

    cpu_after = psutil.cpu_percent(interval=None)

    print(f"Thread {threading.current_thread().name}: CPU Utilization: {cpu_after - cpu_before}%")


# Numbers in a List

# This can be more dynamica by taking input from user

numbers = [2, 4, 8, 32, 256]


# Create threads for calculating squares

threads = []
```

```
for number in numbers:

    thread = threading.Thread(target=cal_num_square, args=(number,),
name=f”Thread-{number}”)

    threads.append(thread)

    thread.start()


# Wait for all threads to finish

for thread in threads:

    thread.join()


# Calculate total CPU utilization

total_cpu_utilization = sum(psutil.cpu_percent(percpu=True, interval=-
None))

print(f”Total CPU Utilization: {total_cpu_utilization}%”)
```

The above code uses `psutil.cpu_percent(interval=None)` to get the CPU utilization before and after the calculation. You would see output as shown in the proceeding **Figure 12.3**

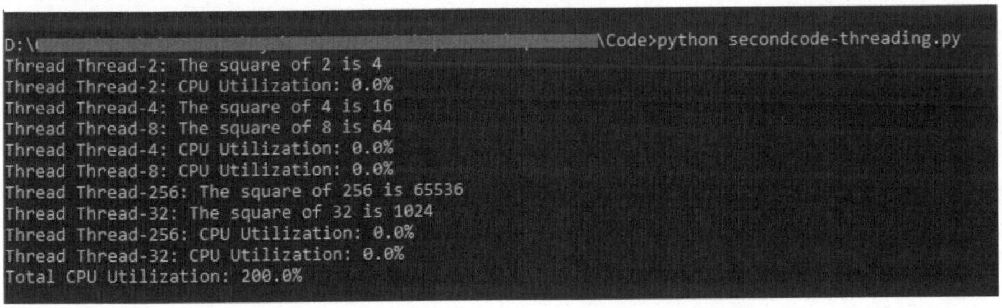

Figure 12.3: *Output of secondcode-threding.py*

Note: If the CPU utilization is showing as 0.00%, it could indicate that the CPU was idle during the interval when the measurement was taken.

To get more precise details about CPU utilization, we can try reducing the interval parameter in the **psutil.cpu_percent()** function. A smaller interval will provide more frequent updates on CPU utilization and may capture activity that occurs within shorter time periods.

Proceeding code is an updated version with a smaller interval for more frequent updates on CPU utilization:

```
import threading

import psutil


# This function calculates square of numbers

def cal_num_square(number):

    # Get CPU utilization before calculation

    cpu_before = psutil.cpu_percent(interval=None)


    # Calculate square

    square = number * number

    print(f"Thread {threading.current_thread().name}: The square of {number} is {square}")


    # Get CPU utilization after calculation

    cpu_after = psutil.cpu_percent(interval=None)

    print(f"Thread {threading.current_thread().name}: CPU Utilization: {cpu_after - cpu_before}%")


# Numbers in a List
```

```
# This can be more dynamica by taking input from user

numbers = [2, 4, 8, 32, 256]


# Create threads for calculating squares

threads = []

for number in numbers:

    thread = threading.Thread(target=cal_num_square, args=(number,), 
name=f"Thread-{number}")

    threads.append(thread)

    thread.start()


# Wait for all threads to finish

for thread in threads:

    thread.join()


# Calculate total CPU utilization

total_cpu_utilization = sum(psutil.cpu_percent(percpu=True, inter-
val=0.1))

print(f"Total CPU Utilization: {total_cpu_utilization}%")
```

The preceding code has a new value of interval parameter in the **psutil.cpu_percent()** function to **0.1**, which means CPU utilization will be measured every 0.1 seconds. Adjust this value as needed to get more frequent updates on CPU utilization.

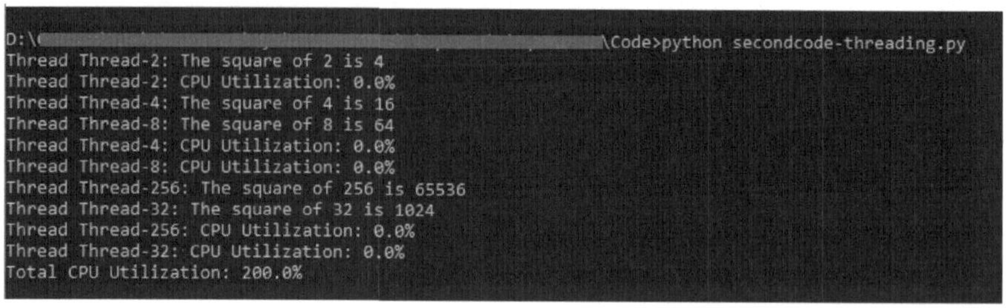

***`Figure 12.4`**: Output of thirdcode-threding.py*

The output shown in `Figure-12.4` may vary depending on CPU state and its utilization.

If the CPU is idle during the execution of the program, it might be challenging to demonstrate CPU utilization accurately. However, we can create a more CPU-intensive task to showcase CPU utilization more effectively. We have written `fourthcode-threading.py` program for your experiment. The demonstration of CPU utilization is beyond the scope of this chapter, so, we are leaving it up to you to experiment with the given code.

Concurrent Execution

Concurrent execution is the ability of a system to perform multiple tasks simultaneously. This approach allows multiple tasks or processes to make progress concurrently, resulting in better resource utilization and improved system responsiveness.

There are various techniques to achieve concurrent execution, such as multiprocessing and multithreading. In multiprocessing, several processes run independently, each with its own memory space and resources. This approach allows tasks to be executed in parallel and takes advantage of multi-core processors, thereby speeding up the overall execution of a program.

Multithreading, on the other hand, involves running multiple threads within a single process. Threads share the same memory space and resources, enabling them to execute concurrently and communicate with each other more efficiently. Multithreading is particularly useful for tasks that can be divided into smaller subtasks that can be executed independently.

Concurrent execution is crucial for building responsive and scalable systems, enabling applications to handle multiple tasks simultaneously without blocking or delaying other tasks. By leveraging concurrent execution, developers can create software that is more efficient, responsive, and capable of handling complex workloads.

For more understanding on Concurrent execution, consider following code:

```
import threading

import time


# Function to print a message

def print_message(message):

    print(message)

    time.sleep(2)  # Simulate a time-consuming task


# Create threads for concurrent execution

thread1 = threading.Thread(target=print_message, args=("I'm Thread 1",))

thread2 = threading.Thread(target=print_message, args=("I'm Thread 2",))


# Start the threads

thread1.start()

thread2.start()


# Wait for the threads to finish

thread1.join()

thread2.join()

print("Execution of Thread 1 and Thread 1 has finished.")
```

In the above code, we created two threads, each executing the **`print_message`** function with a different message. The threads run concurrently, allowing both messages to be printed simultaneously. The **`time.sleep(2)`** statement simulates a time-consuming task to demonstrate the concurrent execution of multiple threads. Finally, we wait for both threads to finish execution before printing a message indicating that they have been completed.

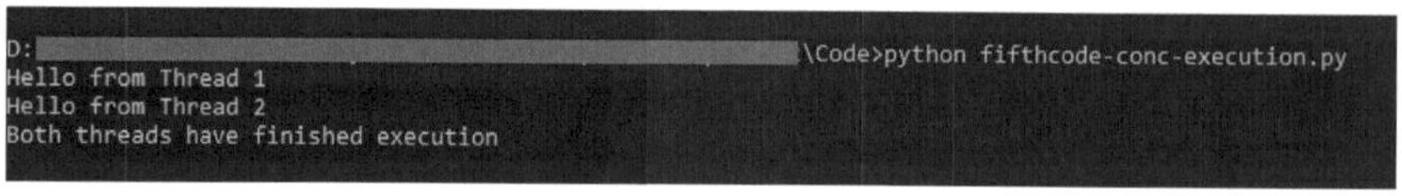

***Figure 12.5**: Output of fifthcode-conc-execution.py*

The preceding **`Figure-12.5`** displayed the output of the program. You can experiment by adding more threads in the above code.

Creating Threads

Creating threads in Python involves using the threading module, which provides a high-level interface for working with threads. Threads allow concurrent execution of tasks within a single process, enabling developers to leverage the power of parallelism in their applications.

To create a thread in Python, you first define a function that represents the task you want the thread to perform. This function will be the target for the thread. You then instantiate a Thread object from the threading module, passing the target function as an argument. Optionally, you can provide arguments to the target function using the args parameter. Once the Thread object is created, you call its `start()` method to begin execution of the thread. The `start()` method initiates the thread's execution, and it begins running the target function concurrently with other threads in the process.

Threads in Python share the same memory space and resources, allowing them to communicate and interact with each other more efficiently. However, this shared access to resources can lead to synchronization issues, such as race conditions and data corruption, which need to be carefully managed using synchronization mechanisms like locks, semaphores, and mutexes.

Using threads in Python enables developers to create responsive and scalable applications by distributing tasks across multiple threads. This concurrency model is particularly useful for tasks that can be divided into smaller subtasks that can be executed independently and concurrently.

Consider following code of simple thread:

```
import threading


# Function to print a message
def print_message(msg):
    print(msg)


#Thread message
message =   "Hi, I'm here from Thread."


# Create a thread
thread = threading.Thread(target=print_message, args=(message,))


# Start the thread
thread.start()
# Wait for the thread to finish
thread.join()
print("Thread has finished execution.")
```

In the preceding code, we defined a function **print_message** that prints a message. We then create a thread **thread** with **print_message** as the target function. We start the thread using the **start()** method and wait for it to finish using the **join()** method. Finally, we print a message indicating that the thread has finished execution.

```
D:                                          \Code>python sixthcode-simple-thread.py
Hi, I'm here from Thread.
Thread has finished execution.
```

Figure 12.6: *Output of sixthcode-simple-thread.py*

The preceding `Figure-12.6` displayed the output of the program. You can experiment by adding more threads and variation of messages in the above code.

Exploring threading module

The threading module in Python provides a high-level interface for working with threads. It offers several methods for creating, managing, and controlling threads. Below, we'll discuss the main methods of the Thread class in the threading module:

- **start()**: This method is used to initiate the execution of a thread. It spawns a new thread and begins running the target function concurrently with other threads in the process.

- **join([timeout])**: The join() method is used to wait for a thread to complete its execution. When called, the calling thread will block until the target thread has finished executing. Optionally, a timeout can be specified to limit the waiting time.

- **is_alive()**: This method checks whether a thread is currently executing. It returns True if the thread is alive (i.e., still executing), and False otherwise.

- **getName(), setName(name)**: These methods are used to get or set the name of a thread. The name is a string identifier for the thread, which can be useful for debugging and logging purposes.

- **daemon, setDaemon(daemonic)**: These methods are used to set a thread as a daemon thread. Daemon threads are background threads that run in the background and do not prevent the program from exiting if they are still running. The daemon attribute can be set to True or False to indicate whether a thread is a daemon thread.

- **ident**: This attribute returns the unique identifier of a thread. It is an integer value assigned to each thread by the operating system.

- **run()**: This method represents the entry point for the thread's execution. It is called when the start() method is invoked and should contain the main logic of the thread's task.

- **enumerate()**: This method returns a list of all active threads currently running in the process. It can be useful for debugging and monitoring the state of threads.
- **isDaemon()**: This method checks whether a thread is a daemon thread. It returns True if the thread is a daemon thread, and False otherwise.
- **sleep(secs)**: The sleep() function is a utility function available in the time module that causes the calling thread to sleep or pause execution for a specified number of seconds.

These methods provide developers with the necessary tools to create, manage, and control threads effectively in Python. By leveraging these methods, developers can build concurrent and parallel applications that take advantage of the available CPU resources and improve performance and scalability.

Consider the following code:

```
import threading

import time


# Function to print a message

def print_message(message):

    print(message)

    time.sleep(3)  # Simulate a time-consuming task


# Create a thread

thread = threading.Thread(target=print_message, args=("I'm here from
thread",), name="CodeThread")
```

```
# Set the thread as a daemon thread
thread.setDaemon(True)

# Start the thread
thread.start()

# Wait for the thread to finish
thread.join()

# Check if the thread is alive
if thread.is_alive():
    print("Thread is still running")
else:
    print("Thread has finished execution")

# Get the name of the thread
print("Thread name:", thread.getName())

# Check if the thread is a daemon thread
if thread.isDaemon():
    print("Thread is a daemon thread")
else:
    print("Thread is not a daemon thread")
```

The preceding code example demonstrates the usage of various methods of the Thread class in the threading module, including **start()**, **join()**, **is_alive()**, **getName()**, **setDaemon()**, and **isDaemon()**. That illustrates how to **create**, **start**, and **manage** threads in Python.

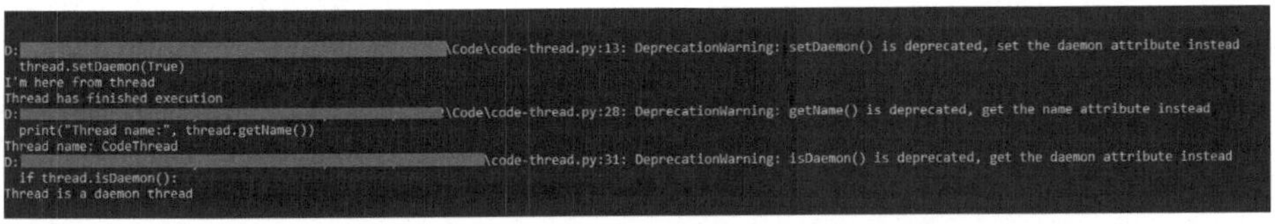

***Figure 12.7**: Output of code-thread.py*

The preceding **Figure-12.7** displayed the output of the program. You can experiment by adding more variations to the above code.

Thread synchronization

Thread synchronization is a critical concept in concurrent programming that ensures orderly access to shared resources among multiple threads. In a multi-threaded environment, where threads execute concurrently, it's essential to coordinate their activities to prevent race conditions, data corruption, and other synchronization issues.

Thread synchronization mechanisms allow threads to coordinate and communicate with each other to ensure the integrity and consistency of shared data. One of the most used synchronization mechanisms is the use of locks, which provide mutual exclusion. Mutual exclusion ensures that only one thread can access a shared resource at any given time, preventing concurrent access and potential conflicts.

Python's threading module provides built-in support for thread synchronization through various synchronization primitives, including Locks, Semaphores, Condition Variables, and Event objects.

Locks, also known as mutexes (mutual exclusion locks), are the simplest form of synchronization mechanism. They allow threads to acquire and release locks to protect critical sections of code, ensuring that only one thread can execute the critical section at a time. Locks can be acquired using the **acquire()** method and released using the **release()** method.

Semaphores are more versatile synchronization primitives that allow multiple threads to access a shared resource simultaneously, up to a specified limit. They maintain a counter that represents the number of available resources. Threads can acquire resources using the `acquire()` method and release them using the `release()` method.

Condition Variables provide a more sophisticated form of synchronization, allowing threads to wait for a certain condition to become true before proceeding. Threads can wait on a condition using the `wait()` method and signal other threads when the condition is satisfied using the `notify()` or `notify_all()` methods.

Event objects are synchronization primitives that allow threads to wait for an event to occur and then proceed. Threads can wait for an event using the `wait()` method and set the event using the `set()` method.

These synchronization primitives provide the building blocks for creating complex synchronization patterns and solving synchronization problems in multi-threaded applications. By carefully designing and implementing synchronization mechanisms, developers can ensure the safety, reliability, and correctness of their multi-threaded programs.

However, improper use of synchronization mechanisms can lead to **deadlocks**, **livelocks**, and other concurrency issues. Therefore, it's essential to understand the principles of thread synchronization and use synchronization primitives judiciously to achieve optimal performance and scalability in multi-threaded applications.

Consider the following code to explain thread synchronization:

```
import threading


# Shared resource

shared_resource = 0


# Lock for synchronization

lock = threading.Lock()
```

```
# Function to increment the shared resource
def increment():
    global shared_resource
    for _ in range(1000000):
        # Acquire the lock
        lock.acquire()
        shared_resource += 1
        # Release the lock
        lock.release()

# Create multiple threads to increment the shared resource
threads = []
for _ in range(5):
    thread = threading.Thread(target=increment)
    threads.append(thread)
    thread.start()

# Wait for all threads to finish
for thread in threads:
    thread.join()
# Print the final value of the shared resource
print("Final value of shared resource:", shared_resource)
```

In the preceding code example,

- shared resource `shared_resource` (initialized to 0) and a `lock` for synchronization using the `threading.Lock()` constructor.
- function `increment()` that increments the `shared_resource` variable by 1 for 1,000,000 times. Inside the function, we acquire the lock using `lock.acquire()` before modifying the shared resource and release the lock using `lock.release()` afterward.
- We create a list threads to hold the thread objects and then create 5 threads, each targeting the `increment()` function. We start each thread using the `start()` method.
- We wait for all threads to finish their execution using the `join()` method to ensure that the main thread waits until all child threads have completed.
- Finally, we print the final value of the shared resource after all threads have finished executing.

In this example, the `lock` ensures that only one thread can modify the `shared_resource` variable at a time. This prevents race conditions and ensures that the final value of the shared resource is consistent and correct. The use of thread synchronization with locks ensures the integrity and consistency of shared data in a multi-threaded environment.

***Figure 12.8**: Output of code-sync.py*

The preceding `Figure-12.8` displayed the output of the program. You can experiment by adding more variations to the above code.

Concepts of Concurrent Programming

Concurrent programming is a programming paradigm that deals with the execution of multiple tasks or processes simultaneously, typically within a single program. It allows developers to write software that can perform multiple operations concurrently, thereby improving performance, responsiveness, and resource utilization.

At its core, concurrent programming aims to make the most efficient use of available resources, such as CPU cycles and memory, by executing multiple tasks concurrently. This is particularly important in today's computing landscape, where multi-core processors are common, and applications are expected to handle increasingly complex workloads.

One of the key concepts in concurrent programming is concurrency, which refers to the ability of a program to make progress on multiple tasks at the same time. Concurrency can be achieved through various techniques, including multi-threading, multiprocessing, asynchronous programming, and parallelism.

Multi-threading is a popular approach to concurrency, where a program is divided into multiple threads of execution. Threads share the same memory space and resources within a process, allowing them to execute independently and communicate with each other more efficiently. This allows developers to create responsive and interactive applications by offloading time-consuming tasks to separate threads, while keeping the main thread free to handle user input and interface updates.

Multiprocessing takes concurrency to the next level by leveraging multiple processes instead of threads. Each process has its own memory space and resources, providing more isolation and fault tolerance compared to threads. Multiprocessing is particularly useful for CPU-bound tasks, where the workload can be distributed across multiple CPU cores to improve performance.

Asynchronous programming is another approach to concurrency, commonly used in event-driven and I/O-bound applications. It allows tasks to run concurrently without blocking the main thread, making it suitable for handling tasks that involve waiting for I/O operations to complete, such as network requests or file I/O.

Parallelism is the concept of executing multiple tasks simultaneously, typically across multiple CPU cores or processors. It is closely related to concurrency but focuses on achieving maximum throughput by parallelizing computations across multiple processing units.

Concurrency introduces several challenges and considerations that developers must address, such as synchronization, race conditions, deadlocks, and resource contention. Synchronization mechanisms, such as locks, semaphores, and condition variables, are used to coordinate access to shared resources and prevent data corruption. Proper synchronization ensures that concurrent threads or processes can safely access and modify shared data without conflicts.

In addition to synchronization, error handling and fault tolerance are critical aspects of concurrent programming. As concurrent programs are more complex and prone to unexpected errors, developers must implement robust error handling mechanisms and strategies for handling failures gracefully.

Concurrency also requires careful design and planning to achieve optimal performance and scalability. Developers must carefully consider factors such as the granularity of tasks, the balance between concurrency and overhead, and the trade-offs between synchronization and parallelism.

Overall, concurrent programming is a powerful paradigm for building efficient, responsive, and scalable software systems. By leveraging concurrency, developers can harness the full potential of modern computing architectures and deliver software that meets the demands of today's increasingly complex and demanding workloads. However, mastering concurrent programming requires a solid understanding of its principles, techniques, and best practices, as well as careful attention to the challenges and considerations involved.

Conclusion

This chapter taught us that threads provide a powerful mechanism for achieving concurrency and parallelism in software applications. Threads enable developers to create responsive, efficient, and scalable systems. However, managing threads effectively requires careful consideration of synchronization, resource sharing, and thread coordination to avoid common pitfalls such as deadlocks and race conditions.

In the next chapter, we will learn more about Regular expressions in Python programming and explore how to use them more precisely.

In the next chapter, we will understand more about Regular expression in Python programming and will explore the way to use Regular expression in more precise way.

Exercise: Test Your Understanding

Answer the following questions and test your understanding of learning from `Chapter 12`:

Q. 1. What is Multithreading?

Q. 2. Write a basic syntax of thread creation.

Q. 3. What is thread synchronization?

Q. 4. Explain the difference between concurrency and parallelism.

Q. 5. Write a simple program of Multithreading.

Notes

Date:

Code Like a Pro
Python's extensive standard library means you have a wealth of modules and tools. Learn to leverage these resources to write efficient and robust programs. Don't reinvent the wheel – use the tools available to you!

Chapter 13
Regular Expression: an overview

This chapter delves into the various concepts of regular expressions in Python, providing readers with a comprehensive overview of this powerful tool for text pattern matching. Regular expressions, commonly referred to as regex, are a fundamental aspect of text processing and manipulation, allowing users to identify and manipulate specific patterns within text data with precision and efficiency.

Throughout this chapter, readers will embark on a journey to understand the intricacies of regular expressions, gaining insights into their significance in various programming tasks. By the end of the chapter, readers will have acquired essential skills in recognizing patterns within text, applying regular expressions to perform text matching, and manipulating text data according to desired patterns.

The chapter begins by laying a solid foundation in understanding regular expressions, elucidating their syntax, and highlighting their importance in text processing tasks. Readers will learn how to construct and interpret regular expression patterns, enabling them to perform sophisticated text manipulations with ease.

Furthermore, the chapter delves into the practical application of regular expressions for text matching. Readers will explore how to utilize regex patterns to search for specific strings, substrings, or patterns within text data, facilitating tasks such as data validation, extraction, and transformation.

As readers progress, they will uncover the vast array of regex metacharacters and quantifiers available for crafting precise and flexible search patterns. Through hands-on examples and exercises, readers will gain proficiency in utilizing these metacharacters and quantifiers to refine their text matching operations.

The chapter also delves into advanced topics such as replacing and extracting text using regular expressions. Readers will learn how to leverage regex patterns to perform targeted replacements and extract relevant information from text data efficiently.

In this chapter, we will cover:

- Understanding Regular Expressions
- Using Patterns for Text Matching
- Regex Metacharacters and Quantifiers
- Replacing and Extracting Text
- Applications of Regular Expressions

Understanding Regular Expressions

Regular expressions, often abbreviated as regex or regexp, are powerful tools for pattern matching and text manipulation in computer science and software engineering. They provide a concise and flexible syntax for defining search patterns within text data, allowing developers to perform complex string operations with ease.

At its core, a regular expression is a sequence of characters that forms a search pattern. These patterns can include literals, such as letters and numbers, as well as metacharacters that represent specific types of characters or character classes. For example, the metacharacter '.' matches any single character, while '\d' matches any digit.

Regular expressions are widely used in various fields, including text processing, data validation, and string manipulation. They can be found in programming languages, text editors, command-line tools, and database systems, making them a versatile and indispensable tool for developers and system administrators alike.

One of the key features of regular expressions is their ability to perform pattern matching and extraction within text data. By specifying a search pattern, developers can search for specific strings, substrings, or patterns within a larger body of text. This allows for tasks such as finding email addresses in a document, extracting phone numbers from a webpage, or validating input data against a predefined format.

Regular expressions also support a wide range of operations, including matching, searching, replacing, splitting, and capturing. These operations enable developers to perform complex text processing tasks efficiently and effectively. For example, the `re.match()` function in Python's re module can be used to check if a string matches a given pattern, while the `re.findall()` function can be used to find all occurrences of a pattern within a string.

Despite their power and versatility, regular expressions can be complex and challenging to master. The syntax of regular expressions can be cryptic, and constructing effective patterns often requires a deep understanding of their capabilities and limitations. Additionally, regular expressions can be prone to errors and unexpected behavior if not used correctly, leading to bugs and security vulnerabilities in software.

To understand the concept, consider the following simple code:

```
import re


# Text containing email addresses

text = """

Regular expressions, often abbreviated as regex or regexp,

are powerful tools for pattern matching and text manipulation in
computer science and software engineering.

Email: gaurav.arora@mail.com

Regular expressions are widely used in various fields, including text
processing, data validation, and string manipulation.

Email: sachin.gupta@mail.com

"""
```

```
# Regular expression pattern for matching email addresses
pattern = r’\b[A-Za-z0-9._%+-]+@[A-Za-z0-9.-]+\.[A-Z|a-z]{2,}\b’

# Find all email addresses in the text
emails = re.findall(pattern, text)

# Print the found email addresses
print(“\nThe input text contains following emails: “)
for email in emails:
    print(email)
```

The preceding code demonstrates how to use regular expressions in Python to search for and extract email addresses from a given text. The regular expression pattern `pattern` accurately captures the structure of email addresses, allowing us to find and extract them from the text efficiently. Regular expressions provide a powerful and flexible tool for pattern matching and text processing in Python, making tasks like finding email addresses in text documents straightforward and efficient.

Figure 13.1: *output of code-regex.py*

The preceding image (**Figure 13.1**) shows the output of the code. You can try more variations by making changes in the regular expression.

The following table depicts the most used Regular expression in Python:

Type	RegEx	Description
Basic Regular Expression	.	(Dot): Matches any single character except newline.
	^	(Caret): Matches the start of the string
	$	(Dollar): Matches the end of the string.
	*	(Asterisk): Matches zero or more occurrences of the preceding character or group.
Meta Characters	+	Matches one or more occurrences
	?	Matches zero or one occurrence.
	\\	Drops the special meaning of the character following it.
	[]	Represents a character class.
	|	Means OR (matches any of the characters separated by it).
	{}	Indicates the number of occurrences of a preceding RegEx to match.
	()	Encloses group of RegEx
Character Classes	[abc]	Matches any character 'a', 'b', or 'c'.
	[0-9]	Matches any digit.

Table 13.1: Regular expression

Using Patterns for Text Matching

Using patterns for text matching is a fundamental aspect of text processing and manipulation in programming. Patterns, also known as regular expressions, provide a powerful and flexible way to search for specific strings, substrings, or patterns within text data. By defining a pattern, developers can instruct the computer to identify and extract desired information from a larger body of text, enabling a wide range of text processing tasks with precision and efficiency.

At its core, text matching involves specifying a pattern that represents the sequence of characters or symbols you want to find within a given text. This pattern can be as simple as a single character or as complex as a sequence of characters with specific properties or constraints. For example, a pattern might represent a word, a phone number, an email address, or any other structured data within text.

Regular expressions, the primary tool for defining patterns in text matching, offer a rich and expressive syntax for constructing complex search patterns. Developers can use a variety of metacharacters, quantifiers, character classes, and other constructs to create patterns that match specific sequences of characters or symbols. For instance, the metacharacter '.' matches any single character, '\d' matches any digit, and '[A-Za-z]+' matches one or more alphabetical characters.

Once a pattern is defined, it can be applied to text data using text matching functions provided by programming languages or libraries. These functions typically accept the pattern and the text to be searched for and return information about matches found within the text. Common text matching functions include `match()`, `search()`, `findall()`, `finditer()`, and `sub()`.

- **The match()** function attempts to match the pattern at the beginning of the text. If a match is found, it returns a match object containing information about the match, such as the matched text and its position within the text. If no match is found, it returns None.
- **The search()** function searches for the first occurrence of the pattern within the text. If a match is found, it returns a match object; otherwise, it returns None.
- **The findall()** function searches for all occurrences of the pattern within the text and returns a list of all matches found.
- **The finditer()** function is similar to findall() but returns an iterator over match objects instead of a list.
- **The sub()** function performs search and replace operations, replacing all occurrences of the pattern within the text with a specified replacement string.

Consider the following code:

```
import re


# Text data containing email addresses

text = "To know more about the Regular Expression you can reach to
author(s) at gaurav.arora@mail.com or sachin.gupta@mail.com."


# Define a search pattern for matching email addresses

pattern = r'\b[A-Za-z0-9._%+-]+@[A-Za-z0-9.-]+\.[A-Za-z]{2,}\b'


# Search for email addresses in the text

matches = re.findall(pattern, text)


# Print the matched email addresses

print("\n\tAuthor(s) email addresses:\n")

for match in matches:

    print("\t",match)
```

In this preceding code-example, we demonstrate text matching using patterns with regular expressions in Python. The regular expression pattern **`pattern`** accurately captures the structure of email addresses, allowing us to find and extract them from the text efficiently. This illustrates how developers can define precise search patterns and apply them to text data to perform sophisticated text matching operations.

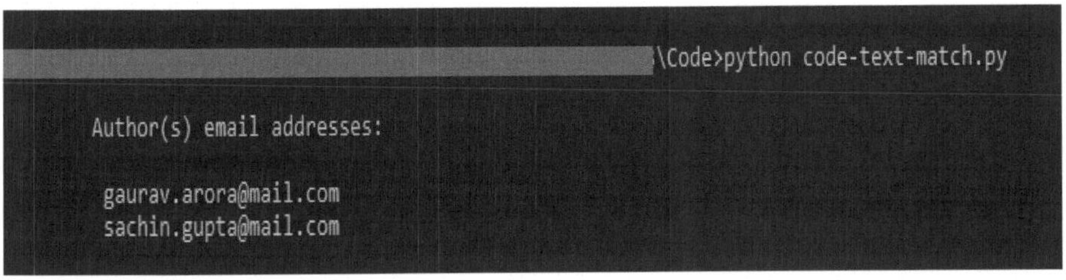

Figure 13.2: *output of code-text-match.py*

The preceding image (`Figure 13.2`) shows the output of the code. You can try more variations by making changes in the regular expression.

Regex Metacharacters and Quantifiers

Regex metacharacters and quantifiers are essential components of regular expressions, providing flexibility and expressiveness in defining search patterns for text matching operations. Metacharacters are special characters with predefined meanings within regular expressions, while quantifiers control the repetition of characters or patterns within the text.

Metacharacters serve various purposes in regular expressions, allowing developers to specify specific types of characters or character classes. For example, the dot (.) metacharacter matches any single character except for newline characters. This allows developers to define patterns that can match a wide range of characters, making regex patterns more versatile and adaptable.

Another important metacharacter is the caret (^), which represents the start of a line or string. When used at the beginning of a regex pattern, the caret ensures that the pattern matches only at the beginning of a line or string, restricting the search to specific positions within the text data.

Similarly, the dollar sign ($) metacharacter represents the end of a line or string. When used at the end of a regex pattern, the dollar sign ensures that the pattern matches only at the end of a line or string, providing precise control over where the pattern can match within the text data.

Quantifiers, on the other hand, control the repetition of characters or patterns within the text. They allow developers to specify how many times a particular character or pattern should be repeated in the text. For example, the asterisk (*) quantifier matches zero or more occurrences of the preceding character or pattern.

This allows developers to define patterns that can match varying lengths of text, making regex patterns more flexible and adaptable to different scenarios.

Another commonly used quantifier is the plus sign (+), which matches one or more occurrences of the preceding character or pattern. This ensures that the pattern must appear at least once in the text data, making it useful for defining patterns that require certain elements to be present.

Additionally, quantifiers such as the question mark (?) provide options for optional matching. The question mark matches zero or one occurrence of the preceding character or pattern, allowing developers to specify optional elements within the text data.

To understand the concept, consider following code:

```
import re


# Text data containing various phone numbers

text = """

Alternatively, you can reach to author(s) via:

Phone: 091-456-7890

Mobile: (456) 789-0123

Alternate: 987.654.3210

"""


# Define a regex pattern to match phone numbers

pattern = r'\b(?:\d{3}[-.\s]?\d{3}[-.\s]?\d{4}|\(\d{3}\)\s?\d{3}[-.\s]?\
d{4})\b'


# Search for phone numbers in the text using the regex pattern

matches = re.findall(pattern, text)
```

```
# Print the matched phone numbers
print("\n\tAuthor(s) phone numbers:\n")
for match in matches:
    print("\t",match)
```

In preceding code-example, we demonstrate the use of regex metacharacters and quantifiers to match phone numbers with different formats within text data. The regular expression pattern `pattern` accurately captures the structure of phone numbers, allowing us to find and extract them from the text efficiently. This illustrates how developers can define precise search patterns using regex metacharacters and quantifiers to perform sophisticated text matching operations.

Figure 13.3: *output of code-metacharacter.py*

The preceding image (**Figure 13.3**) shows the output of the code. You can try more variations by making changes in the regular expression. We got only two contact numbers as an output. While we have three contact numbers in our code. We did not see **Mobile** number in the output, this is because we have a **regex pattern** defined and this pattern does not meet for the format of **Mobile** number, hence this number is not available in the list of matches. Hence, we did not see **Mobile** number in the output.

Replacing and Extracting Text

In Python regular expressions, the concepts of "Replacing" and "Extracting" text involve manipulating strings based on defined patterns. These operations are fundamental for tasks such as text transformation, data cleaning, and information extraction.

Replacing text involves substituting specific patterns within a string with other specified text. This process is useful for tasks like correcting typos, standardizing formats, or removing unwanted characters. Regular expressions provide a powerful mechanism for defining search patterns to identify text that needs replacing. For example, you can use a regular expression pattern to search for all occurrences of a particular word or phrase in a string and replace them with another word or phrase.

Extracting text, on the other hand, involves isolating specific parts of a string that match a given pattern. This process is commonly used to extract relevant information from unstructured text data. Regular expressions enable developers to define precise patterns for extracting desired substrings or data elements from a larger text corpus. For example, you can use a regular expression pattern to extract email addresses, phone numbers, or other structured data from a block of text.

To perform replacing and extracting text using regular expressions in Python, developers typically use the `re.sub()` function for replacing text and the `re.findall()` function for extracting text.

The `re.sub()` function allows you to search for patterns within a string and replace all occurrences of those patterns with a specified replacement string. This function takes three arguments: the regular expression pattern to search for, the replacement string, and the input string. For example, you can use `re.sub()` to replace all occurrences of a word with another word in a string.

The `re.findall()` function, on the other hand, searches for all occurrences of a pattern within a string and returns a list of all matched substrings. This function takes two arguments: the regular expression pattern to search for and the input string. For example, you can use `re.findall()` to extract all email addresses or phone numbers from a block of text.

Consider the following code-example:

```
import re

# Sample text containing phone numbers in different formats
text = """
Alternatively, you can reach to author(s) via:
- Phone: 091-456-7890
- Mobile: (555) 555-5555
- Fax: 123.456.7890
"""

# Regular expression pattern to extract phone numbers
phone_pattern = r'\b(?:\d{3}[-.\s]?)?\d{3}[-.\s]?\d{4}\b'

# Extracting phone numbers from the text using re.findall()
phone_numbers = re.findall(phone_pattern, text)

# Printing the extracted phone numbers
print("Extracted phone numbers:")
for number in phone_numbers:
    print(number)

# Regular expression pattern to replace phone numbers with 'PHONE_
NUMBER'
```

```
replacement = 'PHONE_NUMBER'

replaced_text = re.sub(phone_pattern, replacement, text)


# Printing the text with phone numbers replaced

print("\nText with phone numbers replaced:")

print(replaced_text)
```

In the preceding code-example, we demonstrate replacing and extracting text using regular expressions in Python. The regular expression pattern **phone_pattern** is used to extract phone numbers from the text, while the **re.sub()** function is used to replace these phone numbers with a placeholder string **PHONE_NUMBER**. This illustrates how developers can use regular expressions to perform sophisticated text manipulation operations, such as extracting and replacing specific patterns within text data.

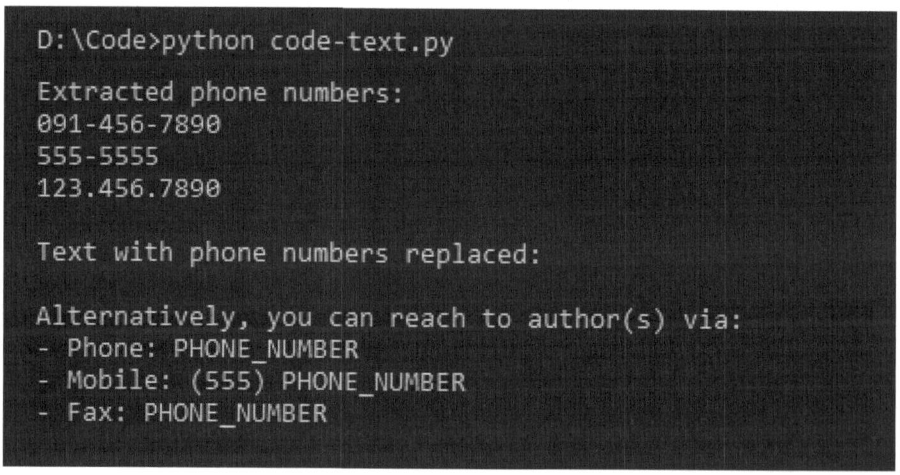

Figure 13.4: *Output of code-text.py*

The preceding image (**Figure 13.4**) shows the output of the code. You can try more variations by making changes in the regular expression.

Applications of Regular Expressions

In this section, we will create a small application based on our fictional use-case.

Imagine we are creating a fictional text-based adventure game set in a medieval fantasy world. In this game, players navigate through various locations, encounter characters, and interact with the environment by typing commands into the game's text interface. As the game developer, we want to enhance the player experience by implementing a natural language processing system that interprets and responds to player commands in a dynamic and flexible manner.

To achieve this, we can leverage regular expressions in Python to parse and interpret player commands. Regular expressions allow us to define patterns that match specific types of commands, enabling us to extract relevant information such as action verbs, target objects, and additional parameters from the player's input.

For example, suppose a player types the command "attack dragon with sword" to engage in combat with a dragon using a sword. We can use regular expressions to parse this command and extract the action ("attack"), target object ("dragon"), and additional parameter ("sword") from the input string.

Furthermore, regular expressions enable us to handle variations and synonyms in player commands effectively. For instance, the command "kill the dragon using the blade" should be interpreted in the same way as "attack dragon with sword." By defining flexible patterns with regular expressions, we can accommodate different phrasings and wordings while still capturing the essential elements of the command.

Additionally, regular expressions allow us to implement error checking and validation for player commands. We can define patterns to detect invalid or nonsensical commands, such as "jump the house" or "fight banana," and provide appropriate feedback to the player to guide them towards valid actions.

Consider the following code:

```
import re

# Regular expression patterns for parsing player commands

command_pattern = r'(?P<action>\w+)\s+(?P<target>\w+)\s+with\
s+(?P<tool>\w+)'
```

```
# Function to interpret player commands
def interpret_command(command):
    match = re.match(command_pattern, command)
    if match:
        action = match.group('action')
        target = match.group('target')
        tool = match.group('tool')
        print(f"Action: {action}")
        print(f"Target: {target}")
        print(f"Tool: {tool}")
    else:
        print("Invalid command. Please try again.")

# Sample player commands
commands = [
    "attack dragon with sword",
    "kill the dragon using the blade",
    "explore the forest",
    "fight banana"
]

# Interpret and process player commands
for command in commands:
```

```
    print(f”Player command: ‘{command}’”)

    interpret_command(command)

    print()
```

In the preceding code, we demonstrate how regular expressions can be applied in a fictional text-based adventure game to parse and interpret player commands dynamically. Regular expressions provide a flexible and powerful tool for processing natural language input, enabling us to create immersive and interactive gaming experiences for players.

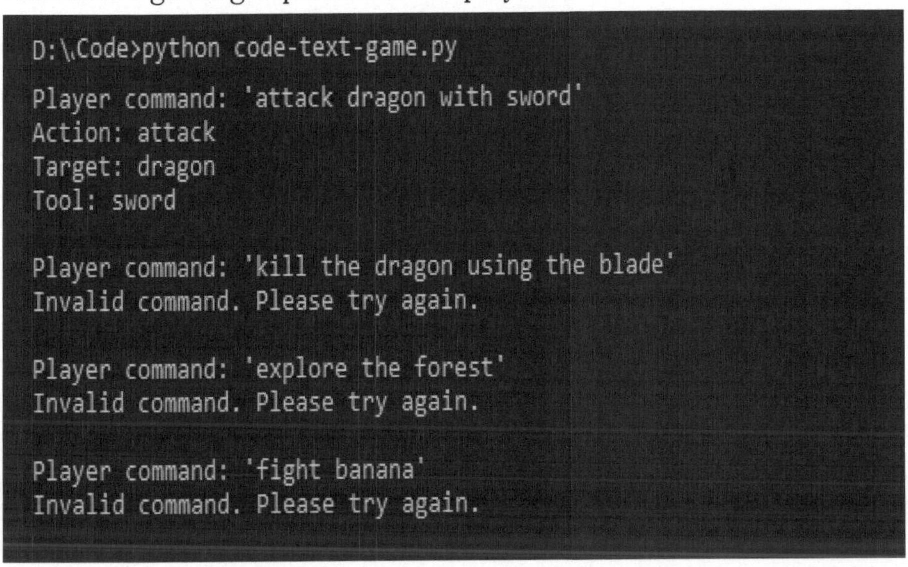
```
D:\.Code>python code-text-game.py
Player command: 'attack dragon with sword'
Action: attack
Target: dragon
Tool: sword

Player command: 'kill the dragon using the blade'
Invalid command. Please try again.

Player command: 'explore the forest'
Invalid command. Please try again.

Player command: 'fight banana'
Invalid command. Please try again.
```

Figure 13.5: *output of code-text-game.py*

The preceding image (`Figure 13.5`) shows the output of the code. This text game is based on the predefined set of commands.

We can make the above text game more interactive by asking user input; consider following code where user input is required to execute the action.

```
import re

# Regular expression patterns for parsing player commands

command_pattern = r’(?P<action>\w+)\s+(?P<target>\w+)\s+with\
s+(?P<tool>\w+)’
```

```
# Function to interpret player commands
def interpret_command(command):
    match = re.match(command_pattern, command)
    if match:
        action = match.group('action')
        target = match.group('target')
        tool = match.group('tool')
        print(f"Action: {action}")
        print(f"Target: {target}")
        print(f"Tool: {tool}")
    else:
        print("Invalid command. Please try again.")

# Interactive mode: continuously accept player commands
print("Welcome to the text adventure game!")
print("Enter commands in the format 'action target with tool'.")
print("For example: 'attack dragon with sword'.")
print("Type 'quit' to exit.")

while True:
    user_input = input("Enter your command: ").lower()

    if user_input == 'quit':
```

```
        print("Exiting game. Goodbye!")

        break


    interpret_command(user_input)

    print()
```

Now, users can interact with the text adventure game by entering commands in the specified format, and the program will interpret and process their commands in real-time. Users can explore the game world, interact with objects and characters, and engage in various activities by typing commands into the text interface. Regular expressions enable us to parse and interpret these commands dynamically, providing a seamless and interactive gaming experience for the players.

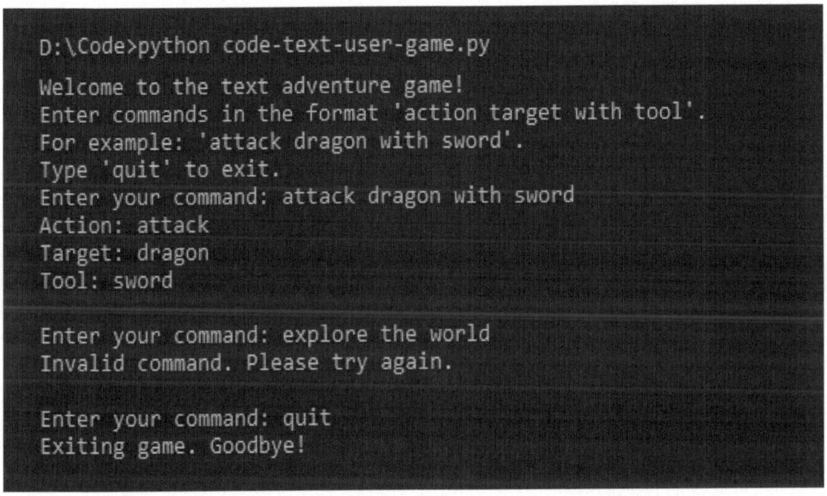

`Figure 13.6`: *output of code-text-game.py*

The preceding image (`Figure 13.6`) shows the output of the code. The out of the code vary as per the user input or command provided by the user.

Conclusion

Regular expressions are a powerful and versatile tool for pattern matching and text manipulation in computer science and software engineering. They enable developers to perform complex string operations with ease, allowing for tasks such as searching, matching, replacing, and extracting text data from a variety of sources. While regular expressions can be challenging to master, they offer immense power and flexibility when used correctly, making them an indispensable tool in the developer's toolkit.

In the next chapter, see the new age concepts like Artificial intelligence and will see how Python is playing an important role in Artificial intelligence.

Exercise: Test Your Understanding

Answer the following questions and test your understanding of learning from `Chapter 13`:

Q. 1. Define regular expression.

Q. 2. Write a `regx` pattern for email.

Q. 3. What do the metacharacters ^ and **$** signify in a regex pattern??

Q. 4. Explain quantifiers `*`, `+`, and `?`.

Q. 5. Replace all **'cat'** from "**The cat sat on the catwalk**." with **'dog'** using a `regx` pattern.

Notes

Date:

Python and Creativity
Programming is a creative process. Use Python to explore your creativity, whether building a unique web application, analyzing interesting datasets, or developing a fun game. The possibilities are endless!

Chapter 14

Basics of Artificial Intelligence

In the modern age of technology, Artificial Intelligence (AI) stands as one of the most transformative and exciting fields, promising to revolutionize various aspects of our lives. This chapter serves as an entry point into AI's vast and fascinating world, focusing specifically on the foundational concepts and principles underpinning AI development using the Python programming language.

Artificial Intelligence, often called AI, encompasses creating intelligent systems that simulate human-like behavior, learn from data, and make decisions autonomously. From virtual assistants like Siri and Alexa to self-driving cars and advanced medical diagnostics, AI has entered numerous industries, drive innovation and reshaping traditional paradigms.

In this chapter, we embark on a journey to explore the basics of Artificial Intelligence. We'll demystify its core concepts and techniques, all while using Python, a versatile and widely used programming language known for its simplicity and readability. Our focus is on empowering readers with the fundamental knowledge and skills needed to understand, implement, and leverage AI solutions using Python.

We begin by laying a solid foundation in understanding Artificial Intelligence and its various subfields, including machine learning, deep learning, natural language processing, and computer vision. Through practical examples and explanations, readers will gain insights into the capabilities and limitations of AI systems and their real-world applications across different domains.

As we delve deeper, we introduce essential Python libraries and frameworks commonly used in AI development, such as NumPy, Pandas, TensorFlow, and scikit-learn. These tools provide the building blocks for creating and training AI models, processing and analyzing data, and solving complex problems like classification, regression, clustering, and more.

Throughout this chapter, we prioritize hands-on learning. You'll find step-by-step tutorials and coding exercises that are designed to reinforce key concepts and foster practical skills. Whether you're a novice exploring AI for the first time or an experienced programmer looking to expand your knowledge, this chapter offers a comprehensive introduction to the Basics of Artificial Intelligence in Python. It's a steppingstone for deeper exploration and mastery in this exciting field.

In this chapter, we will cover:

- Introduction to Artificial Intelligence
- AI Concepts and Applications
- Exploring AI with Python Libraries
- Building Basic AI Models
- Practical Use Cases of AI in Python

Introduction to Artificial Intelligence

Artificial Intelligence, often abbreviated as AI, is a transformative field of computer science that seeks to create intelligent systems capable of performing tasks that typically require human intelligence. These tasks encompass a wide range of activities, including reasoning, learning, problem-solving, perception, and language understanding. At its core, AI aims to replicate and automate cognitive functions, enabling machines to simulate human-like behavior and decision-making processes.

The concept of Artificial Intelligence has captivated the imagination of scientists, researchers, and enthusiasts for decades, inspiring countless works of fiction and driving groundbreaking advancements in technology. From science fiction tales of sentient robots to real-world applications like self-driving cars and virtual assistants, AI continues to push the boundaries of what is possible, revolutionizing industries and reshaping our daily lives.

In essence, Artificial Intelligence can be viewed as the pursuit of creating machines that can think, learn, and adapt in ways that mimic human intelligence. This involves developing algorithms, models, and systems capable of processing vast amounts of data, recognizing patterns, making predictions, and autonomously improving over time.

The field of AI encompasses various subfields and approaches, each addressing different aspects of intelligence and problem-solving. Machine Learning, for example, focuses on developing algorithms that enable computers to learn from data and make predictions or decisions without being explicitly programmed. Deep Learning, a subset of machine learning, involves training neural networks with large datasets to recognize patterns and perform complex tasks such as image recognition and natural language processing.

Natural Language Processing (NLP) is another important area of AI that deals with enabling computers to understand, interpret, and generate human language. NLP powers virtual assistants like Siri and chatbots, allowing users to interact with machines using natural language commands and queries.

As we venture into the world of Artificial Intelligence, we encounter a myriad of opportunities and challenges. While AI holds the promise of revolutionizing industries, enhancing productivity, and improving quality of life, it also raises ethical, societal, and existential questions that require careful consideration.

Python language is one of the best fits for the Artificial Intelligence; to get enhanced this, consider a scenario:

Suppose we have a dataset containing customer reviews of products, and we want to build a machine learning model to classify the sentiment of each review as either positive, negative, or neutral. We can leverage Python and the scikit-learn library to train a classification model using a dataset of labeled reviews.

Before we starts writing code, first install the pandas and scikit-learn libraries along with their dependencies; use the following code:

```
pip install pandas

pip install scikit-learn
```

Once, both the above libraries are installed; write the following code:

```
import pandas as pd

from sklearn.model_selection import train_test_split

from sklearn.feature_extraction.text import TfidfVectorizer
```

```
from sklearn.linear_model import LogisticRegression

from sklearn.metrics import accuracy_score


# Load the dataset

data = pd.read_csv('customer_reviews.csv')


# Split the dataset into training and testing sets

X_train, X_test, y_train, y_test = train_test_split(data['review_text'],
data['sentiment'], test_size=0.2, random_state=42)


# Vectorize the text data using TF-IDF

vectorizer = TfidfVectorizer(max_features=1000)

X_train_vec = vectorizer.fit_transform(X_train)

X_test_vec = vectorizer.transform(X_test)


# Train a logistic regression classifier

classifier = LogisticRegression()

classifier.fit(X_train_vec, y_train)


# Predict the sentiment of test data

y_pred = classifier.predict(X_test_vec)


# Evaluate the model

accuracy = accuracy_score(y_test, y_pred)

print(f"Accuracy: {accuracy}")
```

In preceding code-example, we use Python and scikit-learn to perform sentiment analysis on customer reviews. Here's how the example correlates with the explanation:

- Data Preparation: We load the dataset containing customer reviews into a pandas DataFrame. This step corresponds to the process of acquiring and preprocessing data, a crucial step in any machine learning task.
- Feature Engineering: We split the dataset into training and testing sets to train our model and evaluate its performance. This step is essential for ensuring that our model generalizes well to unseen data.
- Model Building: We use TF-IDF (Term Frequency-Inverse Document Frequency) vectorization to convert the text data into numerical features. Then, we train a logistic regression classifier on the vectorized text data. This step corresponds to the process of building a machine learning model to analyze the sentiment of customer reviews.
- Model Evaluation: We predict the sentiment of the test data using the trained classifier and evaluate the model's performance using accuracy as the evaluation metric. This step helps us assess the effectiveness of our model in classifying the sentiment of customer reviews accurately.

By leveraging Python and machine learning libraries like scikit-learn, we can implement real-world AI applications, such as sentiment analysis, to extract valuable insights from text data and make data-driven decisions. This example demonstrates how Python can be used to apply AI techniques and solve practical problems effectively.

AI Concepts and Applications

Artificial Intelligence (AI) has emerged as a transformative technology with profound implications across various domains, ranging from healthcare and finance to transportation and entertainment. At its core, AI seeks to replicate human-like intelligence in machines, enabling them to perceive, reason, learn, and make decisions autonomously. By leveraging advanced algorithms, data processing techniques, and computational power, AI systems can tackle complex problems and tasks that were once thought to be exclusive to human cognition.

One of the key concepts in AI is machine learning, a subset of AI that focuses on enabling machines to learn from data without being explicitly programmed. Machine learning algorithms analyze large datasets to identify patterns, extract insights, and make predictions or decisions. Supervised learning, unsupervised learning, and reinforcement learning are common approaches in machine learning, each offering unique capabilities for solving different types of problems. For example, in supervised learning, algorithms are trained on labeled data, where each input is associated with a corresponding output, allowing the model to learn from examples and generalize to new, unseen data. On the other hand, unsupervised learning involves discovering hidden patterns or structures within unlabeled data, while reinforcement learning employs a trial-and-error approach to learn optimal behavior through interaction with an environment.

Deep learning, a subfield of machine learning, has gained significant attention and success in recent years, particularly in tasks such as image recognition, natural language processing, and speech recognition. Deep learning models, known as neural networks, are composed of multiple layers of interconnected nodes (neurons) that mimic the structure of the human brain. These models excel at automatically extracting features from raw data and capturing complex relationships, making them highly effective for tasks that involve large amounts of unstructured data.

Beyond machine learning and deep learning, AI encompasses a wide range of techniques and methodologies, including natural language processing (NLP), computer vision, robotics, and expert systems. NLP enables machines to understand, interpret, and generate human language, powering applications such as virtual assistants, sentiment analysis, and language translation. Computer vision enables machines to analyze and interpret visual information from images or videos, enabling tasks like object detection, facial recognition, and autonomous driving.

In practice, AI finds applications across various industries and domains, revolutionizing processes, enhancing decision-making, and unlocking new opportunities for innovation. In healthcare, AI is used for disease diagnosis, personalized treatment recommendations, and drug discovery. In finance, AI powers algorithmic trading, fraud detection, and risk assessment. In transportation, AI enables self-driving cars, traffic optimization, and predictive maintenance.

Overall, AI concepts and applications continue to evolve rapidly, driving advancements in technology and reshaping our world in profound ways. As we embrace the potential of AI, it is essential to consider ethical, societal, and regulatory implications to ensure that AI systems are developed and deployed responsibly for the benefit of humanity.

Exploring AI with Python Libraries

Artificial Intelligence (AI) has rapidly become one of the most dynamic and impactful fields in technology, with Python emerging as a leading programming language for AI development. Python's versatility, simplicity, and extensive ecosystem of libraries make it an ideal choice for implementing AI solutions across a wide range of domains. In this exploration of AI with Python libraries, we'll delve into some of the most commonly used libraries that power AI applications and enable developers to create intelligent systems.

One of the foundational libraries in AI is NumPy, which provides support for numerical computations and efficient array operations in Python. NumPy's array objects and mathematical functions are essential for handling large datasets and performing matrix operations, making it a fundamental building block for many AI algorithms.

Pandas is another indispensable library for AI tasks, offering powerful data structures and data manipulation tools. With Pandas, developers can easily load, clean, transform, and analyze structured data, such as CSV files or database tables. Its DataFrame object provides a convenient way to work with tabular data, making it well-suited for tasks like data preprocessing and exploratory data analysis in AI projects.

For machine learning tasks, scikit-learn stands out as a comprehensive library that provides a wide range of algorithms and utilities for building and deploying machine learning models. From classification and regression to clustering and dimensionality reduction, scikit-learn offers a consistent interface and efficient implementations of popular machine learning algorithms, making it accessible to both beginners and experts alike.

Deep learning, a subset of machine learning that focuses on neural networks, has gained immense popularity in recent years due to its remarkable success in solving complex problems across various domains. TensorFlow and PyTorch are two of the most widely used deep learning frameworks in Python, offering high-level APIs and computational graphs for building and training neural networks. These frameworks provide extensive support for GPU acceleration, distributed computing, and model deployment, making them ideal for developing state-of-the-art deep learning models.

Natural Language Processing (NLP) is another prominent area of AI that deals with understanding and generating human language. The Natural Language Toolkit (NLTK) and spaCy are popular libraries in Python for NLP tasks, offering tools and resources for tokenization, part-of-speech tagging, named entity recognition, sentiment analysis, and more. These libraries enable developers to process and analyze textual data effectively, paving the way for applications like chatbots, language translation, and sentiment analysis.

In addition to these libraries, there are numerous other specialized libraries and tools in Python that cater to specific AI tasks and domains. For example, OpenCV is a powerful computer vision library for image processing and object detection, while Gensim is widely used for topic modeling and document similarity analysis in natural language processing.

In summary, Python's rich ecosystem of libraries plays a pivotal role in advancing AI research and development, providing developers with the tools and resources they need to create intelligent systems that can learn, reason, and interact with the world.

The following is a concise list of possible available or majorly used Python Libraries:

- NumPy: A fundamental library for numerical computations and array operations.
- Pandas: Provides data structures and tools for data manipulation and analysis.
- scikit-learn: Offers a wide range of machine learning algorithms and utilities.
- TensorFlow: An open-source deep learning framework developed by Google.
- PyTorch: A deep learning framework known for its dynamic computation graphs and flexibility.
- Keras: A high-level neural networks API that runs on top of TensorFlow or Theano.
- NLTK (Natural Language Toolkit): A library for natural language processing tasks such as tokenization, stemming, and tagging.
- spaCy: A library for advanced natural language processing tasks and entity recognition.

- OpenCV: A computer vision library for image processing, object detection, and feature extraction.
- Gensim: A library for topic modeling, document similarity analysis, and word embedding.
- Theano: A deep learning library that allows for efficient mathematical expressions and GPU optimization.
- Fastai: A high-level deep learning library built on top of PyTorch, designed for quick experimentation and prototyping.
- XGBoost: An optimized gradient boosting library that provides implementations for gradient boosting algorithms.
- LightGBM: A gradient boosting framework that is designed for distributed and efficient training of large-scale datasets.
- CatBoost: A gradient boosting library that is optimized for categorical features and provides robust performance.
- Hugging Face Transformers: A library for state-of-the-art natural language processing models and pre-trained transformer architectures.
- AllenNLP: A library for deep learning-based natural language processing research, providing modular components for building NLP models.
- MXNet: A deep learning framework known for its scalability and support for distributed training across multiple GPUs and devices.
- Caffe: A deep learning framework developed by Berkeley AI Research (BAIR) that is optimized for computer vision tasks.
- Spark MLlib: A scalable machine learning library built on top of Apache Spark, designed for big data processing and analytics.

These are just some of the many Python libraries available for AI tasks, and the choice of library depends on the specific requirements of the project and the preferences of the developer. Each library has its own strengths and weaknesses, so it's essential to evaluate them based on factors such as performance, ease of use, and suitability for the task at hand.

Building Basic AI Model

To explore the Building Basic AI Model concepts; let's consider one fictional industry use-case:

In the retail industry, managing supply chains efficiently is crucial for optimizing operations, reducing costs, and meeting customer demands. By leveraging artificial intelligence (AI) models, retailers can gain valuable insights into supply chain dynamics, forecast demand more accurately, and make data-driven decisions to improve overall performance. Let's explore how Python concepts can be applied to build a basic AI model for the retail supply chain in a fictional use-case scenario.

Imagine a retail company that operates multiple stores across different locations. The company wants to enhance its supply chain management by predicting future demand for products at each store. By accurately forecasting demand, the company can optimize inventory levels, minimize stockouts, and ensure timely replenishment of goods.

To address this challenge, we'll develop a basic AI model using Python that predicts demand for a specific product at a particular store based on historical sales data and other relevant factors.

Here's how we can approach this:

- **Data Collection**: We start by collecting historical sales data from each store, including information such as product sales, store location, time of sale, promotions, and external factors like weather conditions or holidays. This data will serve as the foundation for training our AI model.
- **Data Preprocessing**: Next, we preprocess the collected data to clean and transform it into a suitable format for model training. This involves handling missing values, encoding categorical variables, scaling numerical features, and splitting the data into training and testing sets.
- **Feature Engineering**: We extract relevant features from the preprocessed data that can help our model capture patterns and relationships in the sales data. This may include features such as day of the week, month, seasonality, promotional periods, and historical sales trends.
- **Model Selection**: We choose an appropriate machine learning algorithm for demand forecasting, such as linear regression, decision trees, or neural networks. We train the selected model on the training data and evaluate its performance using metrics like mean absolute error or root mean squared error.
- **Model Evaluation and Optimization**: We assess the model's performance on the test data and fine-tune its parameters or explore alternative algorithms to improve accuracy. Additionally, we may incorporate additional features or adjust the model architecture to enhance predictive capabilities.

- **Deployment and Monitoring**: Once satisfied with the model's performance, we deploy it into production to generate demand forecasts for each store and product combination in real-time. We continuously monitor the model's predictions and update it as new data becomes available to ensure its accuracy and reliability over time.

By building this basic AI model for demand forecasting in the retail supply chain, our fictional company can gain valuable insights into future demand trends, optimize inventory management, and improve overall supply chain efficiency. This project demonstrates the practical application of Python concepts in solving real-world challenges in the retail industry through AI-driven solutions.

Consider the below code:

```
# Importing necessary libraries

import pandas as pd

from sklearn.model_selection import train_test_split

from sklearn.ensemble import RandomForestRegressor

from sklearn.metrics import mean_squared_error

# Load the historical sales data

sales_data = pd.read_csv('sales_data.csv')

# Preprocessing the data

# Assuming the sales_data.csv contains columns: 'store_id', 'product_id', 'date', 'sales', 'promotion', 'weather', etc.

# Data preprocessing steps such as handling missing values, encoding categorical variables, etc., would be performed here.

# Feature Engineering

# Extracting relevant features from the data

sales_data['date'] = pd.to_datetime(sales_data['date'])

sales_data['day_of_week'] = sales_data['date'].dt.dayofweek

sales_data['month'] = sales_data['date'].dt.month
```

```
sales_data['year'] = sales_data['date'].dt.year

# Other relevant features can be extracted based on the specific use-case

# Splitting the data into training and testing sets

X = sales_data.drop(['sales', 'date'], axis=1)

y = sales_data['sales']

X_train, X_test, y_train, y_test = train_test_split(X, y, test_size=0.2,
random_state=42)

# Building the AI model

model = RandomForestRegressor(n_estimators=100, random_state=42)

model.fit(X_train, y_train)

# Making predictions

y_pred = model.predict(X_test)


# Evaluating the model

mse = mean_squared_error(y_test, y_pred)

print(f"Mean Squared Error: {mse}")


# Deploying the model

# Once satisfied with the model's performance, it can be deployed into
production for generating demand forecasts in real-time.

# Continuous monitoring and updating of the model would be required to
ensure its accuracy and reliability over time.
```

This preceding program demonstrates the basic steps involved in building an AI model for demand forecasting in the retail supply chain use-case.

The program assumes that the sales data is stored in a CSV file named 'sales_data.csv' and contains columns such as 'store_id', 'product_id', 'date', 'sales', 'promotion', 'weather', etc.

Data preprocessing steps such as handling missing values, encoding categorical variables, and feature engineering are crucial but are not included in the provided code snippet due to the specific nature of the data and use-case.

Additionally, the model building, evaluation, and deployment steps are outlined, but the program does not include the actual deployment process, as it may vary depending on the deployment environment and infrastructure.

Practical Use Cases of AI in Python

Artificial Intelligence (AI) has become increasingly prevalent in various industries, revolutionizing processes, enhancing efficiency, and driving innovation. Python, with its rich ecosystem of libraries and frameworks, has emerged as a dominant language for implementing AI solutions due to its simplicity, versatility, and robust community support.

Let's explore some practical use cases of AI in Python across different domains:

- Healthcare: AI-powered healthcare applications leverage Python libraries such as TensorFlow and PyTorch for medical image analysis, disease diagnosis, and patient monitoring. For example, AI algorithms can analyze medical images like X-rays and MRIs to detect anomalies or assist radiologists in identifying tumors and lesions more accurately.
- Finance: In the finance industry, Python is extensively used for algorithmic trading, risk management, fraud detection, and customer analytics. Machine learning algorithms implemented in Python can analyze vast amounts of financial data to identify patterns, predict market trends, and optimize investment strategies.
- Retail: Retailers employ AI solutions to personalize customer experiences, optimize inventory management, and forecast demand. Python libraries like scikit-learn and TensorFlow enable retailers to analyze customer behavior, segment markets, and recommend products tailored to individual preferences based on historical data and real-time interactions.
- Manufacturing: AI-driven predictive maintenance systems use Python for analyzing sensor data from machinery to anticipate equipment failures and minimize downtime. By applying machine learning algorithms, manufacturers can predict maintenance needs, schedule repairs proactively, and optimize production processes for maximum efficiency.
- Transportation: Python plays a crucial role in developing AI applications

for autonomous vehicles, route optimization, and traffic management systems. Machine learning algorithms process data from sensors, cameras, and GPS devices to make real-time decisions, improve navigation, and enhance safety on the roads.

- Marketing: AI-powered marketing tools utilize Python for customer segmentation, sentiment analysis, and personalized content recommendation. By analyzing social media data, online interactions, and purchasing behavior, marketers can target specific audience segments, create more engaging campaigns, and measure campaign effectiveness.
- Agriculture: Python-based AI solutions help farmers improve crop yields, monitor soil conditions, and optimize resource usage. By analyzing satellite imagery, weather data, and soil samples, machine learning models can provide insights into crop health, predict yields, and recommend optimal planting and harvesting times.
- Cybersecurity: Python is widely used for building AI-driven cybersecurity systems that detect and prevent cyber threats in real-time. Machine learning algorithms analyze network traffic, identify anomalous behavior, and mitigate security risks by detecting and responding to malicious activities, such as malware infections and data breaches.
- Energy: In the energy sector, Python facilitates the development of AI applications for energy forecasting, grid optimization, and predictive maintenance of infrastructure. By analyzing historical energy consumption data and environmental factors, machine learning models can predict demand, optimize energy distribution, and reduce costs.
- Education: Python-based AI tools support personalized learning experiences, adaptive tutoring, and educational content recommendation systems. Machine learning algorithms analyze student performance data, learning preferences, and feedback to provide tailored recommendations, assess learning progress, and adapt teaching strategies accordingly.

Use-Case: Customer Segmentation for Targeted Marketing

Customer segmentation is a crucial strategy in marketing that involves dividing customers into groups based on shared characteristics or behaviors. By segmenting customers effectively, marketers can tailor their marketing campaigns, product offerings, and messaging to specific audience segments, thereby improving engagement, conversion rates, and overall marketing ROI.

In this use-case, we'll develop a Python program for customer segmentation based on demographic and transactional data. The program will use machine learning techniques to cluster customers into distinct segments, allowing marketers to target each segment with personalized marketing strategies.

In our example code, we used matplotlib library; if its not installed on your system; install using following command:

```
pip install matplotlib
```

Consider the following code:

```
# Importing necessary libraries

import pandas as pd

from sklearn.preprocessing import StandardScaler

from sklearn.cluster import KMeans

import matplotlib.pyplot as plt


# Load the customer data

customer_data = pd.read_csv('customer_data.csv')


# Preprocessing the data

# Assuming the customer_data.csv contains columns: 'customer_id', 'age', 'income', 'transaction_amount', etc.

# Data preprocessing steps such as handling missing values, encoding categorical variables, etc., would be performed here.


# Selecting relevant features for segmentation

X = customer_data[['age', 'income', 'transaction_amount']]
```

```
# Standardizing the features
scaler = StandardScaler()
X_scaled = scaler.fit_transform(X)

# Determining the optimal number of clusters using the Elbow method
wcss = []
for i in range(1, 11):
    kmeans = KMeans(n_clusters=i, init='k-means++', random_state=42)
    kmeans.fit(X_scaled)
    wcss.append(kmeans.inertia_)

# Plotting the Elbow curve
plt.plot(range(1, 11), wcss)
plt.title('Elbow Method')
plt.xlabel('Number of Clusters')
plt.ylabel('WCSS')
plt.show()

# Applying KMeans clustering with the optimal number of clusters
k = 3  # Assuming 3 clusters based on the Elbow curve
kmeans = KMeans(n_clusters=k, init='k-means++', random_state=42)
y_pred = kmeans.fit_predict(X_scaled)
# Adding the cluster labels to the customer data
customer_data['cluster'] = y_pred
```

```
# Visualizing the clusters

plt.scatter(X_scaled[y_pred == 0, 0], X_scaled[y_pred == 0, 1], s=100, c='red', label='Cluster 1')

plt.scatter(X_scaled[y_pred == 1, 0], X_scaled[y_pred == 1, 1], s=100, c='blue', label='Cluster 2')

plt.scatter(X_scaled[y_pred == 2, 0], X_scaled[y_pred == 2, 1], s=100, c='green', label='Cluster 3')

plt.scatter(kmeans.cluster_centers_[:, 0], kmeans.cluster_centers_[:, 1], s=300, c='yellow', label='Centroids')

plt.title('Customer Segmentation')

plt.xlabel('Age')

plt.ylabel('Income')

plt.legend()

plt.show()



# Outputting the segmented customer data

print(customer_data)
```

This Python program segments customers into distinct clusters based on their age, income, and transaction amount using the KMeans clustering algorithm. The optimal number of clusters is determined using the Elbow method, and the clusters are visualized using a scatter plot. Finally, the segmented customer data, including the assigned cluster labels, is output for further analysis and targeted marketing strategies.

```
D:\Code>python code-customer-segmentation.py
   customer_id  age  income  transaction_amount  cluster
0            1   35   50000                 100        1
1            2   45   60000                 150        2
2            3   30   40000                  80        1
3            4   55   70000                 200        0
4            5   40   55000                 120        2
5            6   50   65000                 180        0
6            7   25   35000                  70        1
7            8   60   75000                 220        0
8            9   28   38000                  75        1
9           10   48   62000                 160        2
```

Figure 14.1: *output of code-customersegmentation.py*

The preceding **`Figure 14.1`** visualizes the clusters based on the data provided in customer_data.csv file.

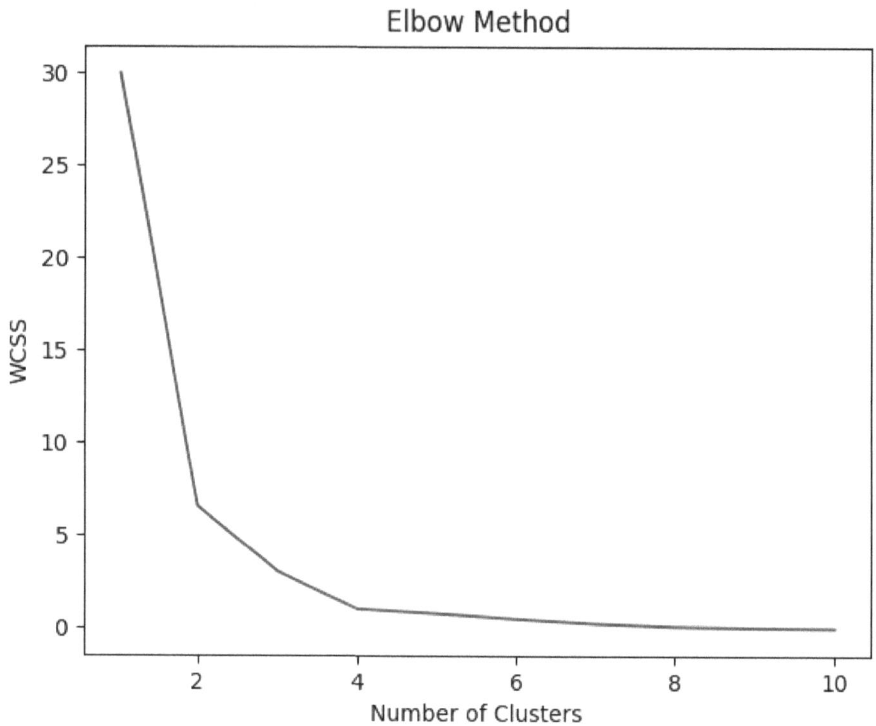

***Figure 14.2**: Visualization of Cluster using Elbow Method*

The preceding **`Figure 14.2`** visualizes the clusters based on the data provided in **`customer_data.csv`** file; it draws using Elbow Method.

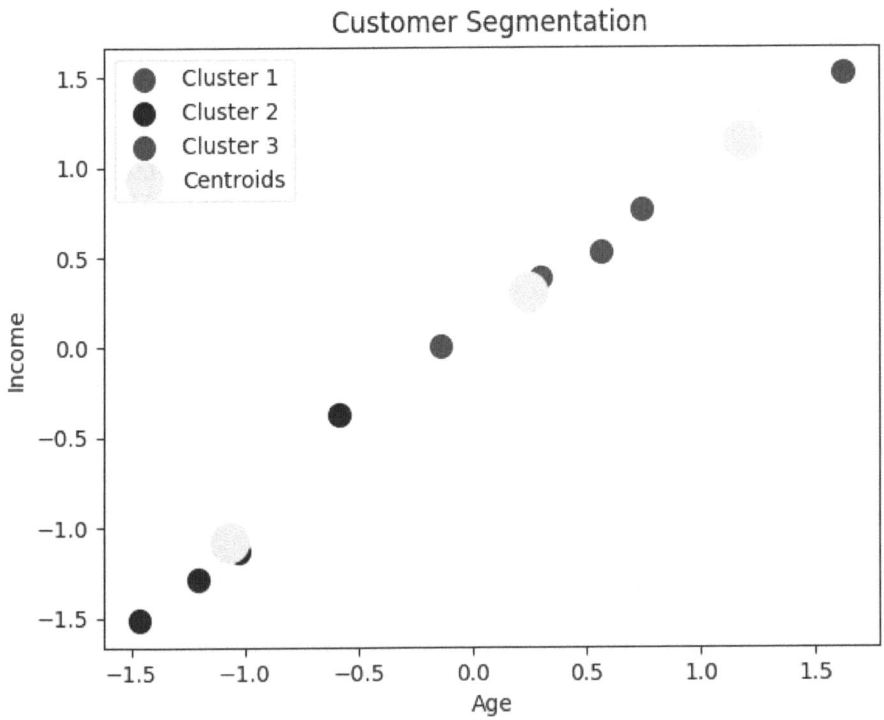

***Figure 14.3**: Customer Segmentation*

The preceding **`Figure 14.3`** visualizes clusters by plotting Customer Segmentation graph of Income and Age as per data provided in **`customer_data.csv`** file.

Conclusion

In this final chapter, we discussed the Basics of Artificial Intelligence in Python, covered the fundamentals of AI concepts, explored various applications of AI, and demonstrated how Python can be leveraged to implement AI in multiple solutions.

We learned the importance of AI in today's technological landscape and its diverse applications across different industries. From healthcare to finance, retail to transportation. With the help of the fundamentals of AI, we understood the value of the potential of AI to solve complex problems, optimize processes, and create value in various domains. In addition to the above, in this chapter, we learned that Python has a rich ecosystem of libraries and tools that help implement AI in solutions efficiently and effectively.

Next Steps: For those eager to embark on a deeper AI journey, the path ahead is filled with exciting opportunities. You can explore advanced AI concepts and techniques and delve into specific AI domains such as computer vision, speech recognition, or recommendation systems. You can learn advanced Python libraries and frameworks like TensorFlow, PyTorch, and scikit-learn..

Exercise: Test Your Understanding

Answer the following questions and test your understanding of learning from `Chapter 14`:

Q. 1. What is Artificial Intelligence?

Q. 2. Brief about the Key concepts of AI.

Q. 3. Briefly explain three popular Python libraries mainly used for AI.

Q. 4. Briefly describe the steps to build a business AI model using Python.

Appendix-A

Answers - Test your understanding

CHAPTER 1

Answers to test your understanding, `Chapter 1`

`Ans.1.` Accepting and embracing transformations can be challenging due to numerous factors, particularly when it comes to shifting mindsets. The most important ones are Uncertainty, Attachment, Beliefs, Fixed Mindset, Loss of Control, Lack of Awareness, etc.

`Ans.2.` Leaders play a vital role in driving and ensuring the success of a transformation. They should exemplify their commitment by actively participating in and embracing the changes themselves. Once leaders have a clear understanding of the transformation, they can provide teams with clear direction. This necessitates effective communication of the vision and the provision of necessary resources and guidance throughout the transformation process. It is important to differentiate between change, transition, and transformation. Leaders need to recognize that the seeds of agility exist in nature and were present long before the evolution of humans. By understanding this, leaders can gain a deeper insight into the essence of agility and its relevance to organizational transformations. With this understanding, leaders can effectively nurture the seeds of agility within their teams and organizations, allowing them to flourish and drive successful transformations.

`Ans.3.` Transition is a process of movement from one state, condition, or phase to another. During a transition, there is often a change in focus or priority.

`Ans.4.` Transformation is a more profound and comprehensive form of change. It involves a fundamental and often radical shift in the underlying nature, structure, or essence of something. Transformation typically involves a rethinking and reconfiguration of the entire system, resulting in a new paradigm or state.

`Ans.5.` For organizational transformations to be successful, it is essential to comprehend the differences between change, transition, and transformation. Transition is the internal psychological and emotional adjustments that people and teams must make to adapt to those changes, whereas change refers to the external modifications made to structures, procedures, or technologies. Transformation, on the other hand, goes deeper; it signifies a profound and lasting shift in the organization's core values, culture, and strategic direction. Recognizing these differences is pivotal because it enables leaders to approach transformations holistically. Organizations may build a more flexible and resilient workforce by addressing not only the structural changes but also concentrating on assisting people through the emotional and psychological shifts. The success of the transformation effort is ultimately attributed to the organization's willingness to embrace transformation as an ongoing cultural shift that guarantees the changes are ingrained in the organization's DNA, making them endure and in line with the long-term strategy.

CHAPTER 2

Answers to test your understanding, **Chapter 2**

Ans.1. Indentation in Python defines the scope of loops, functions, and conditional statements. Unlike many other programming languages that use braces to indicate code blocks, Python uses indentation. Consistent indentation is crucial because incorrect indentation can lead to syntax errors and unexpected behavior.

Ans.2. Consider following simple Python Program:

```
num = 10

if num > 0:

    print("The number is positive")

else:

    print("The number is negative")
```

In the preceding program. variable **num** contains value as **10** which is greater than **0** so, the output will be **The number is positive**

Ans.3. Python supports several built-in data types, including:

Data Type	Description	Example
Int	Integer numbers (whole numbers)	10, -5, 100
float	Floating-point numbers (real numbers with decimals)	3.14, -0.5, 2.0
str	Strings (sequences of characters)	"hello", 'Python', "123"
bool	Boolean values (True or False)	True, False
list	Ordered collections of items (mutable)	[1, 2, 3], ['a', 'b', 'c']
Tuple	Immutable collections of items	(1, 2, 3), ('a', 'b', 'c')
Dict	Key-value pairs	{'name': Sachin, 'age': 30}
Set	Unordered collections of unique elements	{1, 2, 3}, {'a', 'b', 'c'}

Ans.4. Following is a simple program:

```
a = 10

b = 5

sum = a + b

print("The sum is:", sum)
```

In the preceding program, we got the sum of **a** and **b** with the use of addition **+** operator.

Ans.5. The **=** operator is used for assignment, meaning it assigns the value on the right to the variable on the left. For example, **x = 5** assigns the value **5** to the variable **x**. The **==** operator is used for comparison, which checks whether the values on either side are equal. For example, **x == 5** checks if the value of **x** equals **5**.

Ans.6. Consider following simple program:

```
user_input = input("Enter something: ")

print("You entered:", user_input)
```

In the preceding program, the **input()** function takes input from the user, and **print()** displays the output.

CHAPTER 3

Answers to test your understanding, `Chapter 3`

`Ans.1.` A conditional statement is a feature in programming that allows the code to make decisions based on certain conditions. It evaluates an expression and executes a code block if the expression is true. Conditional statements are used to control the flow of a program and make it dynamic and responsive to different inputs and situations.

`Ans.2.` An **`if-else`** statement in Python checks a condition specified in the if part. If the condition is evaluated as **`True`**, the code block inside the **`if`** statement is executed. If the condition is evaluated as **`false`**, the code block inside the **`else`** statement is executed.

Consider the proceeding code example:

```
x = 10

if x > 5:

    print("x is greater than 5")

else:

    print("x is not greater than 5")
```

`Ans.3.` The **`elif`** keyword, short for **`else if`** allows multiple conditions to be checked sequentially. If the initial **`if`** condition is **`False`**, the **`elif`** condition is evaluated. If the **`elif`** condition is **`True`**, its corresponding code block is executed. Multiple **`elif`** statements can be chained to check various conditions.

Consider following code example:

```
x = 10

if x > 15:

    print("x is greater than 15")

elif x > 5:

    print("x is greater than 5 but less than or equal to 15")

else:

    print("x is 5 or less")
```

Ans.4. Nested conditional statements are conditional statements placed within another conditional statement. They are used to evaluate more complex conditions by adding another layer of decision-making.

Ans.5. Logical operators are used to combining multiple conditions within a single conditional statement. The three main logical operators are **and**, **or**, and **not**. These operators allow more complex condition evaluations.

- **and** returns **True** if both conditions are **True**.
- **or** returns **True** if at least one condition is **True**.
- **not** inverts the **boolean** value of a condition.

Consider the following code example:

```
x = 10

y = 20

if x > 5 and y > 15:

    print("Both conditions are true")

if x > 15 or y > 15:

    print("At least one condition is true")

if not (x > 15):

    print("x is not greater than 15")
```

Ans.6. A for loop in Python iterates over a sequence (like a list, tuple, string, or range) and executes a code block for each item in the sequence. It allows you to repeat an action a specific number of times.

Ans.7. A **for** loop iterates over a sequence of elements and stops when the sequence is exhausted. On the other hand, a **while** loop continues to execute as long as its condition remains **true**. while loops are useful for scenarios where the number of iterations is not known beforehand.

Consider the following example:

```
count = 0

while count < 5:
```

```
    print(count)
    count += 1
```

`Ans.8.` The break statement exits a loop prematurely, regardless of the original loop condition. It is often used within conditional statements to stop the loop based on a specific condition.

Consider the following example:

```
for i in range(10):
    if i == 5:
        break
    print(i)
```

`Ans.9.` The continue statement skips the rest of the code inside the loop for the current iteration and moves to the next iteration. It is used to skip certain values in a loop based on a condition.

Consider the following example:

```
for i in range(5):
    if i == 2:
        continue
    print(i)
```

`Ans.10.` An infinite loop occurs when the loop condition always evaluates to **`True`**. It can be created using a **`while`** loop with a condition that never becomes **`False`**. A **`break`** statement is typically used within a conditional statement inside the **`loop`** to break out of an infinite loop.

Consider the following example:

```
while True:
    response = input("Type 'exit' to stop: ")
    if response == 'exit':
        break
    print("You typed:", response)
```

Ans.11. Conditional statements and loops work together to create complex control flows in a program. Conditional statements (**if, elif, else**) allow the program to make decisions and execute different code blocks based on specific conditions. Loops (**for, while**) enable the repetition of code blocks. A program can handle various scenarios and repetitive tasks dynamically by combining these structures.

```
for i in range(10):
    if i % 2 == 0:
        print(f"{i} is even")
    else:
        print(f"{i} is odd")
```

Ans.12. A nested loop is a loop inside another loop. It is used to perform repetitive actions in a multi-dimensional way. For example, nested loops are useful for working with matrices or grids where you need to iterate over rows and columns.

```
for i in range(3):
    for j in range(3):
        print(f"i: {i}, j: {j}")
```

Ans.13. Control flow statements can be used to create a menu-driven program by repeatedly displaying a menu and using conditional statements to execute different actions based on user input.

```
while True:
    print("1. Option 1")
    print("2. Option 2")
    print("3. Exit")
    choice = input("Enter your choice: ")
    if choice == '1':
        print("You selected Option 1")
```

```
    elif choice == '2':

        print("You selected Option 2")

    elif choice == '3':

        break

    else:

        print("Invalid choice, please try again")
```

Ans.14. The else clause in loops executes a block of code after the loop completes its iteration normally, without being interrupted by a break statement. It can be used to run some final code after the loop.

```
for i in range(5):

    if i == 3:

        break

    print(i)

else:

    print("Loop completed without break")
```

Ans.15. Yes, using both types of loops in the same program can help solve more complex problems. For example, you might use a for loop to iterate over a collection of items and a while loop to handle user input:

```
numbers = [1, 2, 3, 4, 5]

for number in numbers:

    print(f"Current number: {number}")

    while True:

        response = input("Type 'next' to proceed or 'stop' to end: ")

        if response ==
```

CHAPTER 4

Answers to test your understanding, `Chapter 4`

`Ans.1.` A function is a reusable block of code designed to perform a specific task.

`Ans.2.` A function is defined using the def keyword, followed by a function name and parentheses containing any parameters.

`Ans.3.` You call a function without parameters by writing the function's name followed by empty parentheses, like **`function_name()`**.

`Ans.4.` The return statement exits the function and optionally passes an expression back to the caller.

`Ans.5.` Yes, a function can return multiple values as a tuple or other data structures.

CHAPTER 5

Answers to test your understanding, `Chapter 5`

`Ans.1.` `TypeError.`

`Ans.2.` `class`.

`Ans.3.` `raise`.

`Ans.4.` Exception.

`Ans.5.` `IndexError`.

CHAPTER 6

Answers to test your understanding, `Chapter 6`

`Ans.1.` The `open()` function.

`Ans.2.` To free up system resources and ensure all data is written to the file.

`Ans.3.` It can lead to memory leaks, and changes may not be saved correctly.

`Ans.4.` Yes, by opening the file in `'r+'` mode.

`Ans.5.` The default mode is read mode, denoted as 'r'.

`Ans.6.` Append mode, denoted as '`a`'.

`Ans.7.` It erases the existing file content and starts fresh.

`Ans.8.` '`w`' overwrites the file, while 'a' appends to the end of the file.

`Ans.9.` '`r`' is for reading only, while 'r+' allows both reading and writing.

`Ans.10.` Adding '`b`' to the mode (like '`rb`' or '`wb`') enables binary file handling.

`Ans.11.` Use the `read()` method on the file object.

`Ans.12.` The `writelines()` method of the file object.

`Ans.13.` Use a for loop to iterate over the file object.

`Ans.14.` It can consume a lot of memory by loading the entire file content into memory.

`Ans.15.` Open the file in append mode (`'a'`) and use the `write()` method.

`Ans.16.` It handles file opening and closing automatically, even in case of errors.

`Ans.17.` Python marks the end of a context manager block for file operations by dedentation of the code. Dedentation refers to the decrease in indentation level that signifies the end of a code block.

`Ans.18.` The `with` keyword.

`Ans.19.` No, the file object is only accessible within the context manager block.

Ans.20. The file is still closed properly, and the error can be caught using try-except.

Ans.21. `FileNotFoundError`.

Ans.22. Catch the **`PermissionError`** using a try-except block.

Ans.23. `IOError`.

Ans.24. Yes, using the **`finally`** block.

Ans.25. By specifying the exception types as a tuple after except.

CHAPTER 7

Answers to test your understanding, `Chapter 7`

`Ans.1.` An iterator is an object that enables a programmer to traverse through all the elements in a collection, regardless of its specific implementation.

`Ans.2.` Generators yield a sequence of values over time, whereas regular functions return a single value and terminate.

`Ans.3.` The two mandatory methods for an iterator are **`__iter__()`** and **`__next__()`**.

`Ans.4.` When a generator function calls yield, it outputs a value and pauses its execution, saving its state for future calls.

`Ans.5.` They are preferred for large datasets because they allow for efficient memory usage by producing values on-the-fly, rather than storing the entire dataset in memory.

`Ans.6.` A generator function is defined as a regular function but uses the yield statement to return values.

`Ans.7.` Generator functions are more memory-efficient as they yield one item at a time and do not store the entire sequence in memory.

`Ans.8.` Yes, generator functions maintain their local variables and execution state between successive calls.

`Ans.9.` A simple example is a function that yields numbers from **`0`** to a given number, defined as:

```
def simple_counter(max): while count < max: yield count; count += 1
```

`Ans.10.` Yes, generator functions can handle complex logic including loops, conditional statements, and state management.

`Ans.11.` The yield statement is used to output a value from a generator function and pause its execution until the next value is requested.

`Ans.12.` **`yield`** pauses the function and saves its state, while return exits the function and sends a value back to the caller.

`Ans.13.` Yes, a generator function can have multiple yield statements in its definition.

`Ans.14.` When a generator function resumes execution, it starts from the point just after the last yield statement.

`Ans.15.` Yes, it's possible to send data back into a generator function using the **`send()`** method.

`Ans.16.` A common method used is the **`for`** loop.

`Ans.17.` Generators are preferable as they are more memory-efficient, generating and processing items one at a time.

`Ans.18.` Yes, iterators can be created for any iterable object in Python, such as lists, tuples, and strings.

`Ans.19.` A generator expression is a more concise way to create generators, similar to list comprehensions but using parentheses.

`Ans.20.` Iterators are particularly useful in scenarios such as reading lines from a large file or processing paginated data.

`Ans.21.` Generators can be used to read large files line by line, which is memory efficient.

`Ans.22.` Generators are ideal for real-time data processing, like handling data from sensors or live feeds.

`Ans.23.` Generators can yield data in chunks, making them suitable for implementing pagination where data is loaded and displayed in parts.

`Ans.24.` An example is using a generator to create an infinite sequence of Fibonacci numbers.

`Ans.25.` Yes, generators can be used to implement coroutines for asynchronous tasks and cooperative multitasking.

CHAPTER 8

Answers to test your understanding, `Chapter 8`

`Ans.1.` A data structure is a way of organizing, managing, and storing data in a computer so that it can be accessed and modified efficiently.

`Ans.2.` Data structures are crucial because they form the foundation for organizing and storing data, directly impacting the performance and efficiency of algorithms and software applications.

`Ans.3.` Lists and dictionaries are two commonly used data structures in Python.

`Ans.4.` The choice of data structure affects how quickly and efficiently operations like data access, search, insertion, and deletion can be performed, thus impacting the overall performance of a program.

`Ans.5.` Primitive data structures hold basic data types like integers and characters, while composite data structures, like arrays or classes, can store collections of items and more complex entities.

CHAPTER 9

Answers to test your understanding, `Chapter 9`

`Ans.1.` It provides specialized container data types, offering alternatives to Python's general-purpose built-in containers like **`dict`**, **`list`**, **`set`**, and **`tuple`**.

`Ans.2.` **`deque`** and **`counter`**.

`Ans.3.` Yes, they are optimized for specific tasks, leading to more efficient code.

`Ans.4.` Yes, **`namedtuple`** is a part of the collections module.

`Ans.5.` Yes, as it has features like equality testing based on order, which regular dictionaries lack.

CHAPTER 10

Answers to test your understanding, `Chapter 10`

`Ans.1.` GUI stands for **`Graphical User Interface`**. Its primary purpose is to provide a user-friendly way for people to interact with software through graphical elements like buttons and menus, rather than text-based commands.

`Ans.2.` Two popular Python libraries for GUI development are **`Tkinter`** and **`PyQt`**.

`Ans.3.` GUI development focuses on creating graphical elements and interfaces for user interaction, whereas command-line interface development involves text-based interaction where users type commands to perform tasks.

`Ans.4.` Python is popular for GUI development due to its simplicity, readability, and the rich set of GUI libraries and tools it offers, making it accessible for both beginners and experienced developers.

`Ans.5.` Event-driven programming is a paradigm in GUI development where the flow of the program is determined by events such as user actions (e.g., mouse clicks, keyboard inputs) or system-generated events.

CHAPTER 11

Answers to test your understanding, `Chapter 11`

`Ans.1.` SQL is used to manage and query relational databases. Python facilitates SQL usage through libraries like **pyodbc** and **SQLAlchemy**, allowing easy database interaction.

`Ans.2.` Preventing SQL injection is crucial to ensure the security of your database interactions in Python. SQL injection occurs when untrusted data from users or external sources is improperly included in SQL queries, allowing attackers to manipulate the query's behavior. To prevent SQL injection in Python, you should use parameterized queries or prepared statements, depending on your library.

Here's how to avoid SQL injection using two shared Python database libraries: **pyodbc**:

Parameterized Queries:

Use placeholders in your SQL queries and provide values separately. The library handles escaping and quoting the data, preventing SQL injection.

```
import pyodbc

connection = pyodbc.connect(connection_string)

cursor = connection.cursor()

product_name = "apple"  # User input or external data

cursor.execute("SELECT name FROM Fruitmaster WHERE name = ?", product_
name)
```

Stored Procedures:

Create and use stored procedures with input parameters. Pass the parameters as separate values when executing the method.

```
cursor.execute("{CALL GetProductByName(?)}", (product_name,))
```

`Ans.3.` Error handling is crucial in database operations for several reasons:

- **Data Integrity**: Databases store critical data, and any unexpected errors during database operations can lead to data corruption or loss. Proper error handling ensures that data remains consistent and intact.
- **Application Stability**: In applications that interact with databases, unhandled errors

can crash the application. Error handling allows the application to gracefully recover or provide informative feedback to users.

- **Security**: Poorly handled errors can expose sensitive information about the database structure, potentially aiding malicious attackers. Proper error handling helps to hide such details from users.

- **Debugging and Maintenance**: Effective error handling provides detailed information about the cause of an issue, simplifying the debugging process and facilitating maintenance tasks.

Custom exceptions in Python are user-defined exception classes that extend Python's built-in Exception class. They are particularly useful in database operations for the following reasons:

- **Customization:** You can create custom exceptions that are specific to your application's needs, making it easier to distinguish between different types of errors. For example, you might define a `DatabaseConnectionError` to handle connection-related issues.

- **Clarity**: Custom exceptions allow you to provide more descriptive error messages, making it easier to understand the nature of the problem. This benefits both developers and users.

- **Hierarchical Structure**: You can create a hierarchy of custom exceptions, with more specific exceptions inheriting from more general ones. This helps in handling errors at different levels of abstraction.

Here's an example of defining and using a custom exception in Python:

```
class DatabaseError(Exception):

    """Base exception for database-related errors."""

    pass

class DatabaseConnectionError(DatabaseError):

    """Exception for database connection issues."""

    pass

class DatabaseQueryError(DatabaseError):

    """Exception for database query issues."""

    pass
```

```
try:

    # Database operation

except DatabaseConnectionError as e:

    print(f'Error in connecting to the database: {e}')

except DatabaseQueryError as e:

    print(f'Error in executing the query: {e}')

except DatabaseError as e:

    print(f'General database error: {e}')

except Exception as e:

    print(f'An unexpected error occurred: {e}')
```

In this example, we've defined a base **DatabaseError** and two more specific exceptions (**DatabaseConnectionError** and **DatabaseQueryError**). When handling errors, you can catch specific exceptions, providing more targeted error messages and handling procedures. This enhances code readability and maintainability, and it allows for better application response to different types of database errors.

Ans.4. A JOIN operation combines data from multiple tables based on a related column. In Python, you can perform a JOIN using SQL queries.

A **JOIN** operation combines data from multiple tables based on a related column. In Python, you can perform a **JOIN** using SQL queries:

```
cursor.execute('SELECT Fruitmaster.name, Suppliermaster.name
FROM Fruitmaster INNER JOIN Suppliermaster ON Fruitmaster.id =
Suppliermaster.id;')
```

.**Ans.5.** Transactions are sequences of database operations that are treated as a single unit. Moreover, transactions ensure data consistency.

```
connection.begin()

try:

    cursor.execute('INSERT INTO Fruitmaster (name, description, type)
```

```
VALUES (?, ?, ?);', ('Orange', 'Citrus fruit', 'fruit'))

    cursor.execute('UPDATE Fruitmaster SET description = ? WHERE name =
?;', ('Sweet and tangy', 'Orange'))

    connection.commit()

except:

    connection.rollback()
```

CHAPTER 12

Answers to test your understanding, `Chapter 12`

`Ans.1.` Multithreading is a technique where multiple threads are created within a single process to execute tasks concurrently. It improves application performance by enabling parallelism, efficiently using CPU resources, and improving responsiveness, especially for applications that involve I/O operations.

`Ans.2.` In Python, you can create a new thread using the threading module. The basic syntax involves defining a function the thread will run and creating a Thread object. Consider following code-snippet for thread creation; it creates a new thread that runs the **`th_function`** function.

```
import threading

def th_function():

    print("Thread is running")

my_thread = threading.Thread(target=th_function)

my_thread.start()
```

`Ans.3.` Thread synchronization is the coordination of thread execution to ensure that shared resources are accessed safely, preventing race conditions. In Python, synchronization can be achieved using locks provided by the **`threading`** module.

For example:

```
import threading

lock = threading.Lock()

def critical_section():

    with lock:

        # Critical section code

        print("Accessing shared resource")

thread1 = threading.Thread(target=critical_section)

thread2 = threading.Thread(target=critical_section)
```

```
thread1.start()

thread2.start()
```

In the example, with a **Lock** ensures that only one thread at a time can execute the code within the **with lock** block.

Ans.4. Concurrency is the ability of a program to manage multiple tasks simultaneously by switching between them, giving the appearance of simultaneous execution. Parallelism, however, involves executing multiple tasks simultaneously using multiple processors or cores. Concurrency is about structure (managing multiple tasks), while parallelism is about execution (doing multiple tasks simultaneously).

Ans.5. The following example is to write a short program that downloads multiple files from the internet simultaneously:

```
import threading

import requests

def download_file(url):

    response = requests.get(url)

    filename = url.split("/")[-1]

    with open(filename, 'wb') as file:

        file.write(response.content)

    print(f"Downloaded {filename}")

urls = [

    'https://arcchieonline.com/file1.zip',

    'https://arcchieonline.com/file2.zip',

    'https://arcchieonline.com/file3.zip'

]

threads = []

for url in urls:

    thread = threading.Thread(turget=download_file, args=(url,))
```

```
    threads.append(thread)
    thread.start()
for thread in threads:
    thread.join()
```

In the preceding small code example, we create a separate thread for each file download, allowing multiple files to be downloaded concurrently and significantly reducing the overall download time.

CHAPTER 13

Answers to test your understanding, `Chapter 13`

`Ans.1.` A regular expression, often abbreviated as regex, is a sequence of characters that defines a search pattern. It helps find, match, and manipulate specific text patterns within larger bodies of text. Regular expressions are powerful tools for text processing tasks such as search and replace operations, data validation, and parsing.

`Ans.2.` **`regex`** pattern to match an email address is:

```
^[a-zA-Z0-9._%+-]+@[a-zA-Z0-9.-]+\.[a-zA-Z]{2,}$
```

This pattern works as below:

- `^[a-zA-Z0-9._%+-]+` matches the beginning of the string and any combination of letters, numbers, and certain special characters before the `@` symbol.
- `@[a-zA-Z0-9.-]+` matches the `@` symbol followed by any combination of letters, numbers, and dots or hyphens.
- `\.[a-zA-Z]{2,}$` matches a dot followed by at least two letters, ensuring the domain part of the email is valid.

`Ans.3.` The metacharacter ^ signifies the start of a string, while **$** means the end of a string.

For example, the regex pattern **`^hello$`** will match the string "**`hello`**" only if it appears as the entire content of the string, with no other characters before or after it..

`Ans.4.` Find below:

- * (asterisk) matches zero or more occurrences of the preceding element.
- + (plus) matches one or more occurrences of the preceding element.
- ? (question mark) matches zero or one occurrence of the preceding element.

`Ans.5.`

```
import re
text = "The cat sat on the catwalk."
new_text = re.sub(r"cat", "dog", text)
print(new_text)
```

CHAPTER 14

Answers to test your understanding, **Chapter 14**

Ans.1. Artificial Intelligence (AI) is the simulation of human intelligence in machines programmed to think and learn like humans. Unlike traditional computing, which follows predefined instructions, AI can learn from experience, recognize patterns, and make decisions. Traditional computing executes tasks based on specific inputs and outputs, whereas AI can adapt to new data and improve its performance over time.

Ans.2. Key concepts in AI include machine learning, natural language processing, neural networks, and computer vision.

These concepts are applied in various fields, such as:

- **Machine Learning**: Used for predictive analytics, recommendation systems, and pattern recognition.
- **Natural Language Processing** (**NLP**): Powers applications like chatbots, language translation, and sentiment analysis.
- **Neural Networks**: Fundamental to deep learning, used in tasks like image and speech recognition.
- **Computer Vision**: Enables facial recognition, autonomous vehicles, and medical image analysis applications.

Ans.3. Mostly used Python libraries for AI:

- **TensorFlow**: An open-source library developed by Google for building and training neural networks, especially for deep learning applications.
- **scikit-learn**: A versatile library for machine learning that equips you with simple and efficient tools for data mining and data analysis, supporting a wide range of supervised and unsupervised learning algorithms.
- **Keras**: A high-level neural networks API, written in Python and capable of running on top of **TensorFlow**, **CNTK**, or **Theano**, designed to enable fast experimentation with deep neural networks.

`Ans.4.` The basic steps to build a simple AI model using Python are:

1. **`Data Collection`**: Gather the data that the model will learn from.

2. **`Data Preprocessing`**: Your role is crucial here. Clean and prepare the data for analysis, including handling missing values and normalizing them. Your efforts make the data ready for the model.

3. **`Model Selection`**: Don't worry; you have many models or algorithms to choose from for the task (e.g., linear regression, decision tree). You are in control of the model selection process. Training the Model: Use the training dataset to teach the model by adjusting its parameters.

4. **`Evaluation`**: Test the model on a separate dataset to assess its performance using accuracy, precision, and recall metrics.

5. **`Optimization`**: Fine-tune the model by adjusting hyperparameters to improve performance.

6. **`Deployment`**: Implement the model into a production environment where it can make predictions on new data.

Next Step

After mastering the basics in this book, consider delving into more advanced topics to enhance your Python skills further. One exciting area to explore is machine learning, which allows you to create algorithms to learn from and make predictions based on data. With Python's powerful libraries like TensorFlow, Keras, and scikit-learn, you can build and train models tackling complex problems, from image recognition to natural language processing.

Another valuable skill is data visualization, which involves creating graphical representations of data to uncover patterns and insights. Python offers several libraries, such as Matplotlib, Seaborn, and Plotly, that make it easy to create various visualizations, including line graphs, bar charts, and interactive plots. Mastering data visualization can help you communicate your findings more effectively and make informed data-based decisions.

Web development is another rewarding area to explore. You can build robust web applications and APIs by learning frameworks like Django and Flask. These frameworks simplify many aspects of web development, from handling HTTP requests to managing databases. Creating web applications with Python allows you to bring your ideas to life and share them with the world.

Additionally, joining communities such as Python Meetup groups can give support, inspiration, and opportunities for collaboration. Keep learning, experimenting, and pushing the boundaries of what you can achieve with Python.

Fun Fact

The Python community is one of the most active and welcoming in the programming world. With numerous forums, mailing lists, and social media groups, you'll always find a place to ask questions, share your progress, and collaborate.

JOIN US ON THE

ARCCHIE PUBLICATIONS

DISCORD SERVER

Connect with fellow readers, authors, and enthusiasts to discuss all things related to our publications and the exciting world of AI, programming, and learning. Share your insights, ask questions, and engage in vibrant discussions to expand your knowledge and inspire creativity. Take advantage of this opportunity to be part of a dynamic community dedicated to exploring the frontiers of technology and innovation. Join our Discord Server today and be part of the ARCCHIE Publications community!

https://discord.gg/z26SenmpEt

Practice, Practice, Practice

The key to becoming proficient in Python is consistent practice. Set aside time daily to code, experiment with new projects, and challenge yourself with exercises. The more you code, the more confident and skilled you'll become.